AFRO-AMERICAN WRITING
AN ANTHOLOGY OF PROSE AND POETRY

AFRO-AMERICAN WRITING

AN ANTHOLOGY OF PROSE AND POETRY

Volume I

Richard A. Long and Eugenia W. Collier
Editors

New York University Press

New York   1972

Acknowledgments

"The Watchers" and "Rhapsody," by William Stanley Braithwaite. Reprinted by permission of Coward-McCann, Inc., from SELECTED POEMS by William Stanley Braithwaite. Copyright 1948 by William Stanley Braithwaite.

"Bad Man Ballad." Collected, adapted and arranged by John A. Lomax and Alan Lomax. Copyright 1934 and renewed 1962 by Ludlow Music, Inc. Reprinted by permission of Ludlow Music, Inc.

"The Prodigal Son" from GOD'S TROMBONES, by James Weldon Johnson. Copyright 1927 by The Viking Press, Inc., renewed 1955 by Grace Nail Johnson. Reprinted by permission of The Viking Press, Inc.

"St. Peter Relates an Incident of the Resurrection Day" from SAINT PETER RELATES AN INCIDENT, by James Weldon Johnson. Copyright 1935 by James Weldon Johnson, renewed 1963 by Grace Nail Johnson. Reprinted by permission of The Viking Press, Inc.

"The Principles of the Universal Negro Improvement Association," "An Appeal to the Conscience of the Black Race to See Itself," "Message from Atlanta Prison," by Marcus Garvey. Reprinted from THE PHILOSOPHY AND OPINIONS OF MARCUS GARVEY by permission of A. Jacques Garvey.

"If We Must Die," "The Lynching," "Flame-Heart," by Claude McKay. Reprinted from SELECTED POEMS OF CLAUDE McKAY, copyright 1953 by Twayne Publishers, Inc., by permission of the Publisher.

"The New Negro in Paris" from A LONG WAY FROM HOME, by Claude McKay. Copyright 1937 by Lee Furman, Inc.; copyright 1970 by Harcourt Brace Jovanovich, Inc. and reprinted with their permission.

"Song of the Son," "Harvest Song," and "Avey" from CANE, by Jean Toomer. Copyright renewed 1951 by Jean Toomer. Reprinted by permission of Liveright Publishers, New York.

"Miss Cynthie," by Rudolph Fisher. Reprinted by permission of Scholastic Magazines, Inc. Copyright 1934, renewed 1962 by Story Magazine, Inc.

For
Arna Bontemps
and
Sterling Brown

poets and pioneers

Contents

PART II: The Civil War to World War I

Foreword

This anthology is designed for varied uses. For the general reader who wishes to gain a historical overview of Afro-American writing, it should be of considerable value. For a one-semester college course, it provides a total of fifty-eight authors, a selection from whom will make possible several different approaches to the material: historical, generic, thematic. The selections also provide complementary reading for varied period courses in American literature.

We are grateful to the New York University Press for patience; to our respective institutions, Atlanta University and Baltimore Community College, we express appreciation for various kinds of help. The following libraries have been useful: Soper Library of Morgan State College, Library of Baltimore Community College, Trevor Arnett Library of Atlanta University, and the Enoch Pratt Free Library of Baltimore. Mrs. Lillian Miles Lewis, curator of special collections at the Trevor Arnett Library, has extended many kindnesses. The staff of the Center of African and African-American Studies (CAAS) of Atlanta University has been of great assistance. Appreciation should be expressed to Misses Rutheen Samuels, Maggie Wanza and Gwendolyn Marshall, CAAS assistants. Special appreciation is due Mrs. Harriette Washington Bell, assistant to the director of CAAS and to Miss Willie Jackson of the Afro-American Studies Program at Atlanta University. This work could scarcely have come to completion in the time available to us without the intelligent and willing collaboration of Miss Thelma Blair, to whom we are both most grateful.

Richard A. Long
Eugenia W. Collier

A SELECT CHRONOLOGY OF AFRO-AMERICAN PROSE AND POETRY, 1760-1970

1760

Jupiter Hammon, "An Evening Thought"

1773

Phillis Wheatley, *Poems on Various Subjects, Religious and Moral*

1778

Jupiter Hammon, "An Address to Miss Phillis Wheatley"

1794

Richard Allen and Absalom Jones, *A Narrative of the Black People during the Late Awful Calamity in Philadelphia*

1829

David Walker, *Appeal*

George Moses Horton, *The Hope of Liberty* (re-issued as *Poems by a Slave* in 1837)

1841

Ann Plato, *Essays* (prose and Poetry)

1845

Narrative of the Life of Frederick Douglass
The Narrative of Lunsford Lane

1846

Narrative of William Hayden

1847

Narrative of William W. Brown, A Fugitive Slave

1848

William W. Brown, *Antislavery Harp*
Narratives of the Sufferings of Lewis and Milton Clarke
W. C. Pennington, *Fugitive Blacksmith*

1849

The Life of Josiah Henson
Narrative of Henry Box Brown
Narrative of the Life and Adventures of Henry Bibb

1850

Narrative of Sojourner Truth

1851

William Nell, *Services of Colored Americans in the Wars of 1776 and 1812*

1852

William W. Brown, *Three Years in Europe*
Martin R. Delany, *The Condition, Elevation, Emigration, and Destiny of the Colored People of the United States*

1853

William W. Brown, *Clotel, or the President's Daughter* (later versions in 1864 and 1867)
Solomon Northrop, *Twelve Years A Slave*

1854

Frances E. Harper, *Poems on Various Subjects*

1855

Frederick Douglass, *My Bondage and My Freedom*
William W. Brown, *Sketches of Places and People Abroad*
William C. Nell, *The Colored Patriots of the American Revolution*
Samuel R. Ward, *The Autobiography of a Fugitive Negro*

1856

Alexander Crummell, *The Duty of a Rising Christian State*

1857

Austin Stewart, *Twenty-Two Years a Slave and Forty Years a Freeman*
Frank J. Webb, *The Garies and Their Friends*

1859

Martin L. Delaney, *Blake, or the Huts of America*
The Rev. J. W. Loguen as a Slave and as a Freeman

1861

Martin R. Delaney, *The Official Report of the Niger Valley Exploring Party*

1863

William W. Brown, *The Black Man*

1866

Jacob Rhodes, *The Nation's Loss*

1867

William W. Brown, *The Negro in the American Rebellion*

1868

Elizabeth Keckley, *Behind the Scenes*

1869

Frances E. Harper, *Moses: A Story of the Nile*

1872

Frances E. Harper, *Sketches of Southern Life*
William Still, *The Underground Railroad*

1873

William W. Brown, *The Rising Son*
Islay Walden, *Miscellaneous Poems*

1874

Frances E. Harper, *Poems on Miscellaneous Subjects*

1877

Albery A. Whitman, *Not a Man, and Yet a Man*

1878

Henry O. Flipper, *The Colored Cadet at West Point*
James M. Trotter, *Music and Some Highly Musical People*

1879

Martin R. Delaney, *Principia of Ethnology*
J. Willis Menard, *Lays in Summer Lands*

1880

William W. Brown, *My Southern Home*

1881

Sam Lucas, *Careful Man Songster*

1882

Alexander Crummell, *The Greatness of Christ and Other Sermons*

1883

George W. Williams, *History of the Negro Race*

1884

Life and Times of Frederick Douglass
T. Thomas Fortune, *Black and White: Land, Labor, and Politics in the South*
Albery A. Whitman, *The Rape of Florida*

1885

T. Thomas Fortune, *The Negro in Politics*

1887

William J. Simmons, *Men of Mark*

1888

Daniel A. Payne, *Recollections of Seventy Years*
George W. Williams, *A History of the Negro Troops in the War of Rebellion*
Joseph T. Wilson, *The Black Phalanx*

1889

Alexander Crummell, *The Race Problem in America*

1891

Archibald H. Grimke, *Life of Charles Sumner*
Archibald H. Grimke, *William Lloyd Garrison*
Irvine G. Penn, *The Afro-American Press*

1893

Paul Laurence Dunbar, *Oak and Ivy*
Frances E. Harper, *Iola Leroy, or Shadows Uplifted*

1894

John Mercer Langston, *From the Virginia Plantation to the National Capital*

1895

James E. Campbell, *Echoes from the Cabin and Elsewhere*
Alexander Crummell, *Incidents of Hope for the Negro Race in America*
Paul Laurence Dunbar, *Majors and Minors*
Frances E. Harper, *Atlanta Offering: Poems*
Alice Moore (later Dunbar-Nelson), *Violets and other Tales*

1896

W. E. B. Du Bois, *The Suppression of the African Slave Trade*
Paul Laurence Dunbar, *Lyrics of Lowly Life*

1897

D. W. Davis, *Weh Down Souf'*

1898

Joseph S. Cotter, *Links of Friendship*
Paul Laurence Dunbar, *Folks from Dixie*
Paul Laurence Dunbar, *The Uncalled*

1899

Charles W. Chesnutt, *The Conjure Woman and Other Tales*
Charles W. Chesnutt, *The Wife of His Youth*
Charles W. Chesnutt, *Frederick Douglass*
W. E. B. Du Bois, *The Philadelphia Negro*
Paul Laurence Dunbar, *Lyrics of the Hearthside*
Sutton E. Griggs, *Imperium in Imperio*

1900

Charles W. Chesnutt, *The House Behind the Cedars*
Paul Laurence Dunbar, *The Love of Landry*
Paul Laurence Dunbar, *The Strength of Gideon*

1901

William S. Braithwaite, *The Canadian*
Charles W. Chesnutt, *The Marrow of Tradition*
Paul Laurence Dunbar, *The Fanatics*
Sutton E. Griggs, *Overshadowed*
Booker T. Washington, *Up From Slavery*
Albery A. Whitman, *An Idyl of the South*

1902

James D. Corothers, *The Black Cat Club*
Paul Laurence Dunbar, *The Sport of the Gods*
Sutton E. Griggs, *Unfettered*

1903

W. E. B. Du Bois, *The Souls of Black Folk*
Paul Laurence Dunbar, *Lyrics of Love and Laughter*
Paul Laurence Dunbar, *In Old Plantation Days*
Booker T. Washington and others, *The Negro Problem*

1904

William S. Braithwaite, *Lyrics of Life and Love*
Paul Laurence Dunbar, *The Heart of Happy Hollow*
Booker T. Washington, *Working With the Hands*

1905

James E. Campbell, *Echoes from the Cabin and Elsewhere*
Charles W. Chesnutt, *The Colonel's Dream*
Paul Laurence Dunbar, *Lyrics of Sunshine and Shadow*
T. Thomas Fortune, *Dreams of Life: Miscellaneous Poems*
Sutton E. Griggs, *The Hindered Hand*

1906

Joseph S. Cotter, *Caleb, the Degenerate*
Frances E. Harper, *Idylls of the Bible*

1907

Booker T. Washington, *The Life of Frederick Douglass*

1908

William S. Braithwaite, *The House of Falling Leaves*
Sutton E. Griggs, *Pointing the Way*
Kelly Miller, *Race Adjustment*

1909

Joseph S. Cotter, *A White Song and A Black One*
W. E. B. Du Bois, *John Brown*
Sutton E. Griggs, *Wisdom's Call*
William Pickens, *Abraham Lincoln*
Booker T. Washington, *The Story of the Negro*

1910

Benjamin Brawley, *The Negro in Literature and Art*
William Pickens, *The Heir of Slaves*

1911

W. E. B. Du Bois, *The Quest of the Silver Fleece*
Booker T. Washington, *My Larger Education*

1912

Joseph S. Cotter, *Negro Tales*
James W. Johnson, *The Autobiography of an Ex-Colored Man*
William Pickens, *Frederick Douglass*
Booker T. Washington, *The Man Farthest Down*

1913

Benjamin Brawley, *A Short History of the American Negro*
William H. Ferris, *The African Abroad*
Fenton Johnson, *A Little Dreaming*
William Pickens, *Fifty Years of Emancipation*

1914

John W. Cromwell, *The Negro in American History*
Kelly Miller, *Out of the House of Bondage*
Alice Dunbar Nelson, *Masterpieces of Negro Eloquence*

1915

W. E. B. Du Bois, *The Negro*
Fenton Johnson, *Visions of the Dusk*
Carter Woodson, *The Education of the Negro Prior to 1861*
John W. Work, *Folk Songs of the American Negro*

1916

Fenton Johnson, *Songs of the Soil*
William Pickens, *The New Negro*

1917

J. W. Johnson, *Fifty Years and Other Poems*
J. A. Rogers, *From Superman to Man*

1918

Benjamin Brawley, *Your Negro Neighbor*
Benjamin Brawley, *The Negro in Literature and Art* (revision)
Benjamin Brawley, *Africa and the War*
Joseph S. Cotter, Jr., *The Band of Gideon*
Maud Cuney-Hare, *The Message of the Trees*
Georgia D. Johnson, *The Heart of a Woman*
Kelly Miller, *An Appeal to Conscience*
Carter Woodson, *A Century of Negro Migration*

1919

William S. Braithwaite, *The Story of the Great War*
Benjamin Brawley, *Women of Achievement*
Kelly Miller, *History of the World War*
Clement Richardson, *National Cyclopedia of the Colored Race*

1920

W. E. B. Du Bois, *Darkwater*
James W. Johnson, *Self-Determining Haiti*
Robert R. Moton, *Finding a Way Out*

1921

Benjamin Brawley, *A Social History of the American Negro*
Leslie P. Hill, *The Wings of Oppression*
Claude McKay, *Spring in New Hampshire*
Kelly Miller, *Booker T. Washington Five Years After* (Pamphlet)
Carter Woodson, *The History of the Negro Church*

1922

Georgia D. Johnson, *Bronze*
James W. Johnson, *The Book of American Negro Poetry*
Claude McKay, *Harlem Shadows*
William Pickens, *The Vengeance of the Gods*
Charles Wesley, *The Collapse of the Confederacy*
Carter Woodson, *The Negro in Our History*

1923

Philosophy and Opinions of Marcus Garvey, ed. Amy Jacques Garvey
William Pickens, *Bursting Bonds*
Jean Toomer, *Cane*

1924

William S. Braithwaite, *Going Over Tindel*
W. E. B. Du Bois, *The Gift of Black Folk*
Jessie Fauset, *There Is Confusion*
Kelly Miller, *The Everlasting Stain*
Walter White, *Fire in the Flint*

1925

Countee Cullen, *Color*
James W. and J. Rosamond Johnson, *The Book of American Negro
    Spirituals*
Alain Locke, *The New Negro*
Carter Woodson, *Negro Orators and Their Orations*

1926

Blues: An Anthology, ed. W. C. Handy
Langston Hughes, *The Weary Blues*
William Pickens, *American Aesop*
Walter A. Roberts, *The Haunting Hand*
Eric Walrond, *Tropic Death*
Charles Wesley, *Negro Labor in the United States*
Walter White, *Flight*

1927

Countee Cullen, *Copper Sun*
Countee Cullen, *Ballad of the Brown Girl*
Countee, Cullen, *Caroling Dusk* (anthology)
Langston Hughes, *Fine Clothes to the Jew*
Charles W. Johnson, *Ebony and Topaz*
James W. Johnson, *God's Trombones*
Alain Locke, *Four Negro Poets*
Charles Wesley, *Negro Labor in the United States*

1928

W. E. B. Du Bois, *Dark Princess*
Jessie Fauset, *Plum Bun*
Rudolph Fisher, *The Walls of Jericho*
Leslie Hill, *Toussaint L'Ouverture*
Nella Larsen, *Quicksand*
Claude McKay, *Home to Harlem*
Carter Woodson, *African Myths with Proverbs*

1929

Countee Cullen, *The Black Christ*
Tyler Gordon, *Born to Be*
Nella Larsen, *Passing*
John F. Matheus, *Ouanga* (libretto)
Claude McKay, *Banjo*
Robert R. Moton, *What the Negro Thinks*
Wallace Thurman, *The Blacker the Berry*

Lorenzo Dow Turner, *Anti-Slavery Sentiment in American Literature*
Walter White, *Rope and Faggot*

POETS OF THE HARLEM RENAISSANCE

The following important poets were published only in magazines and anthologies during the twenties:

Gwendolyn Bennett
Arna Bontemps
Waring Cuney
Jessie Fauset
Frank Horne
Helene Johnson
Anne Spencer

1930

Langston Hughes, *Not Without Laughter*
Charles W. Johnson, *The Negro in American Civilization*
James W. Johnson, *Black Manhattan*
James W. Johnson, *St. Peter Relates An Incident*
Eslanda Goode Robeson, *Paul Robeson, Negro*
Carter G. Woodson, *The Rural Negro*

1931

Arna Bontemps, *God Sends Sunday*
Eva Dykes, Otelia Cromwell and Lorenzo Turner, *Readings From Negro Authors*
Jessie Fauset, *The Chinaberry Tree*
Langston Hughes, *Dear, Lovely Death*
James W. Johnson, *The Book of American Negro Poetry* (revision)
George Schuyler, *Black No More*
George Schuyler, *Slaves Today*

1932

Sterling Brown, *Southern Road*
Countee Cullen, *One Way to Heaven*

Rudolph Fisher, *The Conjure Man Dies*
Langston Hughes, *Scottsboro Limited*
Langston Hughes, *The Dream Keeper*
Langston Hughes and Arna Bontemps, *Popo and Fifine*
Claude McKay, *Gingertown*
Wallace Thurman, *Infants of the Spring*

1933

J. Mason Brewer, *Negrito: Negro Dialect Poems of the Southwest*
Jessie Fauset, *Comedy: American Style*
James W. Johnson, *Along This Way*
Alain Locke, *The Negro in America* (bibliography)
Claude McKay, *Banana Bottom*
Carter Woodson, *The Miseducation of the Negro*

1934

Horace M. Bond, *The Education of the Negro in the American Social Order*
D. O. W. Holmes, *The Evolution of the Negro College*
Langston Hughes, *The Ways of White Folks*
Zora Neale Hurston, *Jonah's Gourd Vine*
Charles Johnson, *Shadow of the Plantation*
James W. Johnson, *Negro Americans, What Now?*
Negro: An Anthology, ed. Nancy Cunard

1935

Benjamin Brawley, *Early Negro Writers*
Countee Cullen, *The Medea and Other Poems*
Frank Marshall Davis, *Black Man's Verse*
W. E. B. Du Bois, *Black Reconstruction*
George W. Henderson, *Ollie Miss*
Zora Neale Hurston, *Mules and Men*
Charles Wesley, *Richard Allen. Apostle of Freedom*

1936

Ralph J. Bunche, *A World View of Race*
Arna Bontemps, *Black Thunder*

Benjamin Brawley, *Paul Lawrence Dunbar*
Charles Johnson, *A Preface to Racial Understanding*
Alain Locke, *The Negro and His Music*
Carter G. Woodson, *The African Background Outlined*

1937

Arna Bontemps, *Sad-Faced Boy*
Benjamin Brawley, *The Negro Genius*
Sterling Brown, *The Negro in American Fiction*
Sterling Brown, *Negro Poetry and Drama*
Frank Marshall Davis, *I Am the American Negro*
Angelo Herndon, *Let Me Live*
Zora Neale Hurston, *Their Eyes Were Watching God*
George W. Lee, *River George*
Claude McKay, *A Long Way From Home*
Waters E. Turpin, *These Low Grounds*

1938

Benjamin Brawley, ed. *The Best Short Stories of P. L. Dunbar*
Frank Marshall Davis, *Through Sepia Eyes*
Langston Hughes, *A New Song*
Zora Neale Hurston, *Tell My Horse*
Georgia Douglass Johnson, *An Autumn Love Cycle*
Richard Wright, *Uncle Tom's Children*

1939

William Attaway, *Let Me Breathe Thunder*
Horace M. Bond, *Negro Education in Alabama*
Arna Bontemps, *Drums at Dusk*
W. E. B. Du Bois, *Black Folk: Then and Now*
E. Franklin Frazier, *The Negro Family in the United States*
Zora Neale Hurston, *Moses, Man of the Mountain*
Saunders Redding, *To Make A Poet Black*
Waters E. Turpin, *O Canaan!*
Carter Woodson, *African Heroes and Heroines*

1940

Countee Cullen, *The Lost Zoo*
W. E. B. Du Bois, *Dusk of Dawn*
Langston Hughes, *The Big Sea*
Alain Locke, *The Negro in Art*
Rayford W. Logan, *The Diplomatic Relations of the United States
    with Haiti*
McKay, Claude, *Harlem: Negro Metropolis*
Mary Church Terrell, *A Colored Woman in A White World*
Richard Wright, *Native Son*

1941

William Attaway, *Blood on the Forge*
Sterling Brown, Arthur P. Davis and Ulysses Lee, *The Negro Caravan*
W. C. Handy, *Father of the Blues: An Autobiography*
Richard Wright, *Twelve Million Black Voices*

1942

Eva Dykes, *The Negro in English Romantic Thought*
Lorenzo J. Greene, *The Negro in Colonial New England*
Langston Hughes, *Shakespeare in Harlem*
Zora Neale Hurston, *Dust Tracks on a Road*
George W. Lee, *Beale Street Sundown*
Saunders Redding, *No Day of Triumph*
Margaret Walker, *For My People*

1943

Langston Hughes, *Freedom's Plow*
Charles Johnson, *Patterns of Negro Segregation*
Carl R. Offord, *The White Face*
Roi Ottley, *New World A-Coming*
James A. Porter, *Modern Negro Art*
Chancellor Williams, *The Raven*

1944

Arthur H. Fauset, *Black Gods of the Metropolis*
Melvin B. Tolson, *Rendezvous with America*

1945

Gwendolyn Brooks, *A Street in Bronzeville*
St. Clair Drake and Horace Cayton, *Black Metropolis*
W. E. B. Du Bois, *Color and Democracy*
Chester Himes, *If He Hollers, Let Him Go*
Adam Clayton Powell, *Marching Blacks*
Richard Wright, *Black Boy*

1946

Brailsford K. Brazeal, *The Brotherhood of Sleeping Car Porters*
Owen Dodson, *Powerful Long Ladder*
Katherine Dunham, *Journey to Accompong*
Shirley Graham, *Paul Robeson, Citizen of the World*
George W. Henderson, *Jule*
Ann Petry, *The Street*
Era Bell Thompson, *American Daughter*
Robert C. Weaver, *Negro Labor*
Frank Yerby, *The Foxes of Harrow*

1947

W. E. B. Du Bois, *The World and Africa*
Chester Himes, *Lonely Crusade*
Langston Hughes, *Fields of Wonder*
Willard Motley, *Knock on Any Door*
Ann Petry, *Country Place*

1948

William S. Braithwaite, *Selected Poems*
Frank Marshall Davis, *47th Street Poems*
Hugh M. Gloster, *Negro Voices in American Fiction*
Zora Neale Hurston, *Seraph on the Suwanee*
Roi Ottley, *Black Odyssey*

Benjamin Quarles, *Frederick Douglass*
William Gardner Smith, *Last of the Conquerers*
Dorothy West, *The Living is Easy*

1949

Gwendolyn Brooks, *Annie Allen*
Shirley Graham, *Your Most Humble Servant* (Benjamin Banneker)
Robert Hayden and Myron O'Higgins, *The Lion and the Archer*
Langston Hughes, *One-Way Ticket*
Langston Hughes and Arna Bontemps, *The Poetry of the Negro,
1746-1949*

1950

William Demby, *Beetlecreek*
Langston Hughes, *Simple Speaks His Mind*
Saunders Redding, *Stranger and Alone*
Saunders Redding, *They Came in Chains*
William Gardner Smith, *Anger at Innocence*

1951

Arna Bontemps, *Chariot in the Sky*
Owen Dodson, *Boy at the Window*
Langston Hughes, *Montage of a Dream Deferred*
Saunders Redding, *On Being Negro In America*

1952

Helen M. Chesnutt, *Charles W. Chesnutt: Pioneer of the Color Line*
Ralph Ellison, *Invisible Man*
Langston Hughes, *Laughing to Keep From Crying*

1953

James Baldwin, *Go Tell It On The Mountain*
Gwendolyn Brooks, *Maud Martha*
Langston Hughes, *Simple Takes A Wife*
Claude McKay, *Selected Poems*
Ann Petry, *The Narrows*

Melvin B. Tolson, *Libretto for the Republic of Liberia*
Richard Wright, *The Outsider*

1954

Chester Himes, *The Third Generation*
John O. Killens, *Youngblood*
Carl R. Offord, *The Naked Fear*
William Gardner Smith, *South Street*
Richard Wright, *Black Power*

1955

James Baldwin, *Notes of A Native Son*
Robert E. Hayden, *Figure of Time*
Roi Ottley, *The Lonely Warrior* (Robert S. Abbott)

1956

James Baldwin, *Giovanni's Room*
Margaret Butcher, *The Negro in American Culture*
John H. Franklin, *From Slavery to Freedom*
Langston Hughes, *I Wonder As I Wander*
Pauli Murray, *Proud Shoes*
Richard Wright, *The Color Curtain*

1957

W. E. B. Du Bois, *The Ordeal of Mansart*
E. Franklin Frazier, *Black Bourgeosie*
E. Franklin Frazier, *The Negro in the United States*
Langston Hughes, *Simple Stakes A Claim*
Julian Mayfield, *The Hit*
Waters E. Turpin, *The Rootless*
Richard Wright, *Pagan Spain*
Richard Wright, *White Man, Listen!*

1958

Otelia Cromwell, *Lucretia Mott*
Benjamin Davis, *Communist Councilman From Harlem: An Auto-
biography*
Langston Hughes, *Tambourines to Glory*
Martin Luther King, Jr., *Stride Toward Freedom*
Julian Mayfield, *The Long Night*
Saunders Redding, *The Lonesome Road*
Richard Wright, *The Long Dream*

1959

Frank L. Brown, *Turnbull Park*
Philip Butcher, *George W. Cable: The Northhampton Years*
W. E. B. Du Bois, *Mansart Builds A School*
Katherine Dunham, *A Touch of Innocence*
Paule Marshall, *Brown Girl, Brownstones*
Lawrence Reddick, *Crusader Without Violence* (Martin L. King, Jr.)
Gladys B. Sheppard, *Mary Church Terrell*

1960

Gwendolyn Brooks, *The Bean Eaters*
Owen Dodson, *The Confession Stone*
May Miller, *Into the Clearing*
John A. Williams, *The Angry Ones*

1961

James Baldwin, *Nobody Knows My Name*
Waring Cuney, *Puzzles*
Margaret Danner, *Impressions of African Art Forms*
W. E. B. Du Bois, *Worlds of Color*
Langston Hughes, *Ask Your Mama*
LeRoi Jones, *Preface to a 20 Volume Suicide Note*
Paule Marshall, *Soul Clap Hands and Sing*
Julian Mayfield, *The Grand Parade*
Benjamin Quarles, *The Negro in the American Revolution*
John A. Williams, *Night Song*
Richard Wright, *Eight Men*

1962

James Baldwin, *Another Country*
Robert Hayden, *A Ballad of Remembrance*
Langston Hughes, *Fight for Freedom: The Story of the N.A.A.C.P.*
William Melvin Kelly, *A Different Drummer*
Lewis E. Lomax, *The Negro Revolt*
May Miller, *Poems*
Benjamin Quarles, *Lincoln and the Negro*

1963

James Baldwin, *The Fire Next Time*
Arna Bontemps, *Personals*
Frank Horne, *Haverstraw*
Langston Hughes, *Something in Common and Other Stories*
John O. Killens, *And Then We Heard The Thunder*
Gordon Parks, *The Learning Tree*
Conrad Kent Rivers, *These Black Bodies and This Sunburnt Face*
William G. Smith, *The Stone Face*
Mary E. Vroman, *Esther*
Charles Wright, *The Messenger*
Richard Wright, *Lawd, Today*

1964

Lerone Bennett, *Confrontations in Black and White*
Ralph Ellison, *Shadow and Act*
Ernest J. Gaines, *Catherine Carmier*
Lorraine Hansberry, *The Movement*
Kristin Hunter, *God Bless the Child*
LeRoi Jones, *The Dead Lecturer*
William Melvin Kelly, *Dancers on the Shore*
Benjamin Quarles, *The Negro in the Making of America*

1965

James Baldwin, *Going to Meet the Man*
Lerone Bennett, *The Negro Mood*
Claude Brown, *Manchild in the Promised Land*
William Demby, *The Catacombs*

Ronald Fair, *Many Thousand Gone*
Autobiography of Malcolm X (with Alex Haley)
Langston Hughes, *Simple's Uncle Sam*
LeRoi Jones, *The System of Dante's Hell*
William Melvin Kelly, *A Drop of Patience*
John O. Killens, *Black Man's Burden*
Naomi Long Madgett, *Star by Star: Poems*
A. B. Spellman, *The Beautiful Days*
Howard Thurman, *The Luminous Darkness*
Melvin B. Tolson, *Harlem Gallery*
Henry Van Dyke, *Ladies of the Rachmaninoff Eyes*
Richard Wright, *Savage Holiday*

1966

Ronald L. Fair, *Hog Butcher*
Sam Greenlee, *The Spook Who Sat By The Door*
Rosa Guy, *Bird At My Window*
Robert Hayden, *Selected Poems*
Kristin Hunter, *The Landlord*
LeRoi Jones, *Home*
Loren Miller, *The Petitioners* (the Supreme Court and the Negro)
A. B. Spellman, *Four Lives in the Bebop Business*
Margaret Walker, *Jubilee*
Charles Wright, *The Wig*

1967

Stokely Carmichael and Charles V. Hamilton, *Black Power*
Harold Cruse, *The Crisis of the Negro Intellectual*
James A. Emmanuel, *Langston Hughes*
Langston Hughes, *The Panther and the Lash*
Frank Hercules, *I Want A Black Doll*
LeRoi Jones, *Tales*
William Melvin Kelly, *Dem*
John O. Killens, *'Sippi*
Charlene Hatcher Polite, *The Flagellants*
Ishmael Reed, *The Free Lance Pall Bearers*
John A. Williams, *The Man Who Cried I Am*

1968

James Baldwin, *Tell Me How Long the Train's Been Gone*
Gwendolyn Brooks, *In the Mecca*
Eldridge Cleaver, *Soul on Ice*
Harold Cruse, *Rebellion or Revolution*
W. E. B. Du Bois, *Autobiography*
James A. Emmanuel, *The Treehouse and Other Poems*
Mari Evans, *Where Is All the Music?*
Ernest Gaines, *Bloodline*
Nikki Giovanni, *Black Feeling, Black Talk*
Etheridge Knight, *Poems from Prison*
Jewel C. Latimore, *Black Essence*
Don L. Lee, *Black Pride*
Don L. Lee, *Think Black*
Audre Lorde, *First Cities*
Dudley Randall, *Cities Burning*
Dudley Randall and Margaret Danner, *Poem Counterpoem*
Mary E. Vroman, *Harlem Summer*

1969

Lerone Bennett, *Pioneers in Protest*
Gwendolyn Brooks, *Riot*
Lucille Clifton, *Good Times*
Mercer Cook and Stephen Henderson, *The Militant Black Writer*
W. Edward Farrison, *William Wells Brown*
Nikki Giovanni, *Black Judgment*
Ted Joans, *Black Pow-Wow; Jazz Poems*
Don L. Lee, *Don't Cry, Scream!*
James McPherson, *Hue and Cry*
Larry Neal, *Black Boogaloo*
Ishmael Reed, *Yellow Back Radio Broke Down*
Sonia Sanchez, *Homecoming*
John A. Williams, *Sons of Darkness, Sons of Light*
Sarah E. Wright, *This Child's Gonna Live*
Frank Yerby, *Speak Now*

1970

Maya Angelou, *I Know Why The Caged Bird Sings*
Robert H. Brisbane, *The Black Vanguard*
Cecil Brown, *The Life and Loves of Mr. Jiveass Nigger*
Mari Evans: *I Am A Black Woman*
Ronald L. Fair, *World of Nothing*
Ted Joans, *Afrodisia*
Don L. Lee, *We Walk the Way of the New World*
Paule Marshall, *The Chosen Place, The Timeless People*
Louise Meriwether, *Daddy Was A Number Runner*
Pauli Murray, *Dark Testament and Other Poems*
William G. Smith, *Return to Black America*

Introduction

The cries of "Black Power!" that echoed down a dusty Southern road in the early 1960s, drowning out the strains of "We Shall Overcome," announced the beginning of a new age of awareness for Black Americans. The turmoil and trouble of the sixties, the tragedy and the triumph, resulted in a renewed emphasis on blackness—its meaning and its significance and the new direction in which America must turn. Thus, Afro-Americans emerged rather suddenly from their invisibility and became visible in many domains. This visibility is not an unmixed blessing. The distortions of overemphasis are as brutal as those of underemphasis. Today on every hand, strident voices, black and white, are bringing us up to date on what the Afro-American was and is.

Definitions are increasingly important. The survival of a culture —any culture—depends in large measure on the nature of its definitions of itself and of those aspects of life on which its survival depends: for example, what the past implies, what freedom means, who the enemy is. The literature of a culture is a totality of its definitions, a self-portrait of that culture. Knowledge of a literature, then, yields valuable insight into the culture that produced it. In this crucial and often mystifying age, Afro-American literature is involved in a general rage for scrutiny and redress. It is necessary for those who are devoted to the study of this literature to conceptualize a view of the Afro-American literary experience, if they are to relate effectively the reality of the past with the perplexities of the present, in the task of preparing for the uncertainty of the future.

First, then, what is to be included in the Afro-American literary experience? All writings by Americans of African descent, whether or not they write about that which is uniquely black? Writings by nonblacks which treat the Afro-American experience with insight or sympathy? Patronizing works by nonblacks? The philosophical issues posed by these questions have never been resolved to anybody's satisfaction. But some type of resolution is vital here in an anthology purporting to deal with the literature of black Americans.

It is our conviction that Afro-American literature is grounded in Afro-American life and that anyone who partakes of this life is molded by it. Even one who minimizes his blackness and writes from a Euro-American perspective is responding in his way to his experience as a black person. The works of William Stanley Braithwaite, for example, may be counted as part of the Afro-American literary experience, as well as the militantly black works of Malcolm X and Amiri Baraka (LeRoi Jones). A strange but legitimate bedfellow is the body of black folk tales collected and recorded by white Georgian Joel Chandler Harris.

There is a rationale for confining the study of the Afro-American literary experience to the works of Afro-American writers. At the moment of social crisis through which we are passing, such a study is of the highest existential relevance. There is no wall between the academy and the street. Our books are our weapons and the only ones which are likely to enable us to survive. Therefore, we must distinguish, as never before, between the profound and the superficial, between the felt and the observed, between soul and slick. We must scrutinize our heritage with sharper eyes than ever for those segments of truth which will be our passports into the future.

And here Euro-American works are not helpful. Writings by nonblacks are likely to be about the "American" experience; writings by blacks are almost certain to be from the Afro-American experience. And it is the depths of that experience which must now concern us. It is not surprising that most white writers dealing with Afro-American experience succeed in obtaining only a negative relevance, if indeed they are not irrelevant. It would indeed be strange if it were otherwise, for they neither have nor choose to have the perspective of the Afro-American. And what they report is shaped to the expectations of the white majority. Hence it is not a matter of wonder that most bestsellers about Afro-Americans have been written by whites. And those few bestsellers written by Afro-Americans have been largely misunderstood by whites. In other words, their success is a result of a collapse in communication.

The Afro-American literary experience, then, is contained in the writings that embody the Afro-American's spiritual journeying.

And that experience is today germane to any full consideration of the Afro-American in all of his dimensions.

What are the directions apparent in the literature of black Americans? We discern in the Afro-American literary experience two essential modes, two categories of vision: the simplistic and the oracular. Both may be associated with either hope or despair—the two poles around which Afro-American works cluster. Two classics of Afro-American literature illustrate the simplistic and oracular modes: *Up from Slavery* and *The Souls of Black Folk*. *Up from Slavery* presents the simplistic vision. It is not merely a question of the so-called Washington philosophy or of Washington's moral vision. There is a coalescence of form and content which serves to underscore the simplistic nature of the work. The underlying pattern is of the Horatio Alger myth based on the Calvinistic idea of wealth being a reward for work. *Up from Slavery* is filled with simplistic themes: uprightness, cleanliness, mother-love. It is optimistic. All will be well, though the where, when, and how are only obscurely hinted at.

In *The Souls of Black Folk* we find the oracular mode illustrated. Here all is complex; the canvas is crowded. The very language of DuBois, modelled on nineteenth-century rhetoric, is intended to suggest the manifold dimensions of the Afro-American experience. The metaphor of the veil, and the two-ness of the black man's vision are the leitmotivs of a varied collection, one that includes historical and social essays and a short story. Most appropriately, the work embodies a conscious reply to the simplistic rhetoric and ideology of Booker T. Washington.

The further importance of these two works is that in addition to illustrating the two modes, the simplistic and the oracular, they each illustrate a major genre of Afro-American literature. These two genres, the life-story and the oration, were dominant before the Civil War. There were the slave narrative and the antislavery polemic, both of which reached their masterful pinnacle in the work of Frederick Douglass, sadly neglected as a literary master. The slave narrative attained a sort of climax in Douglass' *Narrative* and then received, as it were, the kiss of death, both historically and artistically, in *Up from Slavery*. Douglass, of course, practiced the oracular mode throughout his life. His editorial "Nemesis" fulfills all the demands the rhetoricians would place upon such a work, a work that is in fact an oration. DuBois' work falls into the tradition of these orations, though they are the orations of the study rather than of the meeting hall. His eloquence is marshalled to move with passion and indignation the thinking man in his study rather than a crowd at a public meeting.

In addition to the two genres, the life-story and the oration, there also existed before the Civil War a rich folklore or popular literature for whose shape and content we are dependent upon tardy reporters with varying degrees of proficiency. Afro-American folklore, possessing as it does strong African roots, simply eludes attempts to cast it into Euro-American frames. It surfaced in the pre-Civil War epoch most prominently in an essentially poetic form—the biblical sermon. This was the true literature of the folk. It had its themes, its artifices, its almost universal public. And in spite of James Weldon Johnson's fears in 1927, it lives still, and has indeed acquired a secular lease on life.

Since the Civil War other genres have arisen. The essay assumed prominence during the dark years at the turn of the century when black thinkers wrestled with what was then known as the Negro Problem, and again during the twenties when black scholars assessed the place of the black artist in the scheme of things, and again in the fifties and sixties when every aspect of the black man's experience in America had to be scrutinized, and black thinkers wrestled with what had become known as the White Problem. Fiction also became increasingly important as an art form, as the image of the black man changed from Charles Chesnutt's conniving, obsequious Uncle Julius to the many faces of the Harlem Renaissance to Richard Wright's victimized Bigger Thomas to Ralph Ellison's faceless Invisible Man to the very strong, very black hero of the sixties. Poetry probed the innermost recesses of blackness, flowering most profusely in the Harlem Renaissance of the twenties and then again in the Black Renaissance of the sixties. In all genres the thrust has been increasingly toward the oracular rather than the simplistic mode as writers have discovered the materials of art in the varied nuances of Afro-American life.

Certain time cycles emerge. We distinguish the larger periods as

I. To the Civil War: the literature of the slave culture; art as an expression of suffering and an affirmation of manhood in the quest for freedom.

II. From the Civil War to the era of World War I: the literature of the newly freed citizens; the struggle for identity as reflected in literature.

III. From World War I to the era of World War II: the first flowering of Afro-American literature as high art, the Harlem Renaissance, its precursers and immediate descendants.

IV. From the mid-forties to the present: from protest to the Black Arts movement; new forms and expanded use of language as the quest for identity changes to self-discovery.

All such divisions are, of course, artificial. Some writers extend over two or even three of the periods; some adhere only casually to the dominant thrust of the period. But time periods are convenient and economical, and they provide a workable taking-off point.

We must now turn our attention to a critical issue and an issue of criticism. This is the condemnation frequently made that Afro-American writers are lacking in universality, bound up as so many of them are by the theme of race and race-conflict, which is local, limited, parochial. Obviously, there are themes which are universal in some sense or other: love, death, and nature, for example. But any extensive treatment of such themes outside of lyric poetry has to be circumstantial, set in a given time and place. And no given time and place are universal. What is inherently universal about Dante's ten heavens and limbo, about Homer's libations to the gods and his funeral pyres of heroes, about Shakespeare's feudal kings? The answer is, very little. Or Melville's whaling ship or Mark Twain's river towns? The answer is, nothing.

The demand for universality in the writings of the Afro-American cloaks a disapproval which the critic cannot articulate: The writing of the Afro-American is the stain in the literature of this country which seriously challenges the myth of American perfection. Even the most liberal critic turns out to be a racist at this point. Fundamental wrong, fundamental error, fundamental injustice disturb the picture. And yet it is fundamental wrong, fundamental error, fundamental injustice that Afro-American literature must reflect to be true to itself, for it is a literature of oppression, it is a cry from the soul of an oppressed people. It is also a literature of protest, a cry for redress. And in its most recent manifestation it is preeminently a literature of liberation.

This, then, is the cycle of Afro-American literature; this is its dynamic course: from oppression through protest to liberation. This experience is a proper object of study and criticism both in itself and as a part of the larger pattern of the literature of the United States and the literature of the world. Only by seeing this experience as an entity, a totality, and then confronting it with other literary traditions will it be possible to draw from it what inheres therein, the vital and profound truths of the tragic dilemma of democracy and freedom denied in the plenitude of its unending assertion.

Part I

To the Civil War

Conventional accounts of the American experience present the American Revolution as the seed time of that peculiarly American blessing, liberty. Here we encounter the beginning of the almost continuous divergence of the black experience from the mainstream tradition, for the American Revolution modified the position of the blacks, who made up nearly one fourth of the population, mainly by transferring the ultimate authority for the maintenance of slavery from the British crown to the new republic. The change was imperceptible to the blacks. Though blacks were to be found, both slave and free, in most of the colonies at the time of the Revolution, it is Virginia which best encapsulates the history of the black man in the colonies. It was at Jamestown that the first blacks arrived in 1619 as indentured servants, the only form of servitude then known there. It was there in 1662 that slavery was declared hereditary, thus providing legal sanction for the sad history that ensued. Over a hundred years later, Thomas Jefferson of Virginia composed the Declaration of Independence, from which he was forced to delete a disapproval of slavery in order to have it adopted. However, by this time enlightened Virginians, at least, saw little future for slavery in the new United States, and Pennsylvania had gone one step further to organize an Abolition Society in 1775, a year before the emasculated Declaration.

In the colonies still further north, New York and Massachusetts, two literate domestic slaves had emerged, singing the blessedness of

Christian salvation. On Long Island, New York, Jupiter Hammon as early as 1760 wrote:

> Salvation comes by Christ alone,
> The only Son of God
> Redemption now to every one
> That loves his holy word.

It would be stretching the point to perceive in this any element distinctly Afro-American: Hammon was little more than a moral versifier. With Phillis Wheatley, Boston's prodigy, much more talent is in evidence, but her references to slavery are rare and illustrative, as in the poem "To the Right Honorable William, Earl of Dartmouth":

> Should you, my lord, while you pursue my song,
> Wonder from whence my love of Freedom sprung,
> Whence flow these wishes for the common good,
> By feeling hearts alone best understood,
> I, young in life, by seeming cruel fate
> Was snatch'd from Afric's fancy'd happy seat:
> What pangs excrutiating must molest,
> What sorrows labour in my parent's breast?
> Steel'd was the soul and by no misery mov'd
> That from a father seiz'd his babe belov'd
> Such, such my case. And can I then but pray
> Others may never feel tyrannic sway?

Both Hammon and Wheatley were to be used to bolster the claims of succeeding generations of abolitionists, black and white, that given the opportunity to pursue Christian pursuits and to develop pious personalities, blacks would be found not at all wanting in these respects.

Slavery began to expand rapidly and to reveal itself as the scourge it was to become in 1793, when a New England Yankee residing in Georgia invented the cotton gin, thus making a peculiar institution of dubious value an exceedingly profitable one. In the same year a Fugitive Slave Law was passed sanctioning the institution on a national level. Virginia again became a focus of Afro-American history with Gabriel's Revolt in 1800, chronicled in Arna Bontemps' novel *Black Thunder* (1936). From this point the lines were clearly drawn in the politics and pragmatics of slavery and freedom, and slavery, which was the condition of the overwhelming number of blacks, was the inexorable context for those who were free, North and South. Against this developing canvas the slave poet of North Carolina, George Moses Horton, uttered plaintively "The Slave's Complaint":

> Am I sadly cast aside,
> On misfortune's rugged tide?
> Will the world my pains deride
> Forever?
>
> Must I dwell in Slavery's night,
> And all pleasure take its flight,
> Far beyond my feeble sight,
> Forever?

The answer to Horton's query given by the slave power and its eloquent spokesmen, such as John C. Calhoun, was a profound echo; forever and ever. In their view black slavery was a blessing both for them and for the blacks, and only the scum of the earth could be opposed to such an idyllic system.

The real substance of Afro-American writing in the period between the development of the cotton kingdom and the passing of the Thirteenth Amendment is the protest against slavery. The most outright protest was David Walker's *Appeal* (1829), the rhetoric of which was so stinging that the pamphlet was outlawed in the South and a reward offered for the assassination of the author. Yet, it did not actually call for insurrection; it merely listed in emotional terms the nature of the blacks' oppression. Whether or not Walker's *Appeal* had any direct part in Nat Turner's famed revolt of 1831, Nat's own confession gives no clue, but the connection was surely made by his proslavery contemporaries, who feared the pen as much as the sword.

As interesting as David Walker's *Appeal* and closely associated with it in tone and spirit was *An Address to the Slaves of the United States of America*, written by Henry Highland Garnet and proposed for adoption to a national convention of free blacks in 1843. The essay, rejected by the convention as too provocative, was subsequently printed by Garnet and received wide circulation. Garnet's argument to his brothers in bondage, that it was sinful to submit voluntarily to slavery and that to do so incurred the penalty of eternal damnation, was an artful twisting of the proslavery argument urging submission with the prospect of eternal bliss.

One solution offered to the problem of blacks and to the problem of slavery (not always the same, since there were hundreds of thousands of free blacks) was that of colonization outside of the United States, preferably in Africa, though occasionally Haiti and other places were mentioned. The American Colonization Society had been founded in 1816. As early as 1822 it had sent settlers to what was to become, in 1847, Liberia. Actually, it was the free blacks who were the object of the colonization schemes. It was their troublesome presence which many whites, North and South, found most undesirable. The lure of colonization had limited appeal for Afro-Americans, and many whites who backed the scheme did so from the most ignoble motive—the elimination of the free blacks so that they could not influence those in slavery to aspire to liberty. Pro-colonization attracted little of the literary energies of Afro-Americans before the Civil War.

The most characteristic genre of Afro-American expression during the period before the Civil War was the slave narrative. Some of these were dictated to friendly antislavery whites. But many represented the individual effort of the author himself. Among those of considerable importance we should note the *Narrative of William Wells Brown* (1847) and Samuel R. Ward's, *The Autobiography of A Fugitive Slave* (1855). Ward's own experience in slavery was brief. His slave parents escaped with him from Maryland when he was a child of three. He was widely known as an antislavery lecturer. Exiled to Canada because of his antislavery activities, he found time there to compose his autobiography as a document in the struggle.

William Wells Brown, who achieved considerable fame in the pre-Civil War period as a writer, was another of the antislavery lecturers known both in the United States and in England. While in London for a five year period he published a novel, *Clotel; or the President's Daughter* (1853), which was subsequently revised and republished twice by him in the United States. He also wrote and published in 1858 a play, *The Escape: or a Leap for Freedom.* Both novel and play join his antislavery work and his *Narrative* in a common theme: protest against slavery.

The most brilliant figure to emerge in the struggle against slavery was Frederick Douglass, an escaped slave. His career as an antislavery lecturer began in 1841, and his oratorical skill and magnificent physical presence were themselves telling arguments against a system that denied liberty to such a man. In 1845 the *Narrative of the Life of Frederick Douglass* appeared and immediately became a popular work. With consummate literary skill Douglass told the story of his life as a slave and his escape from servitude. A revised version appeared in 1855 under the title *My Bondage and My Freedom*. Meanwhile Douglass lectured, edited a newspaper, and kept up a large correspondence with antislavery supporters in the United States and England.

The 1850s saw the lines being drawn more tightly between that part of the nation committed to eternal slavery for the black man and those who wished the institution (and usually also the blacks) out of the country. Black protest took many forms: conventions passing resolutions; support of the Underground Railroad, whose legendary figure is Harriet Tubman; and interminable lectures, usually before the converted. Among the remarkable platform speakers was the poet Frances E. W. Harper, whose career continued into the twentieth century and whose public declamations of her poems in the 1850s caused her audiences to buy her published poems by the thousands. One of her poems, "Eliza Harris," describes the character of that name from Harriet Beecher Stowe's antislavery novel *Uncle Tom's Cabin* (1852), itself the single most potent work in the annals of antislavery. Mrs. Harper's poem concludes:

But she's free!—yes, free from the land where the slave
From the hand of oppression must rest in the grave;
Where bondage and torture, where scourges and chains
Have plac'd on our banner indelible stains.

The bloodhounds have miss'd the scent of her way;
The hunter is rifled and foil'd of his prey;
Fierce jargon and cursing, with clanking of chains
Make sounds of strange discord on Liberty's plains.

With the rapture of love and fulness of bliss,
She placed on his brow a mother's fond kiss:—
O poverty, danger and death she can brave,
For the child of her love is no longer a slave!

The political events of the fifties ended the hopes for a non-violent abolition of slavery. The Missouri Compromise was repealed in 1854 by the Kansas and Nebraska Act, thus encouraging the expansion of slavery. The Supreme Court rendered in 1857 the Dred Scott Decision, which sanctioned slavery in federal territory. John Brown's Raid of 1859, an armed attempt to free the slaves in West Virginia, ended disastrously with his execution. The acts of Secession, which followed the election of the pro-Union antislavery candidate Abraham Lincoln in 1860, brought about a situation in which the forcible abolition of slavery could be proposed as a matter of political and military expediency, and it was on this narrow ground that the stage was set for the Emancipation Proclamation and the Thirteenth Amendment.

PHILLIS WHEATLEY

(?1753-1784)

It is as a frail black child standing on a slave block in puritan Boston in 1761 that Phillis Wheatley enters the annals of American history. Purchased as a domestic servant by John Wheatley and christened by his family, she rapidly acculturated herself to her environment and was considered a prodigy. An ability to versify using the models available, chiefly adaptations of psalms and neo-classical poetry, brought her such acclaim that when she accompanied members of the Wheatley family to England in 1773 she was received by many distinguished people, and the Lord Mayor of London presented her with an edition of Paradise Lost. *It was in London in 1773 that* Poems, on Various Subjects, Religious and Moral *was published.*

Colonial America, a literary province of England, could hardly have been expected to produce many poets. Phillis Wheatley ranks with the best three or four who emerged between the colonization and the Revolution. Her achievement is, however, only relative, and she must be considered a minor English poet of her time whose interest for Afro-American literature is minimal. There was neither an Afro-American society for her to reflect nor an Afro-American audience to address. Nevertheless, the propaganda value of her achievement in the struggle of blacks in the United States has been extraordinary. The countless institutions and organizations named for her since early in the nineteenth century attest to the prestige of her attainment.

Of the poems presented here, "On Imagination" is simply a set piece in the manner of the English poetry of the time, utilizing the Miltonic diction that is normal for the genre. "To the University of Cambridge, in New England" (Harvard) is a greeting or compli-

mentary *poem of occasion. "On Being Brought from Africa to America"* offers, together with a passage on freedom in the poem which she addressed to Lord Dartmouth, one of the few allusions made by Phillis to her African home, of which she had probably blotted out all recollection. Her poems have been edited several times, notably by Heartman (1915), Ruth Wright (1930) and Julian D. Mason, Jr. (1966). Heartman's edition also includes her surviving letters.

On Imagination

Thy various works, imperial queen, we see.
How bright their forms! how decked with pomp by thee!
Thy wondr'ous acts in beauteous order stand,
And all attest how potent is thine hand.

From Helicon's refulgent heights attend,
Ye sacred choir, and my attempts befriend:
To tell her glories with a faithful tongue.
Ye blooming graces, triumph in my song.

Now here, now there, the roving Fancy flies,
Till some loved object strikes her wand'ring eyes,
Whose silken fetters all the senses bind,
And soft captivity involves the mind.

Imagination! who can sing thy force?
Or who describe the swiftness of thy course?
Soaring through air to find the bright abode,
Th' empyreal palace of the thundering God,
We on thy pinions can surpass the wind,
And leave the rolling universe behind:
From star to star the mental optics rove,
Measure the skies, and range the realms above.
There in one view we grasp the mighty whole,
Or with new worlds amaze th' unbounded soul.

Though Winter's frowns to Fancy's raptured eyes
The fields may flourish, and gay scenes arise;
The frozen deeps may break their iron bands,
And bid their waters murmur o'er the sands.
Fair Flora may resume her fragrant reign,
And with her flow'ry riches deck the plain;
Sylvanus may diffuse his honors round,
And all the forest may with leaves be crowned;
Show'rs may descend, and dews their gems disclose,
And nectar sparkle on the blooming rose.

Such is thy pow'r, nor are thine orders vain,
Oh, thou, the leader of the mental train;
In full perfection all thy works are wrought,
And thine the sceptre o'er the realms of thought.
Before thy throne the subject-passions bow,
Of subject-passions sov'reign ruler Thou;
At thy command joy rushes on the heart,
And through the glowing veins the spirits dart.

Fancy might now her siken pinions try
To rise from earth, and sweep th' expanse on high;
From Tithon's bed now might Aurora rise,
Her cheeks all glowing with celestial dies,
While a pure stream of light o'erflows the skies.

The monarch of the day I might behold,
And all the mountains tipped with radiant gold,
But I reluctant leave the pleasing views,
Which Fancy dresses to delight the Muse;
Winter austere forbids me to aspire,
And northern tempests damp the rising fire;
They chill the tides of Fancy's flowing sea,
Cease then, my song, cease th' unequal lay.

To the University of Cambridge, in New England

WHILE an intrinsic ardor prompts to write,
The muses promise to assist my pen;
'Twas not long since I left my native shore
The land of errors, and Egyptians gloom:
Father of mercy, 'twas thy gracious hand
Brought me in safety from those dark abodes.

Students, to you 'tis giv'n to scan the heights
Above, to traverse the ethereal space,
And mark the systems of revolving worlds.
Still more, ye sons of science, ye receive
The blissful news by messengers from heav'n,
How *Jesus'* blood for your redemption flows.
See him with hands outstretched upon the cross;
Immense compassion in his bosom glows;
He hears revilers, nor resents their scorn:
What matchless mercy in the Son of God!
When the whole human race by sin had fall'n,
He deign'd to die that they might rise again,
And share with him in the sublimest skies,
Life without death, and glory without end.

Improve your privileges while they stay,
Ye pupils, and each hour redeem, that bears
Or good or bad report of you to heav'n.
Let sin, that baneful evil to the soul,
By you be shunned, nor once remit your guard;
Suppress the deadly serpent in its egg.
Ye blooming plants of human race divine,
An *Ethiope* tells you 'tis your greatest foe;
Its transient sweetness turns to endless pain,
And in immense perdition sinks the soul.

On Being Brought from Africa to America

'Twas mercy brought me from my *Pagan* land,
Taught my benighted soul to understand
That there's a God, that there's a *Saviour* too:
Once I redemption neither sought nor knew.
Some view our race with scornful eye,
"Their color is a diabolic die."
Remember, Christians, Negroes, black as Cain,
May be refined, and join th' angelic train.

JUPITER HAMMON

(? 1720-1800)

The slave-poet Jupiter Hammon is more a colonial curiosity than an authentic monument of Afro-American literature. His poetry is occasional, inspired by pious sentiment, and reflects acquiescence in an essentially benign divine order. Not enough is known of the circumstances of his life to relate any of his surviving broadsides to it. As a domestic servant with a literary bent living on rural Long Island, it may be supposed that his life was one of uneventful labor, reading and churchgoing.

Poems such as "An Evening Thought" (1761) and "A Winter Piece" (1782) reflect a bucolic piety in no way different from that of Euro-American writers of similar talents and temperament. Only in "An Address to Miss Phillis Wheatley" (1778) is there possibility of a quickened interest in Hammon's work. Expectation, however, is dashed in the wake of the poem's metred moralizing.

An Address to Miss Phillis Wheatley

1.

O, come, you pious youth! adore
   The wisdom of thy God,
In bringing thee from distant shore,
   To learn His holy word,

2.

Thou mightst been left behind,
   Amidst a dark abode;
God's tender mercy still combined,
   Thou hast the holy word.

3.

Fair Wisdom's ways are paths of peace,
   And they that walk therein,
Shall reap the joys that never cease,
   And Christ shall be their King.

4.

God's tender mercy brought thee here;
   Tossed o'er the raging main;
In Christian faith thou hast a share,
   Worth all the gold of Spain.

5.

While thousands tossed by the sea,
 And others settled down,
God's tender mercy set thee free
 From dangers that come down.

6.

That thou a pattern still might be,
 To youth of Boston town,
The blessed Jesus set thee free
 From every sinful wound.

7.

The blessed Jesus, who came down,
 Unveiled his sacred face,
To cleanse the soul of every wound,
 And give repenting grace.

8.

That we poor sinners may obtain
 The pardon of our sin,
Dear Blessed Jesus, now constrain,
 And bring us flocking in.

9.

Come, you, Phillis, now aspire,
 And seek the living God,
So step by step thou mayst go higher,
 Till perfect in the word.

10.

While thousands moved to distant shore,
 And others left behind,
The blessed Jesus still adore;
 Implant this in thy mind.

11.

Thou hast left the heathen shore;
　Through mercy of the Lord,
Among the heathen live no more;
　Come magnify thy God.

12.

I pray the living God may be,
　The shepherd of thy soul;
His tender mercies still are free,
　His mysteries to unfold.

13.

Thou, Phillis, when thou hunger hast,
　Or pantest for thy God,
Jesus Christ is thy relief,
　Thou hast the holy word.

14.

The bounteous mercies of the Lord
　Are hid beyond the sky,
And holy souls that have His word
　Shall taste them when they die.

15.

The bounteous mercies are from God,
　The merits of His Son;
The humble soul that loves His word
　He chooses for his own.

16.

Come, dear Phillis, be advised
　To drink Samaria's flood;
There nothing that shall suffice
　But Christ's redeeming blood.

17.

While thousands muse with earthly toys,
   And range about the street,
Dear Phillis, seek for heaven's joys,
   Where we do hope to meet.

18.

When God shall send his summons down,
   And number saints together,
Blessed angels chant (triumphant sound),
   Come live with me forever.

19.

The humble soul shall fly to God,
   And leave the things of time,
Start forth as 'twere at the first word,
   To taste things more divine.

20.

Behold! the soul shall waft away,
   Whene'er we come to die,
And leave its cottage made of clay,
   In twinkling of an eye.

21.

Now glory be to the Most High,
   United praises given,
By all on earth, incessantly,
   And all the host of heaven.

DAVID WALKER
(1785-1830)

Little is known of the man, but David Walker reveals himself in his Appeal *as one of the most passionate and radical of evangelists against the evil of slavery as an institution. The* Appeal *was printed in Boston in 1829. Its distribution and fame were sufficient to have it banned in several of the Southern states. Walker's own violent and mysterious death may have been a result of the tremors which his words evoked in the slave power.*

Walker was himself born in slavery in North Carolina, and like the many antislavery pamphleteers and lecturers who were to follow, he had personal experience of the institution he damned so resoundingly. The spirit of Walker's Appeal *animated his successors such as Douglass and Ward.*

From *David Walker's Appeal*

PREAMBLE.

My dearly beloved Brethren and Fellow Citizens:

Having travelled over a considerable portion of these United States, and having, in the course of my travels taken the most accurate observations of things as they exist—the result of my observations has warranted the full and unshakened conviction, that we, (colored people of these United States) are the most degraded, wretched, and abject set of beings that ever lived since the world began, and I pray God, that none like us ever may live again until time shall be no more. They tell us of the Israelites in Egypt, the Helots in Sparta, and of the Roman Slaves, which last, were made up from almost every nation under heaven, whose sufferings under those ancient and heathen nations were, in comparison with ours, under this enlightened and christian nation, no more than a cypher—or in other words, those heathen nations of antiquity, had but little more among them than the name and form of slavery, while wretchedness and endless miseries were reserved, apparently in a phial, to be poured out upon our fathers, ourselves and our children by *christian* Americans!

These positions, I shall endeavour, by the help of the Lord, to demonstrate in the course of this *appeal*, to the satisfaction of the most incredulous mind—and may God Almighty who is the father of our Lord Jesus Christ, open your hearts to understand and believe the truth.

The *causes*, my brethren, which produce our wretchedness and miseries, are so very numerous and aggravating, that I believe the pen only of a Josephus or a Plutarch, can well enumerate and explain them. Upon subjects, then, of such incomprehensible magnitude, so impenetrable, and so notorious, I shall be obliged to omit a large class of, and content myself with giving you an exposition of a few of those, which do indeed rage to such an alarming pitch, that they cannot but be a perpetual source of terror and dismay to every reflecting mind.

I am fully aware, in making this appeal to my much afflicted and suffering brethren, that I shall not only be assailed by those whose greatest earthly desires are, to keep us in abject ignorance and wretchedness, and who are of the firm conviction that heaven has designed us and our children to be slaves and *beasts of burden* to them and their children.—I say, I do not only expect to be held up to the public as an ignorant, impudent and restless disturber of the public peace, by such avaricious creatures, as well as a mover of insubordination—and perhaps put in prison or to death, for giving a superficial exposition of our miseries, and exposing tyrants. But I am persuaded, that many of my brethren, particularly those who are ignorantly in league with slave-holders or tyrants, who acquire their daily bread by the blood and sweat of their more ignorant brethren—and not a few of those too, who are too ignorant to see an inch beyond their noses, will rise up and call me cursed—Yea, the jealous ones among us will perhaps use more abject subtlety by affirming that this work is not worth perusing; that we are well situated and there is no use in trying to better our condition, for we cannot. I will ask one question here.—Can our condition be any worse?—Can it be more mean and abject? If there are any changes, will they not be for the better, though they may appear for the worst at first? Can they get us any lower? Where can they get us? They are afraid to treat us worse, for they know well, the day they do it they are gone. But against all accusations which may or can be preferred against me, I appeal to heaven for my motive in writing—who knows that my object is, if possible, to awaken in the breasts of my afflicted, degraded and slumbering brethren, a spirit of enquiry and investigation respecting our miseries and wretchedness in this *Republican Land of Liberty!!!!!*

The sources from which our miseries are derived and on which I shall comment, I shall not combine in one, but shall put them under distinct heads and expose them in their turn; in doing which, keeping truth on my side, and not departing from the strictest rules of morality, I shall endeavor to penetrate, search out, and lay them open for your inspection. If you cannot or will not profit by them, I shall have done *my* duty to you, my country and my God.

And as the inhuman system of *slavery*, is the *source* from which most of our miseries proceed, I shall begin with that *curse to nations;* which has spread terror and devastation through so many nations of antiquity, and which is raging to such a pitch at the present day in Spain and in Portugal. It had one tug in England, in France, and in the United States of America; yet the inhabitants thereof, do not learn wisdom, and erase it entirely from their dwellings and from all with whom they have to do. The fact is, the labor of slaves comes so cheap to the avaricious usurpers, and is (as they think) of such great utility to the country where it exists, that those who are actuated by sordid avarice only, overlook the evils, which will as sure as the Lord lives, follow after the good. In fact, they are so happy to keep in ignorance and degradation, and to receive the homage and the labor of the slaves, they forget that God rules in the armies of heaven and among the inhabitants of the earth, having his ears continually open to the cries, tears and groans of his oppressed people; and being a just and holy Being will at one day appear fully in behalf of the oppressed, and arrest the progress of the avaricious oppressors; for although the destruction of the oppressors God may not effect by the oppressed, yet the Lord our God will bring other destructions upon them—for not unfrequently will he cause them to rise up one against another, to be split and divided, and to oppress each other, and sometimes to open hostilities with sword in hand. Some may ask, what is the matter with this enlightened and happy people?—Some say it is the cause of political usurpers, tyrants, oppressors, &c. But has not the Lord an oppressed and suffering people among them? Does the Lord condescend to hear their cries and see their tears in consequence of oppression? Will he let the oppressors rest comfortably and happy always? Will he not cause the very children of the oppressors to rise up against them, and oftimes put them to death? "God works in many ways his wonders to perform."

I will not here speak of the destructions which the Lord brought upon Egypt, in consequence of the oppression and consequent groans of the oppressed—of the hundreds and thousands of Egyptians whom God hurled into the Red Sea for afflicting his people in their land—of the Lord's suffering people in Sparta or Lacedemon, the land of the truly famous Lycurgus—nor have I time to comment upon the cause which produced the fierceness with which Sylla usurped the title, and absolutely acted as dictator of the Roman people—the conspiracy of

Cataline—the conspiracy against, and murder of Caesar in the Senate house—the spirit with which Marc Antony made himself master of the commonwealth—his associating Octavius and Lipidus with himself in power,—their dividing the provinces of Rome among themselves—their attack and defeat on the plains of Phillipi the last defenders of their liberty, (Brutus and Cassius)—the tyranny of Tiberius, and from him to the final overthrow of Constantinople by the Turkish Sultan, Mahomed II., A. D. 1453. I say, I shall not take up time to speak of the *causes* which produced so much wretchedness and massacre among those heathen nations, for I am aware that you know too well, that God is just, as well as merciful!—I shall call your attention a few moments to that *christian* nation, the Spaniards, while I shall leave almose unnoticed that avaricious and cruel people, the Portuguese, among whom all true hearted christians and lovers of Jesus Christ, must evidently see the judgments of God displayed. To show the judgments of God upon the Spaniards I shall occupy but little time, leaving a plenty of room for the candid and unprejudiced to reflect.

All persons who are acquainted with history, and particularly the Bible, who are not blinded by the God of this world, and are not actuated solely by avarice—who are able to lay aside prejudice long enough to view candidly and impartially, things as they were, are, and probably will be, who are willing to admit that God made man to serve him *alone*, and that man should have no other Lord or Lords but himself—that God Almighty is the *sole proprietor* or *master* of the whole human family, and will not on any consideration admit of a colleague, being unwilling to divide his glory with another.—And who can dispense with prejudice long enough to admit that we are men, notwithstanding our *improminent noses* and *woolly heads,* and believe that we feel for our fathers, mothers, wives and children as well as they do for theirs.—I say, all who are permitted to see and believe these things, can easily recognize the judgments of God among the Spaniards. Though others may lay the cause of the fierceness with which they cut each other's throats, to some other circumstances, yet they who believe that God is a God of justice, will believe that SLAVERY *is the principal cause.*

While the Spaniards are running about upon the field of battle cutting each other's throats, has not the Lord an afflicted and suffering people in the midst of them whose cries and groans in consequence of oppression are continually pouring into the ears of the God of justice? Would they not cease to cut each others throats if they could? But how can they? The very support which they draw from government to aid them in perpetrating such enormities, does it not arise in a great degree from the wretched victims of oppression among them? And yet they are calling for *Peace!—Peace ! !* Will any peace be given unto them? Their destruction may indeed be procrastinated awhile, but can it continue long while they are oppressing the Lord's people? Has He not the hearts of all men in His hand? Will he suffer one part of his creatures to go on oppressing another like brutes always, with impunity? And yet those avaricious wretches are calling for *Peace ! ! ! !* I declare it does appear to me, as though some nations think God is asleep, or that he made the Africans for nothing else but to dig their mines and work their farms, or they cannot believe history, sacred or profane. I ask every man who has a heart and is blessed with the privilege of believing—Is not God a God of justice to all his creatures? Do you say he is? Then if he gives peace and tranquility to tyrants, and permits them to keep our fathers, our mothers, ourselves and our children in eternal ignorance and wretchedness to support them and their families, would he be to us a God of *justice?* I ask O ye *christians ! ! !* who hold us and our children, in the most abject ignorance and degradation, that ever a people were afflicted with since the world began—I say, if God gives you peace and tranquility, and suffers you thus to go on afflicting us and our children, who have never given you the least provocation,— Would he be to us *a God of justice?* If you will allow that we are MEN, who feel for each other, does not the blood of our fathers and of us their children, cry aloud to the Lord of Sabaoth against you, for the cruelties and murders with which you have, and do continue to afflict us. But it is time for me to close my remarks on the suburbs, just to enter more fully into the interior of this system of cruelty and oppression.

HENRY HIGHLAND GARNET

(1815-1882)

Like Douglass, Garnet was born in slavery on the Eastern shore of Maryland. Like Ward, his parents took him as a child in their escape from slavery to New York, where he attended school with Ward and others who were to achieve fame in the cause of black liberation. Garnet's most famous work is An Address to the Slaves of the United States of America *(1843), a truly radical document.*

Garnet toured Europe, speaking against slavery, and was a missionary in Jamaica. After the abolition of slavery he achieved a certain degree of official approval and was named United States Representative to Liberia.

Alexander Crummell, who had been one of his schoolmates in New York, wrote The Eulogy of Henry Highland Garnet *(1882).*

An Address to the Slaves of the United States of America

PREFACE.

The following Address was first read at the National Convention held at Buffalo, N. Y., in 1843. Since that time it has been slightly modified, retaining, however, all of its original doctrine. The document elicited more discussion than any other paper that was ever brought before that, or any other deliberative body of colored persons, and their friends. Gentlemen who opposed the Address, based their objections on these grounds. 1. That the document was war-like, and encouraged insurrection; and 2. That if the Convention should adopt it, that those delegates who lived near the borders of the slave states, would not dare to return to their homes. The Address was rejected by a small majority; and now in compliance with the earnest request of many who heard it, and in conformity to the wishes of numerous friends who are anxious to see it, the author now gives it to the public, praying God that this little book may be borne on the four winds of heaven, until the principles it contains shall be understood and adopted by every slave in the Union.   H. H. G.

Troy, N. Y., April 15, 1848.

ADDRESS TO THE SLAVES OF THE U.S.

BRETHREN AND FELLOW CITIZENS:

Your brethren of the north, east, and west have been accustomed to meet together in National Conventions, to sympathize with each other, and to sweep over your unhappy condition. In these meetings we have addressed all classes of the free, but we have never until this time, sent a word of consolation and advice to you. We have been contented in sitting still and mourning over your sorrows, earnestly hoping that before this day, your sacred liberties would have been restored. But, we have hoped in vain. Years have rolled on, and tens of thousands have been borne on streams of blood, and tears, to the shores of eternity. While you have been oppressed, we have also been partakers with you; nor can we be free while you are enslaved. We therefore write to you as being bound with you.

Many of you are bound to us, not only by the ties of a common humanity, but we are connected by the more tender relations of parents, wives, husbands, children, brothers, and sisters, and friends. As such we most affectionately address you.

Slavery has fixed a deep gulf between you and us, and while it shuts out from you the relief and consolation which your friends would willingly render, it afflicts and persecutes you with a fierceness which we might not expect to see in the fiends of hell. But still the Almighty Father of Mercies has left to us a glimmering ray of hope, which shines out like a lone star in a cloudy sky. Mankind are becoming wiser, and better—the oppressor's power is fading, and you, every day, are becoming better informed, and more numerous. Your grievances, brethren, are many. We shall not attempt, in this short address, to present to the world, all the dark catalogue of this nation's sins, which have been committed upon an innocent people. Nor is it indeed, necessary, for you feel them from day to day, and all the civilized world look upon them with amazement.

Two hundred and twenty-seven years ago, the first of our injured race were brought to the shores of America. They came not with glad spirits to select their homes, in the New World. They came not with their own consent, to find an unmolested enjoyment of the blessings of this fruitful soil. The first dealings which they had with men calling themselves Christians, exhibited to them the worst features of corrupt and sordid hearts; and convinced them that no cruelty is too great, no villainy, and no robbery too abhorrent for even enlightened men to perform, when influenced by avarice, and lust. Neither did they come flying upon the wings of Liberty, to a land of freedom. But, they came with broken hearts, from their beloved native land, and were doomed to unrequited toil, and deep degradation. Nor did the evil of their bondage end at their emancipation by death. Succeeding generations inherited their chains, and millions have come from eternity into time, and have returned again to the world of spirits, cursed, and ruined by American Slavery.

The propagators of the system, or their immediate ancestors very soon discovered its growing evil, and its tremendous wickedness, and secret promises were made to destroy it. The gross inconsistency of a people holding slaves, who had themselves "ferried o'er the wave," for freedom's sake, was too apparent to be entirely overlooked. The voice of Freedom cried, "emancipate your Slaves." Humanity supplicated with tears, for the deliverance of the children of Africa. Wisdom urged her solemn plea. The bleeding captive plead his innocence, and pointed to Christianity who stood weeping at the cross. Jehovah frowned upon the nefarious institution, and thunderbolts, red with vengeance, struggled to leap forth to blast the guilty wretches who maintained it. But all was vain. Slavery had stretched its dark wings of death over the land, the Church stood silently by— the priests prophesied falsely, and the people loved to have it so. Its throne is established, and now it reigns triumphantly.

Nearly three millions of your fellow citizens, are prohibited by law, and public opinion, (which in this country is stronger than law), from reading the Book of Life. Your intellect has been destroyed as much as possible, and every ray of light they have attempted to shut out from your minds. The oppressors themselves have become involved in the ruin. They have become weak, sensual, and rapacious. They have cursed you—they have cursed themselves—they have cursed the earth which they have trod. In the language of a Southern statesman, we can truly say, "even the wolf, driven back long since by the approach of man, now returns after the lapse of a hundred years, and howls amid the desolations of slavery."

The colonists threw the blame upon England. They said that the mother country entailed the evil upon them, and that they would rid themselves of it if they could. The world thought they were sincere, and the philanthropic pitied them. But time soon tested their sincerity. In a few years, the colonists grew strong and severed themselves from the British Government. Their Independence was declared, and they took their station among the sovereign powers of the earth. The declaration was a glorious document. Sages admired it, and the patriotic of every nation reverenced the Godlike sentiments which it contained. When the power of Government returned to their hands, did they emancipate the slaves? No; they rather added new links to our chains. Were they ignorant of the principles of

Liberty? Certainly they were not. The sentiments of their revolutionary orators fell in burning eloquence upon their hearts, and with one voice they cried, LIBERTY OR DEATH. O, what a sentence was that! It ran from soul to soul like electric fire, and nerved the arm of thousands to fight in the holy cause of Freedom. Among the diversity of opinions that are entertained in regard to physical resistance, there are but a few found to gainsay that stern declaration. We are among those who do not.

SLAVERY! How much misery is comprehended in that single word. What mind is there that does not shrink from its direful effects? Unless the image of God is obliterated from the soul, all men cherish the love of Liberty. The nice discerning political economist does not regard the sacred right, more than the untutored African who roams in the wilds of Congo. Nor has the one more right to the full enjoyment of his freedom than the other. In every man's mind the good seeds of liberty are planted, and he who brings his fellow down so low, as to make him contented with a condition of slavery, commits the highest crime against God and man. Brethren, your oppressors aim to do this. They endeavor to make you as much like brutes as possible. When they have blinded the eyes of your mind—when they have embittered the sweet waters of life—when they have shut out the light which shines from the word of God—then, and not till then has American slavery done its perfect work.

To SUCH DEGRADATION IT IS SINFUL IN THE EXTREME FOR YOU TO MAKE VOLUNTARY SUBMISSION. The divine commandments, you are in duty bound to reverence, and obey. If you do not obey them you will surely meet with the displeasure of the Almighty. He requires you to love him supremely, and your neighbor as yourself—to keep the Sabbath day holy—to search the Scriptures—and bring up your children with respect for his laws, and to worship no other God but him. But slavery sets all these at naught, and hurls defiance in the face of Jehovah. The forlorn condition in which you are placed does not destroy your moral obligation to God. You are not certain of Heaven, because you suffer yourselves to remain in a state of slavery, where you cannot obey the commandments of the Sovereign of the universe. If the ignorance of slavery is a passport to heaven, then it is a blessing, and no curse, and you should rather desire its perpetuity than its abolition. God will not receive slavery, nor ignorance, nor any other state of mind, for love, and obedience to him. Your condition does not absolve you from your moral obligation. The diabolical injustice by which your liberties are cloven down, NEITHER GOD, NOR

ANGELS, OR JUST MEN, COMMAND YOU TO SUFFER FOR A SINGLE MOMENT. THEREFORE IT IS YOUR SOLEMN AND IMPERATIVE DUTY TO USE EVERY MEANS, BOTH MORAL, INTELLECTUAL, AND PHYSICAL, THAT PROMISE SUCCESS. If a band of heathen men should attempt to enslave a race of Christians, and to place their children under the influence of some false religion, surely, heaven would frown upon the men who would not resist such aggression, even to death. If, on the other hand, a band of Christians should attempt to enslave a race of heathen men and to entail slavery upon them, and to keep them in heathenism in the midst of Christianity, the God of heaven would smile upon every effort which the injured might make to disenthral themselves.

Brethren, it is as wrong for your lordly oppressors to keep you in slavery, as it was for the man thief to steal our ancestors from the coast of Africa. You should therefore now use the same manner of resistance, as would have been just in our ancestors, when the bloody foot prints of the first remorseless soul thief was placed upon the shores of our fatherland. The humblest peasant is as free in the sight of God, as the proudest monarch that ever swayed a sceptre. Liberty is a spirit sent out from God, and like its great Author, is no respector of persons.

Brethren, the time has come when you must act for yourselves. It is an old and true saying, that "if hereditary bondmen would be free, they must themselves strike the blow." You can plead your own cause, and do the work of emancipation better than any others. The nations of the old world are moving in the great cause of universal freedom, and some of them at least, will ere long, do you justice. The combined powers of Europe have placed their broad seal of disapprobation upon the African slave trade. But in the slave holding parts of the United States, the trade is as brisk as ever. They buy and sell you as though you were brute beasts. The North has done much—her opinion of slavery in the abstract is known. But in regard to the South, we adopt the opinion of the New York Evangelist—"We have advanced so far, that the cause apparently waits for a more effectual door to be thrown open than has been yet." We are about to point you to that more effectual door. Look around you, and behold the bosoms of your loving wives, heaving with untold agonies! Hear the cries of your poor children! Remember the stripes your fathers bore. Think of the torture and disgrace of your noble mothers. Think of your wretched sisters, loving virtue and purity, as they are driven into concubinage, and are exposed to the unbridled lusts of incarnate devils. Think of the undying glory that hangs around the ancient name of Africa:—and forget not that you are native-born American citizens, and as such, you are justly entitled to all the rights that are granted to the freest. Think how many tears you have poured out upon the soil which you have cultivated with unrequited toil, and enriched with your blood; and then go to your lordly enslavers, and tell them plainly, that YOU ARE DETERMINED TO BE FREE. Appeal to their sense of justice, and tell them that they have no more right to oppress you, than you have to enslave them. Entreat them to remove the grievous burdens which they have imposed upon you, and to remunerate you for your labor. Promise them renewed diligence in the cultivation of the soil, if they will render to you an equivalent for your services. Point them to the increase of happiness and prosperity in the British West Indies, since the act of Emancipation. Tell them in language which they cannot misunderstand, of the exceeding sinfulness of slavery, and of a future judgment, and of the righteous retributions of an indignant God. Inform them that all you desire, is FREEDOM, and that nothing else will suffice. Do this, and for ever after cease to toil for the heartless tyrants, who give you no other reward but stripes and abuse. If they then commence the work of death, they, and not you, will be responsible for the consequences. You had far better all die—*die immediately*, than live slaves, and entail your wretchedness upon your posterity. If you would be free in this generation, here is your only hope. However much you and all of us may desire it, there is not much hope of Redemption without the shedding of blood. If you must bleed, let it all come at once—rather, *die freemen, than live to be slaves*. It is impossible, like the children of Israel, to make a grand Exodus from the land of bondage. THE PHARAOHS ARE ON BOTH SIDES OF THE BLOOD-RED WATERS! You cannot remove en masse, to the dominions of the British Queen—nor can you pass through Florida, and overrun Texas, and at last find peace in Mexico. The propagators of American slavery are spending their blood and treasure, that they may plant the black flag in the heart of Mexico, and riot in the halls of the Montezumas. In the language of the Rev. Robert Hall, when addressing the volunteers of Bristol, who were rushing forth to repel the invasion of Napoleon, who threatened to lay waste the fair homes of England, "Religion is too much interested in your behalf, not to shed over you her most gracious influences."

You will not be compelled to spend much time in order to become inured to hardships. From the first moment that you breathed the air of heaven, you have been accustomed to nothing else but hardships. The heroes of the American Revolution were never put upon harder fare, than a peck of corn, and a few herrings per week. You have not become enervated by the luxuries of life. Your sternest energies have been beaten out upon the anvil of severe trial. Slavery has done this, to make you subservient to its own purposes; but it has done more than this, it has prepared you for any emergency. If you receive good treatment, it is what you could hardly expect; if you meet with pain, sorrow, and even death, these are the common lot of the slaves.

Fellow-men! patient sufferers! behold your dearest rights crushed to the earth! See your sons murdered, and your wives, mothers, and sisters, doomed to prostitution! In the name of the merciful God! and by all that life is worth, let it no longer be a debateable question, whether it is better to choose LIBERTY or DEATH!

In 1822, Denmark Veazie, of South Carolina, formed a plan for the liberation of his fellow men. In the whole history of human efforts to overthrow slavery, a more complicated and tremendous plan was never formed. He was betrayed by the treachery of his own people, and died a martyr to freedom. Many a brave hero fell, but History, faithful to her high trust, will transcribe his name on the same monument with Moses, Hampden, Tell, Bruce, and Wallace, Toussaint L'Ouverture, Lafayette and Washington. That tremendous movement shook the whole empire of slavery. The guilty soul thieves were overwhelmed with fear. It is a matter of fact, that at that time, and in consequence of the threatened revolution, the slave states talked strongly of emancipation. But they blew one blast of the trumpet of freedom, and then laid it aside. As these men became quiet, the slaveholders ceased to talk about emancipation: and now, behold your condition today! Angels sigh over it, and humanity has long since exhausted her tears in weeping on your account!

The patriotic Nathaniel Turner followed Denmark Veazie. He was goaded to desperation by wrong and injustice. By Despotism, his name has been recorded on the list of infamy, but future generations will number him among the noble and brave.

Next arose the immortal Joseph Cinque, the hero of the Amistad. He was a native African, and by the help of God he emancipated a whole ship-load of his fellow men on the high seas. And he now sings of liberty on the sunny hills of Africa, and beneath his native palm trees, where he hears the lion roar, and feels himself as free as that king of the forest. Next arose Madison Washington, that bright star of freedom, and took his station in the constellation of freedom.

He was a slave on board the brig Creole, of Richmond, bound to New
Orleans, that great slave mart, with a hundred and four others. Nineteen struck for liberty or death. But one life was taken, and the whole
were emancipated, and the vessel was carried into Nassau, New Providence. Noble men! Those who have fallen in freedom's conflict,
their memories will be cherished by the true hearted, and the God-
fearing, in all future generations; those who are living, their names
are surrounded by a halo of glory.

We do not advise you to attempt a revolution with the sword,
because it would be INEXPEDIENT. Your numbers are too small, and
moreover the rising spirit of the age, and the spirit of the gospel, are
opposed to war and bloodshed. But from this moment cease to labor
for tyrants who will not remunerate you. Let every slave throughout
the land do this, and the days of slavery are numbered. You cannot
be more oppressed than you have been—you cannot suffer greater
cruelties than you have already. RATHER DIE FREEMEN, THAN LIVE TO
BE SLAVES. Remember that you are THREE MILLIONS.

It is in your power so to torment the God cursed slaveholders,
that they will be glad to let you go free. If the scale was turned and
black men were the masters, and white men the slaves, every destruc-
tive agent and element would be employed to lay the oppressor low.
Danger and death would hang over their heads day and night. Yes, the
tyrants would meet with plagues more terrible than those of Pharaoh.
But you are a patient people. You act as though you were made for
the special use of these devils. You act as though your daughters were
born to pamper the lusts of your masters and overseers. And worse
than all, you tamely submit, while your lords tear your wives from
your embraces, and defile them before your eyes. In the name of
God we ask, are you men? Where is the blood of your fathers? Has
it all run out of your veins? Awake, awake; millions of voices are
calling you! Your dead fathers speak to you from their graves.
Heaven, as with a voice of thunder, calls on you to arise from the
dust.

Let your motto be RESISTANCE! RESISTANCE! RESISTANCE!— No
oppressed people have ever secured their liberty without resistance.
What kind of resistance you had better make, you must decide by the
circumstances that surround you, and according to the suggestion
of expediency. Brethren, adieu. Trust in the living God. Labor for
the peace of the human race, and remember that you are three
millions.

GEORGE HORTON
(c.1800-c.1880)

The third of the slave-poets known to American literature was curiously enough a campus figure. The proximity (and accessibility) of books on the campus of the University of North Caroline at Chapel Hill served to make of George Horton a minor poet, adept at writing poems of dalliance commissioned by amorous undergraduates. He had, however, more serious concerns, his freedom being the major one. This gifted man received his freedom only with the abolition of slavery, in spite of a bizarre effort to raise enough money to buy his freedom by the sale of his verse.

Poems by a Slave (1837), Poetical Works (1845) and the Naked Genius (1865) contain the works of Horton known to us. Of his verse William H. Robinson, Jr., says, in Early Black American Poets: "There is not much thought in most of his work, his best pieces being those that plead for his freedom with a sincerity that is believable, despite the conventionally stilted syntax and the abstract language."

To Eliza

Eliza, tell thy lover why
Or what induced thee to deceive me?
   Fare thee well—away I fly—
I shun the lass who thus will grieve me.

Eliza, still thou art my song,
Although by force I may forsake thee;
   Fare thee well, for I was wrong
To woo thee while another take thee.

Eliza, pause and think awhile—
Sweet lass! I shall forget thee never:
   Fare thee well: although I smile,
I grieve to give thee up forever.

Eliza, I shall think of thee—
My heart I shall ever twine about thee;
   Fare thee well—but think of me,

Compell'd to live and die without thee,
   "Fare thee well!—and if forever,[1]
"Still forever fare thee well!"

The Art of a Poet

True nature first inspires the man,
But he must after learn to scan,
    And mark well every rule;
Gradual the climax then ascend,
And prove the contrast in the end,
    Between the wit and fool.

A fool tho' blind, may write a verse,
And seem from folly to emerge,
    And rime well every line;
One lucky, void of light, may guess
And safely to the point may press,
    But this does not refine.

Polish mirror, clear to shine,
And streams must run if they refine,
    And widen as they flow;
The diamond water lies concealed,
Till polished it is ne'er revealed,
    Its glory bright to show.

A bard must traverse o'er the world,
Where things concealed must rise unfurled,
    And tread the feet of yore;
Tho' he may sweetly harp and sing,
But strictly prune the mental wing,
    Before the mind can soar.

Slavery

When first my bosom glowed with hope,
   I gazed as from a mountain top
     On some delightful plain;
But oh! how transient was the scene—
It fled as though it had not been,
     And all my hopes were vain.

How oft this tantalyzing blaze
     Has led me through deception's maze;
     My friends became my foe—
Then like a plaintive dove I mourned;
To bitter all my sweets were turned,
     And tears began to flow.

Why was the dawning of my birth
Upon this vile, accursed earth,
     Which is but pain to me?
Oh! that my soul had winged its flight,
When I first saw the morning light,
     To worlds of liberty!

Come, melting Pity, from afar,
And break this vast, enormous bar
     Between a wretch and thee;
Purchase a few short days of time,
And bid a vassal rise sublime
     On wings of liberty.

Is it because my skin is black,
That thou should'st be so dull and slack,
   And scorn to set me free?
Then let me hasten to the grave,
The only refuge for the slave,
   Who mourns for liberty.

The wicked cease from troubling there;
No more I'd languish or despair—
   The weary there can rest!
Oppression's voice is heard no more,
Drudg'ry and pain and toil are o'er,
   Yes! there I shall be blest!

WILLIAM WELLS BROWN
(1815-1884)

Like Douglass and Ward a leading antislavery lecturer, William Wells Brown turned to the novel as an extension of his platform activity against slavery. He was born in Lexington, Kentucky, as a slave. From St. Louis, where he was working, he fled to Canada in 1834. While in England on a five-year stay he published the first of four versions of his novel, Clotel; or the President's Daughter *(1853) (later versions published in the United States were* Clotelle: A Tale of the Southern States *[1864] and* Clotelle; or the Colored Heroine *[1867]). Earlier, Brown had written the narrative of his own life in slavery in 1847.*

Brown also wrote and lectured on the history of the black man. He had lectured in Boston on the Revolution in Haiti as early as 1855. Published works included The Black Man *(1863) and* The Negro in the American Rebellion *(1867). In a more personal vein he wrote* The Rising Son *(1874) and* My Southern Home *(1880).*

A comprehensive study of Brown as a pioneer figure in black literature has been written by W. Edward Farrison (1969) and is indispensable for knowing Brown and his period.

From *Clotel, or the President's Daughter*

CHAPTER XIX

ESCAPE OF CLOTEL

"The fetters galled my weary soul—
  A soul that seemed but thrown away:
I spurned the tyrant's base control,
  Resolved at least the man to play.

No country has produced so much heroism in so short a time, connected with escapes from peril and oppression, as has occurred in the United States among the fugitive slaves, many of whom show great shrewdness in their endeavours to escape from this land of bondage. A slave was one day seen passing on the high road from a border town in the interior of the state of Virginia to the Ohio river. The man had neither hat upon his head or coat upon his back. He was driving before him a very nice fat pig, and appeared to all who saw him to be a labourer employed on an adjoining farm. "No negro is permitted to go at large in the Slave States without a written pass from his or her master, except on business in the neighbourhood." "Where do you live, my boy?" asked a white man of the slave, as he passed a white house with green blinds. "Jist up de road, sir," was the answer. "That's a fine pig." "Yes, sir, marser like dis choat berry much." And the negro drove on as if he was in great haste. In this way he and the pig travelled more than fifty miles before they reached the Ohio river. Once at the river they crossed over; the pig was sold; and nine days after the runaway slave passed over the Niagara river, and, for the first time in his life, breathed the air of freedom. A few weeks later, and, on the same road, two slaves were seen passing; one was on horseback, the other was walking before him with his arms tightly bound, and a long rope leading from the man on foot to the one on horseback. "Oh, ho, that's a runaway rascal, I suppose," said a farmer, who met them on the road. "Yes, sir, he bin runaway, and I got him fast. Marser will tan his jacket for him nicely when he gets him." "You are a trustworthy fellow, I imagine," continued the farmer. "Oh yes, sir; marser puts a heap of confidence in this nigger." And the slaves travelled on. When the one on foot was fatigued they would change positions, the other being tied and driven on foot. This they called "ride and tie." After a journey of more than two hundred miles they reached the Ohio river, turned the horse loose, told him to go home, and proceeded on their way to Canada. However they were not to have it all their own way. There are men in the Free States, and especially in the states adjacent to the Slave States, who make their living by catching the runaway slave, and returning him for the reward that may be offered. As the two slaves above mentioned were travelling on towards the land of freedom, led by the North Star, they were set upon by four of these slave-catchers, and one of them unfortunately captured. The other escaped. The captured fugitive was put under the torture, and compelled to reveal the name of his owner and his place of residence. Filled with delight, the kidnappers started back with their victim. Overjoyed with the prospect of receiving a large reward, they gave themselves up on the third night to pleasure. They put up at an inn. The negro was chained to the bed-post, in the same room with his captors. At dead of night, when all was still, the slave arose from the floor upon which he had been lying, looked around, and saw that the white men were fast asleep. The brandy punch had done its work. With palpitating heart and trembling limbs he viewed his position. The door was fast, but the warm weather had compelled them to leave the window open. If he could but get his chains off, he might escape through the window to the piazza, and reach the ground by one of the posts that supported the piazza. The sleeper's clothes hung upon chairs by the bedside; the slave thought of the padlock key, examined the pockets and found it. The chains were soon off, and the negro stealthily making his way to the window: he stopped and said to himself, "These men are villains, they are enemies to all who like me are trying to be free. Then why not I teach them a lesson?" He then undressed himself, took the clothes of one of the men, dressed himself in them, and escaped through the window, and, a moment more, he was on the high road to Canada. Fifteen days later, and the writer of this gave him a passage across Lake Erie, and saw him safe in her Britannic Majesty's dominions.

We have seen Clotel sold to Mr. French in Vicksburgh, her hair cut short, and everything done to make her realise her position as a servant. Then we have seen her re-sold, because her owners feared she would die through grief. As yet her new purchaser treated her with respectful gentleness, and sought to win her favour by flattery and presents, knowing that whatever he gave her he could take back again. But she dreaded every moment lest the scene should change, and trembled at the sound of every footfall. At every interview with her new master Clotel stoutly maintained that she had left a husband in Virginia, and would never think of taking another. The gold watch and chain, and other glittering presents which he purchased for her, were all laid aside by the quadroon, as if they were of no value to her. In the same house with her was another servant, a man, who had from time to time hired himself from his master. William was his name. He could feel for Clotel, for he, like her, had been separated from near and dear relatives, and often tried to console the poor woman. One day the quadroon observed to him that her hair was growing out again. "Yes," replied William, "you look a good deal like a man with your short hair." "Oh," rejoined she, "I have often been told that I would make a better looking man than a woman. If I had the money," continued she, "I would bid farewell to this place." In a moment more she feared that she had said too much, and smilingly remarked, "I am always talking nonsense." William was a tall, full-bodied negro, whose very countenance beamed with intelligence. Being a mechanic, he had, by his own industry, made more than what he paid his owner; this he laid aside, with the hope that some day he might get enough to purchase his freedom. He had in his chest one hundred and fifty dollars. His was a heart that felt for others, and he had again and again wiped the tears from his eyes as he heard the story of Clotel as related by herself. "If she can get free with a little money, why not give her what I have?" thought he, and then he resolved to do it. An hour after, he came into the quadroon's room, and laid the money in her lap, and said, "There, Miss Clotel, you said if you had the means you would leave this place; there is money enough to take you to England, where you will be free. You are much fairer than many of the white women of the South, and can easily

pass for a free white lady." At first Clotel feared that it was a plan
by which the negro wished to try her fidelity to her owner; but she
was soon convinced by his earnest manner, and the deep feeling with
which he spoke, that he was honest. "I will take the money only on
one condition," said she; "and that is, that I effect your escape as well
as my own." "How can that be done?" he inquired. "I will assume the
disguise of a gentleman and you that of a servant, and we will take
passage on a steamboat and go to Cincinnati, and thence to Canada.
Here William put in several objections to the plan. He feared detection, and he well knew that, when a slave is once caught when attempting to escape, if returned is sure to be worse treated than before.
However, Clotel satisfied him that the plan could be carried out if
he would only play his part.

The resolution was taken, the clothes for her disguise procured,
and before night everything was in readiness for their departure. That
night Mr. Cooper, their master, was to attend a party, and this was
their opportunity. William went to the wharf to look out for a boat,
and had scarcely reached the landing ere he heard the puffing of a
steamer. He returned and reported the fact. Clotel had already packed
her trunk, and had only to dress and all was ready. In less than an
hour they were on board the boat. Under the assumed name of "Mr.
Johnson," Clotel went to the clerk's office and took a private state
room for herself, and paid her own and servant's fare. Besides being
attired in a neat suit of black, she had a white silk handkerchief tied
round her chin, as if she was an invalid. A pair of green glasses covered her eyes; and fearing that she would be talked to too much and
thus render her liable to be detected, she assumed to be very ill. On
the other hand, William was playing his part well in the servants' hall;
he was talking loudly of his master's wealth. Nothing appeared as
good on the boat as in his master's fine mansion. "I don't like dees
steamboats no how," said William; "I hope when marser goes on a
journey agin he will take de carriage and de hosses." Mr. Johnson
(for such was the name by which Clotel now went) remained in his
room, to avoid, as far as possible, conversation with others. After a
passage of seven days they arrived at Louisville, and put up at Gough's
Hotel. Here they had to await the departure of another boat for the
North. They were now in their most critical position. They were still
in a slave state, and John C. Calhoun, a distinguished slave-owner, was
a guest at this hotel. They feared, also, that trouble would attend their
attempt to leave this place for the North, as all persons taking negroes
with them have to give bail that such negroes are not runaway slaves.

The law upon this point is very stringent: all steamboats and other public conveyances are liable to a fine for every slave that escapes by them, besides paying the full value for the slave. After a delay of four hours, Mr. Johnson and servant took passage on the steamer Rodolph, for Pittsburgh. It is usual, before the departure of the boats, for an officer to examine every part of the vessel to see that no slave secretes himself on board, "Where are you going?" asked the officer of William, as he was doing his duty on this occasion. "I am going with marser," was the quick reply. "Who is your master?" "Mr. Johnson, sir, a gentleman in the cabin." "You must take him to the office and satisfy that captain that all is right, or you can't go on this boat." William informed his master what the officer had said. The boat was on the eve of going, and no time could be lost, yet they knew not what to do. At last they went to the office, and Mr. Johnson, addressing the captain, said, "I am informed that my boy can't go with me unless I give security that he belongs to me." "Yes," replied the captain, "that is the law." "A very strange law indeed," rejoined Mr. Johnson, "that one can't take his property with him." After a conversation of some minutes, and a plea on the part of Johnson that he did not wish to be delayed owing to his illness, they were permitted to take their passage without farther trouble, and the boat was soon on its way up the river. The fugitives had now passed the Rubicon, and the next place at which they would land would be in a Free State. Clotel called William to her room, and said to him, "We are now free, you can go on your way to Canada, and I shall go to Virginia in search of my daughter." The announcement that she was going to risk her liberty in a Slave State was unwelcome news to William. With all the eloquence he could command, he tried to persuade Clotel that she could not escape detection, and was only throwing her freedom away. But she had counted the cost, and made up her mind for the worst. In return for the money he had furnished, she had secured for him his liberty, and their engagement was at an end.

After a quick passage the fugitives arrived at Cincinnati, and there separated. William proceeded on his way to Canada, and Clotel again resumed her own apparel, and prepared to start in search of her child. As might have been expected, the escape of those two valuable slaves created no little sensation in Vicksburgh. Advertisements and messages were sent in every direction in which the fugitives were thought to have gone. It was soon, however, known that they had left the town as master and servant; and many were the communications which appeared in the newspapers, in which the writers thought, or pretended, that they had seen the slaves in their disguise. One was to the effect that they had gone off in a chaise; one as master, and the other as servant. But the most probable was an account given by a correspondent of one of the Southern newspapers, who happened to be a passenger in the same steamer in which the slaves escaped, and which we here give:—

"One bright starlight night, in the month of December last, I found myself in the cabin of the steamer Rodolph, then lying in the port of Vicksburgh, and bound to Louisville. I had gone early on board, in order to select a good berth, and having got tired of reading the papers, amused myself with watching the appearance of the passengers as they dropped in, one after another, and I being a believer in physiognomy, formed my own opinion of their characters.

"The second bell rang, and as I yawningly returned my watch to my pocket, my attention was attracted by the appearance of a young man who entered the cabin supported by his servant, a strapping negro.

"The man was bundled up in a capacious overcoat; his face was bandaged with a white handkerchief, and its expression entirely hid by a pair of enormous spectacles.

"There was something so mysterious and unusual about the young man as he sat restless in the corner, that curiosity led me to observe him more closely.

"He appeared anxious to avoid notice, and before the steamer had fairly left the wharf, requested, in a low, womanly voice, to be shown his berth, as he was an invalid, and must retire early: his name he gave as Mr. Johnson. His servant was called, and he was put quietly to bed. I paced the deck until Tybee light grew dim in the distance, and then went to my berth.

"I awoke in the morning with the sun shining in my face; we were then just passing St. Helena. It was a mild beautiful morning, and most of the passengers were on deck, enjoying the freshness of the air, and stimulating their appetites for breakfast. Mr. Johnson soon made his appearance, arrayed as on the night before, and took his seat quietly upon the guard of the boat.

"From the better opportunity afforded by daylight, I found that he was a slight built, apparently handsome young man, with black hair and eyes, and of a darkness of complexion that betokened Spanish extraction. Any notice from others seemed painful to him; so to satisfy my curiosity, I questioned his servant, who was standing near, and gained the following information.

"His master was an invalid—he had suffered for a long time under a complication of diseases, that had baffled the skill of the best physicians in Mississippi he was now suffering principally with the 'rheumatism,' and he was scarcely able to walk or help himself in any way. He came from Vicksburgh, and was now on his way to Philadelphia, at which place resided his uncle, a celebrated physician, and through whose means he hoped to be restored to perfect health.

"This information communicated in a bold, off-hand manner, enlisted my sympathies for the sufferer, although it occurred to me that he walked rather too gingerly for a person afflicted with so many ailments."

After thanking Clotel for the great service she had done him in bringing him out of slavery, William bade her farewell. The prejudice that exists in the Free States against coloured persons, on account of their colour, is attributable solely to the influence of slavery, and is but another form of slavery itself. And even the slave who escapes from the Southern plantations, is surprised when he reaches the North, at the amount and withering influence of this prejudice. William applied at the railway station for a ticket for the train going to Sandusky, and was told that if he went by that train he would have to ride in the luggage-van. "Why?" asked the astonished negro. "We don't send a Jim Crow carriage but once a day, and that went this morning." The "Jim Crow" carriage is the one in which the blacks have to ride. Slavery is a school in which its victims learn much shrewdness, and William had been an apt scholar. Without asking any more questions, the negro took his seat in one of the first-class carriages. He was soon seen and ordered out. Afraid to remain in the town longer, he resolved to go by that train; and consequently seated himself on a goods' box in the luggage-van. The train started at its proper time, and all went on well. Just before arriving at the end of the journey, the conductor called on William for his ticket. "I have none," was the reply. "Well, then, you can pay your fare to me," said the officer. "How much is it?" asked the black man. "Two dollars." "What do you charge those in the passenger-carriage?" "Two dollars." "And do you charge me the same as you do those who ride in the best carriages?" asked the negro. "Yes," was the answer. "I shan't pay it," returned the man. "You black scamp, do you think you can ride on this road without paying your fare?" "No, I don't want to ride for nothing; I only want to pay what's right." "Well, launch out two dollars, and that's right." "No, I shan't; I will pay what I ought, and won't pay any more." "Come, come, nigger, your fare and be done with it," said the conductor, in a manner that is never used except by Americans to blacks. "I won't pay you two dollars, and that enough," said William. "Well, as you have come all the way in the luggage-van, pay me a dollar and a half and you may go." "I shan't do any such thing." "Don't you mean to pay for riding?" "Yes, but I won't pay a dollar and a half for riding up here in the freight-van. If you had let me come in the carriage where others ride, I would have paid you two dollars." "Where were you raised? You seem to think yourself as good as white folks." "I want nothing more than my rights." "Well, give me a dollar, and I will let you off." "No, sir, I shan't do it." "What do you mean to do then—don't you wish to pay anything?" "Yes, sir, I want to pay you the full price." "What do you mean by full price?" "What do you charge per hundred-weight for goods?" inquired the negro with a degree of gravity that would have astonished Diogenes himself. "A quarter of a dollar per hundred," answered the conductor. "I weigh just one hundred and fifty pounds," returned William, "and will pay you three eighths of a dollar." "Do you expect that you will pay only thirty-seven cents for your ride?" "This, sir, is your own price. I came in a luggage-van, and I'll pay for luggage." After a vain effort to get the negro to pay more, the conductor took the thirty-seven cents, and noted in his cash-book, "Received for one hundred and fifty pounds of luggage, thirty-seven cents." This, reader, is no fiction; it actually occurred in the railway above described.

Thomas Corwin, a member of the American Congress, is one of the blackest white men in the United States. He was once on his way to Congress, and took passage in one of the Ohio river steamers. As he came just at the dinner hour, he immediately went into the dining saloon, and took his seat at the table. A gentleman with his whole party of five ladies at once left the table. "Where is the captain," cried the man in an angry tone. The captain soon appeared, and it was sometime before he could satisfy the old gent, that Governor Corwin was not a nigger. The newspapers often have notices of mistakes made by innkeepers and others who undertake to accommodate the public, one of which we give below.

On the 6th inst., the Hon. Daniel Webster and family entered Edgartown, on a visit for health and recreation. Arriving at the hotel, without alighting from the coach, the landlord was sent for to see if suitable accommodation could be had. That dignitary apppearing, and surveying Mr. Webster, while the hon. senator addressed him, seemed woefully to mistake the dark features of the traveller as he sat back in the corner of the carriage, and to suppose him a *coloured man*, particularly as there were two coloured servants of Mr. W. outside. So he promptly declared that there was no room for him and his family, and he could not be accommodated there—at the same time suggesting that he might perhaps find accommodation at some of the huts "up back," to which he pointed. So deeply did the prejudice of looks possess him, that he appeared not to notice that the stranger introduced himself to him as Daniel Webster, or to be so ignorant as not to have heard of such a personage; and turning away, he expressed to the driver his astonishment that he should bring *black* people there for *him* to take in. It was not till he had been repeatedly assured and made to understand that the said Daniel Webster was a real live senator of the United States, that he perceived his awkward mistake and the distinguished honour which he and his house were so near missing.

In most of the Free States, the coloured people are disfranchised on account of their colour. The following scene, which we take from a newspaper in the state of Ohio, will give some idea of the extent to which this prejudice is carried.

"The whole of Thursday last was occupied by the Court of Common Pleas for this county in trying to find out whether one Thomas West was of the VOTING COLOUR, as some had very *constitutional doubts* as to whether his colour was orthodox, and whether his hair was of the official crisp! Was it not a dignified business? Four profound judges, four acute lawyers, twelve grave jurors, and I don't know how many venerable witnesses, making in all about thirty men, perhaps, all engaged in the profound, laborious, and illustrious business, of finding out whether a man who pays tax, works on the road, and is an industrious farmer, has been born according to the republican, Christian constitution of Ohio—so that he can vote! And they wisely, gravely, and 'JUDGMATICALLY' decided that he should not vote! What wisdom—what research it must have required to evolve this truth! It was left for the Court of Common Pleas for Columbian county, Ohio, in the United States of North America, to find out what Solomon never dreamed of—the courts of all civilised, heathen, or Jewish countries, never contemplated. Lest the wisdom of our courts should be circumvented by some such men as might be named, who are so near being born constitutionally that they might be taken for white by sight, I would suggest that our court be invested with SMELLING powers, and that if a man don't exhale the constitutional smell, he shall not vote! This would be an additional security to our liberties."

William found, after all, that liberty in the so-called Free States was more a name than a reality; that prejudice followed the coloured man into every place that he might enter. The temples erected for the worship of the living God are no exception. The finest Baptist church in the city of Boston has the following paragraph in the deed that conveys its seats to pewholders:

"And it is a further condition of these presents, that if the owner or owners of said pew shall determine hereafter to sell the same, it shall first be offered, in writing, to the standing committee of said society for the time being, at such price as might otherwise be obtained for it; and the said committee shall have the right, for ten days after such offer, to purchase said pew for said society, at that price, first deducting therefrom all taxes and assessments on said pew then remaining unpaid. And if the said committee shall not so complete such purchase within said ten days, then the pew may be sold by the owner or owners thereof (after payment of all such arrears) to any one respectable *white person*, but upon the same conditions as are contained in this instrument; and immediate notice of such sale shall be given in writing, by the vendor, to the treasurer of said society."

Such are the conditions upon which the Rowe Street Baptist Church, Boston, disposes of its seats. The writer of this is able to put that whole congregation, minister and all, to flight, by merely putting his coloured face in that church. We once visited a church in New York that had a place set apart for the sons of Ham. It was a dark, dismal looking place in one corner of the gallery, grated in front like a hencoop, with a black border around it. It had two doors; over one was B. M.—black men; over the other B. W.—black women.

(1853)

FREDERICK DOUGLASS
(1817-1895)

Douglass, who was born a slave on a plantation in Maryland, is one of the giants of world history. The magnitude of his achievement is frequently overlooked by those who see him only as a great leader of the antislavery movement. A careful reading of his life and a study of his mind as reflected in the vast amount of writing he left will reveal a towering genius. He left three distinct autobiographies, each of which reveals the growth of a mind, and each of which is a triumph of literary art: Narrative of the Life of Frederick Douglass *(1845);* My Bondage and My Freedom *(1855);* Life and Times of Frederick Douglass *(1881-1892).*

As the editor of his own antislavery newspaper from 1847 to 1860, Douglass wrote regularly on a wide range of questions. Contributors to his paper included such other black reformers as Samuel Ward, William Wells Brown, and Martin Delany, as well as aspiring poets and essayists.

The position of Douglass in black esteem at the abolition of slavery was equalled only by that of Lincoln. He continued for three decades to be a central figure in the consciousness of black people. In a sense the leadership role, more symbolic than real, played by Douglass was assumed by Booker T. Washington, whose Atlanta speech was spoken, significantly, in the year of Douglass' death. Douglass, however, would have found the views of the Great Compromiser unacceptable.

Many eminent Afro-Americans have eulogized and written about

Douglass: Chesnutt wrote a biography of Douglass (1899), as did Booker T. Washington (1907) and William Pickens (1912). Students go today to the biography by the noted historian Benjamin Quarles (1948) and to the four-volume collection of Douglass' writings edited by Phillip Foner (1950-1955).

The Right to Criticize American Institutions

Speech before the American Anti-Slavery Society, May 11, 1847

I am very glad to be here. I am very glad to be present at this Anniversary, glad again to mingle my voice with those with whom I have stood identified, with those with whom I have laboured, for the last seven years, for the purpose of undoing the burdens of my brethren, and hastening the day of their emancipation.

I do not doubt but that a large portion of this audience will be disappointed, both by the *manner* and the *matter* of what I shall this day set forth. The extraordinary and unmerited eulogies, which have been showered upon me, here and elsewhere, have done much to create expectations which, I am well aware, I can never hope to gratify. I am here, a simple man, knowing what I have experienced in Slavery, knowing it to be a bad system, and desiring, by all Christian means, to seek its overthrow. I am not here to please you with an eloquent speech, with a refined and logical address, but to speak to you the sober truths of a heart overborne with gratitude to God that we have in this land, cursed as it is with Slavery, so noble a band to second my efforts and the efforts of others, in the noble work of undoing the yoke of bondage, with which the majority of the States of this Union are now unfortunately cursed.

Since the last time I had the pleasure of mingling my voice with the voices of my friends on this platform, many interesting and even trying events have occurred to me. I have experienced, within the last eighteen or twenty months, many incidents, all of which it would be interesting to communicate to you, but many of these I shall be compelled to pass over at this time, and confine my remarks to giving a general outline of the manner and spirit with which I have been hailed abroad, and welcomed at the different places which I have visited during my absence of twenty months.

You are aware, doubtless, that my object in going from this country, was to get beyond the reach of the clutch of the man who claimed to own me as his property. I had written a book, giving a history of that portion of my life spent in the gall and bitterness and degradation of Slavery, and in which, I also identified my oppressors as the perpetrators of some of the most atrocious crimes. This had deeply incensed them against me, and stirred up within them the purpose of revenge, and, my whereabouts being known, I believed it necessary for me, if I would preserve my liberty, to leave the shores of America, and take up my abode in some other land, at least until the clamor had subsided. I went to England, monarchical England, to get rid of Democratic Slavery; and I must confess that at the very threshold I was satisfied that I had gone to the right place. Say what you will of England—of the degradation—of the poverty—and there is much of it there,—say what you will of the oppression and suffering going on in England at this time, there is Liberty there, not only for the white man, but for the black man also. The instant that I stepped upon the shore, and looked into the faces of the crowd around me, I saw in every man a recognition of my manhood, and an absence, a perfect absence, of everything like that disgusting hate with which we are pursued in this country. [Cheers.] I looked around in vain to see in any man's face a token of the slightest aversion to me on account of my complexion. Even the cabmen demeaned themselves to me as they did to other men, and the very dogs and pigs of old England treated me as a man! I cannot, however, my friends, dwell upon this anti-prejudice, or rather the many illustrations of the absence of prejudice against colour in England, but will proceed, at once, to defend the right and duty of invoking English aid and English sympathy for the overthrow of American Slavery, for the education of coloured Americans, and to forward, in every way, the interests of humanity; inasmuch as the right of appealing to England for aid in overthrowing Slavery in this country has been called in question, in public meetings and by the press, in this city.

I cannot agree with my friend Mr. Garrison, in relation to my love and attachment to this land. I have no love for America, as such; I have no patriotism. I have no country. What country have I? The institutions of this country do not know me, do not recognize me as a man. I am not thought of, spoken of, in any direction, out of the anti-slavery ranks, as a man. I am not thought of, or spoken of, except as a piece of property belonging to some *Christian* slave-holder, and all the religious and political institutions of this country, alike pronounce me a slave and a chattel. Now, in such a country as this, I cannot have patriotism. The only thing that links me to this land is my family, and the painful consciousness that here there are three millions of my fellow-creatures, groaning beneath the iron rod of the worst despotism that could be devised, even in Pandemonium; that here are men and brethren, who are identified with me by their complexion, identified with me by their hatred of Slavery, identified with me by their love and aspirations for liberty, identified with me by the stripes upon their backs, their inhuman wrongs and cruel sufferings. This, and this only, attaches me to this land, and brings me here to plead with you, and with this country at large, for the dis-enthralment of my oppressed countrymen, and to overthrow this system of Slavery which is crushing them to the earth. How can I love a country that dooms three millions of my brethren, some of them my own kindred, my own brothers, my own sisters, who are now clanking the chains of Slavery upon the plains of the South, whose warm blood is now making fat the soil of Maryland and of Alabama, and over whose crushed spirits rolls the dark shadow of oppression, shutting out and extinguishing forever, the cheering rays of that bright sun of Liberty lighted in the souls of all God's children by the Omnipotent hand of Deity itself? How can I, I say, love a a country thus cursed, thus bedewed with the blood of my brethren? A country, the Church of which, and the Government of which, and the Constitution of which, is in favour of supporting and perpetuating this monstrous system of injustice and blood? I have not, I cannot have, any love for this country, as such, or for its Constitution. I desire to see its overthrow as speedily as possible, and its Constitution shivered in a thousand fragments, rather than this foul curse should continue to remain as now. [Hisses and Cheers.]

In all this, my friends, let me make myself understood. I do not hate America as against England, or against any other country, or land. I love humanity all over the globe. I am anxious to see right-eousness prevail in all directions. I am anxious to see Slavery over-thrown here; but, I never appealed to Englishmen in a manner calculated to awaken feelings of hatred or disgust, or to influence their prejudices towards America as a nation, or in a manner pro-vocative of national jealousy or ill-will; but I always appealed to their conscience—to the higher and nobler feelings of the people of that country, to enlist them in this cause. I always appealed to their manhood, that which preceded their being Englishmen, (to quote an expression of my friend Phillips,) I appealed to them as men, and I had a right to do so. They are men, and the slave is a man, and we have a right to call upon all men to assist in breaking his bonds, let them be born when, and live where they may.

But it is asked, "What good will this do?" or "What good has it done?" "Have you not irritated, have you not annoyed your American friends, and the American people rather, than done them good?" I admit that we have irritated them. They deserve to be irritated. I am anxious to irritate the American people on this question. As it is in physics, so in morals, there are cases which demand irritation, and counter irritation. The conscience of the American public needs this irritation. And I would *blister it all over, from centre to circumference,* until it gives signs of a purer and better life than it is now manifesting to the world.

But why expose the sins of one nation in the eyes of another? Why attempt to bring one people under the odium of another people? There is much force in this question. I admit that there are sins in almost every country which can be best removed by means confined exclusively to their immediate locality. But such evils and such sins pre-suppose the existence of a moral power in this immediate locality sufficient to accomplish the work of renovation. But where, pray, can we go to find moral power in this nation, sufficient to overthrow Slavery? To what institution, to what party shall we apply for aid? I say, we admit that there are evils which can be best removed by influences confined to their immediate locality. But in regard to American Slavery, it is not so. It is such a giant crime, so darkening to the soul, so blinding in its moral influence, so well calculated to blast and corrupt all the humane principles of our nature, so well adapted to infuse its own accursed spirit into all around it, that the people among whom it exists have not the moral power to abolish it. Shall we go to the Church for this influence? We have heard its character described. Shall we go to politicians or political parties? Have they the moral power necessary to accomplish this mighty task? They have not. What are they doing at this moment? Voting supplies for Slavery—voting supplies for the extension, the stability, the perpetuation of Slavery in this land. What is the Press doing? The same. The pulpit? Almost the same. I do not flatter myself that there is moral power in the land sufficient to overthrow Slavery, and I welcome the aid of England. And that aid will come. The growing intercourse between England and this country, by means of steam-navigation, the relaxation of the protective system in various countries in Europe, gives us an opportunity to bring in the aid, the moral and Christian aid of those living on the other side of the Atlantic. We welcome it, in the language of the resolution. We entreat our British friends to continue to send in their remonstrances across the deep, against Slavery in this land. And these remonstrances will have a powerful effect here. Sir, the Americans may tell of their ability, and I have no doubts they have it, to keep back the invader's hosts, to repulse the strongest force that its enemies may send against this country. It may boast, and it may *rightly* boast, of its capacity to build its ramparts so high that no foe can hope to scale them, to render them so impregnable as to defy the assault of the world. But, Sir, there is one thing it cannot resist, come from what quarter it may. It cannot resist TRUTH. You cannot build your forts so strong, nor your ramparts so high, nor arm yourself so powerfully, as to be able to withstand the overwhelming MORAL SENTIMENT against Slavery now flowing into this land. For example; prejudice against color is continually becoming weaker in this land and more and more consider this sentiment as unworthy a lodgment in the breast of an enlightened community. And the American abroad dare not now, even in a public conveyance, to lift his voice in defence of this disgusting prejudice.

I do not mean to say that there are no practices abroad which deserve to receive an influence favourable to their extermination, from America. I am most glad to know that Democratic freedom—not the bastard democracy, which, while loud in its protestations of regard for liberty and equality, builds up Slavery, and, in the name of Freedom, fights the battles of Despotism—is making great strides in Europe. We see abroad, in England especially, happy indications of the progress of American principles. A little while ago England was cursed by a Corn monopoly—by the giant monopoly, which snatched from the mouths of the famishing poor the bread which you sent them from this land. The community, the *people* of England, demanded its destruction, and they have triumphed. We have aided them, and they aid us, and the mission of the two nations, henceforth, is *to serve each other.*

Sir, it is said that, when abroad, I misrepresented my country on this question. I am not aware of any misrepresentation. I stated facts, and facts only. A gentleman of your own city, Rev. Dr. Cox, has taken particular pains to stigmatize me as having introduced the subject of Slavery illegitimately into the World's Temperance Convention. But what was the fact? I went to that Convention, not as a delegate. I went into it by the invitation of the Committee of the Convention. I suppose most of you know the circumstances, but I wish to say one word in relation to the spirit and the principle which animated me at the meeting. I went into it at the invitation of the Committee, and spoke not only at their urgent request, but by public announcement. I stood on the platform on the evening referred to, and heard some eight or ten Americans address the seven thousand people assembled in that vast Hall. I heard them speak of the temperance movement in this land. I heard them eulogize the temperance societies in the highest terms, calling on England to follow their example; (and England may follow them with advantage to herself;) but I heard no reference made to the 3,000,000 of people in this country who are denied the privileges, not only of temperance, but of all other societies. I heard not a word of the American slaves, who, if seven of them were found together at a temperance meeting, or any other place, would be scourged and beaten by their cruel tyrants. Yes, nine-and-thirty lashes is the penalty required to be inflicted by the law if any of the slaves get together in a number exceeding seven, for any purpose however peaceable or laudable. And while these American gentlemen were extending their hands to me, and saying, "How do you do, Mr. Douglass? I am most happy to meet you here," &c. &c. I knew that, in America, they would not have touched me with a pair of tongs. I felt, therefore, that that was the place and the time to call to remembrance the 3,000,000 of slaves, whom I aspired to represent on that occasion. I did so, not maliciously, but with a desire, only, to subserve the best interests of my race. I besought the American delegates, who had at first responded to my speech with shouts of applause, when they should arrive at home to extend the borders of their temperance societies so as to include the 500,000 coloured people in the Northern States of the Union. I also called to mind the facts in relation to the mob that occurred in the city of Philadelphia, in the year 1842. I stated these facts to show to the British public how difficult it is for a coloured man in this country to do anything to elevate himself or his race from the state of degradation in which they are plunged; how difficult it is for him to be virtuous or temperate, or anything but a menial, an outcast. You all remember the circumstances of the mob to which I have alluded. A number of intelligent, philanthropic, manly coloured men, desirous of snatching their coloured brethren from the fangs of intemperance, formed themselves into a procession, and walked through the streets of Philadelphia with appropriate banners and badges and mottoes. I stated the fact that that procession was not allowed to proceed far, in the city of Philadelphia—the American city of Brotherly Love, the city of all others loudest in its boasts of freedom and liberty—before these noble-minded men were assaulted by the citizens, their banners torn in shreds and themselves trampled in the dust, and inhumanly beaten, and all their bright and fond hopes and anticipations, in behalf of their friends and their race, blasted by the wanton cruelty of their white fellow-citizens. And all this was done for no other reason than that they had presumed to walk through the street with temperance banners and badges, like human beings.

The statement of this fact caused the whole Convention to break forth in one general expression of intense disgust at such atrocious and inhuman conduct. This disturbed the composure of some of our American representatives, who, in serious alarm, caught hold of the skirts of my coat, and attempted to make me desist from my exposition of the situation of the coloured race in this country. There was one Doctor of Divinity there, the ugliest man that I ever saw in my life, who almost tore the skirts of my coat off, so vehement was he in his *friendly* attempts to induce me to yield the floor. But fortunately the audience came to my rescue, and demanded that I should go on, and I did go on, and, I trust, discharged my duty to my brethren in bonds and the cause of human liberty, in a manner not altogether unworthy the occasion.

I have been accused of *dragging* the question of Slavery into the Convention. I had a right to do so: It was the *World's* convention—not the Convention of any sect, or number of sects—not the Convention of any particular nation—not a man's or a woman's Convention, not a black man's nor a white man's Convention, but the *World's* Convention, the Convention of ALL, black as well as *white, bond* as well as *free*. And I stood there, as I thought, a representative of the 3,000,000 of men whom I had left in rags and wretchedness, to be devoured by the accused institution which stands by them, as with a drawn sword, ever ready to fall upon their devoted and defenceless heads. I felt, as I said to Dr. Cox, that it was demanded of me by conscience, to speak out boldly in behalf of those whom I had left behind. [Cheers.] And, Sir, (I think I may say this, without subjecting myself to the charge of egotism,) I deem it very fortunate for the friends of the slave, that Mr. Garrison and myself were there just at that time. Sir, the churches in this country have long repined at the position of the churches in England on the subject of Slavery. They have sought many opportunities to do away the prejudices of the English churches against American Slavery. Why, Sir, at this time there were not far from seventy ministers of the Gospel from Christian America, in England, pouring their leprous pro-slavery distilment into the ears of the people of that country, and by their prayers, their conversation, and their public speeches, seeking to darken the British mind on the subject of Slavery, and to create in the English public the same cruel and heartless apathy that prevails in this country in relation to the slave, his wrongs and his rights. I knew them by their continuous slandering of my race; and at this time, and under these circumstances, I deemed it a happy interposition of God, in behalf of my oppressed and misrepresented and slandered people, that one of their number should burst up through the dark incrustation of malice, and hate, and degradation, which had been thrown over them, and stand before the British public to open to them the secrets of the prison-house of bondage in America. [Cheers.] Sir, the slave sends no delegates to the Evangelical Alliance. [Cheers.] The slave sends no delegates to the World's Temperance Convention. Why? Because chains are upon his arms and fetters fast bind his limbs. He must be driven out to be sold at auction by some *Christian* slaveholder, and the money for which his soul is bartered must be appropriated to spread the Gospel among the heathen.

Sir, I feel that it is good to be here. There is always work to be done. Slavery is everywhere. Slavery goes everywhere. Slavery was in the Evangelical Alliance, looking saintly in the person of the Rev. Dr. Smythe; it was in the World's Temperance Convention in the person of the Rev. Mr. Kirk. Dr. Marsh went about saying, in so many words, that the unfortunate slaveholders in America were so peculiarly situated, so environed by uncontrollable circumstances, that they could not liberate their slaves; that if they were to emancipate them they would be, in many instances, cast into prison. Sir, it did me good to go around on the heels of this gentleman. I was glad to follow him around for the sake of my country, for the country is not, after all, so bad as the Rev. Dr. Marsh represented it to be.

My fellow-countrymen, what think ye he said of you, on the other side of the Atlantic? He said you were not only pro-slavery, but that you actually aided the slaveholder in holding his slaves securely in his grasp; that, in fact, you compelled him to be a slaveholder. This I deny. You are not so bad as that. You do not compel the slaveholder to be a slaveholder.

And Rev. Dr. Cox, too, talked a great deal over there; and among other things he said, "that many slaveholders—dear Christian men!—were sincerely anxious to get rid of their slaves"; and to show how difficult it is for them to get rid of their human chattels, he put the following case: A man living in a State, the laws of which compel all persons emancipating their slaves to remove them beyond its limits, wishes to·liberate his slaves, but he is too poor to transport them beyond the confines of the State in which he resides; therefore he cannot emancipate them—he is necessarily a slaveholder. But, Sir, there was one fact, which I happened, fortunately, to have on hand just at that time, which completely neutralized this very affecting statement of the Doctor's. It so happens that Messrs. Gerrit Smith and Arthur Tappan have advertised for the especial benefit of this afflicted class of slaveholders that they have set apart the sum of $10,000 to be appropriated in aiding them to remove their emancipated slaves beyond the jurisdiction of the State, and that the money would be forthcoming on application being made for it; but *no such application was ever made!* This shows that, however truthful the statements of these gentlemen may be concerning the things of the world to come, they are lamentably reckless in their statements concerning things appertaining to this world. I do not mean to say that they would designedly tell that which is false, but they did make the statements I have ascribed to them.

And Dr. Cox and others charge me with having stirred up warlike feelings while abroad. This charge, also, I deny. The whole of my arguments and the whole of my appeals, while I was abroad, were in favour of anything else than war. I embraced every opportunity to propagate the principles of peace while I was in Great Britain. I confess, honestly, that were I not a peace-man, were I a believer in fighting at all, I should have gone through England, saying to Englishmen, as Englishmen, there are 3,000,000 of men across the Atlantic who are whipped, scourged, robbed of themselves, denied every privilege, denied the right to read the Word of the God who made them, trampled under foot, denied all the rights of humanbeings; go to their rescue; shoulder your muskets, buckle on your knapsacks, and in the invincible cause of Human Rights and Universal Liberty, go forth, and the laurels which you shall win will be as fadeless and as imperishable as the eternal aspirations of the human soul after that freedom which every being made after God's image instinctively feels is his birth-right. This would have been my course had I been a war man. That such was not my course, I appeal to my whole career while abroad to determine.

> *Weapons of war we have cast from the battle;*
>   TRUTH *is our armour, our watch-word is* LOVE;
> *Hushed be the sword, and the musketry's rattle,*
>   *All our equipments are drawn from above.*
>   *Praise then the God of Truth,*
>   *Hoary age and ruddy youth,*
>   *Long may our rally be*
>   *Love, Light and Liberty,*
> *Ever our banner the banner of Peace*

From *My Bondage and My Freedom*

CHAPTER IV.

A GENERAL SURVEY OF THE SLAVE PLANTATION.

It is generally supposed that slavery, in the state of Maryland, exists in its mildest form, and that it is totally divested of those harsh and terrible peculiarities, which mark and characterize the slave system, in the southern and south-western states of the American union. The argument in favor of this opinion, is the contiguity of the free states, and the exposed condition of slavery in Maryland to the moral, religious and humane sentiment of the free states.

I am not about to refute this argument, so far as it relates to slavery in that State, generally; on the contrary, I am willing to admit that, to this general point, the argument is well grounded. Public opinion is, indeed, an unfailing restraint upon the cruelty and barbarity of masters, overseers, and slave-drivers, whenever and wherever it can reach them; but there are certain secluded and out-of-the way places, even in the state of Maryland, seldom visited by a single ray of healthy public sentiment—where slavery, wrapt in its own congenial, midnight darkness, *can*, and *does* develop all its malign and shocking characteristics; where it can be indecent without shame, cruel without shuddering, and murderous without apprehension or fear of exposure.

Just such a secluded, dark, and out-of-the-way place, is the "home plantation" of Col. Edward Lloyd, on the Eastern Shore, Maryland. It is far away from all the great thoroughfares, and is proximate to no town or village. There is neither school-house, nor town-house in its neighborhood. The school-house is unnecessary, for there are no children to go to school. The children and grand-children of Col. Lloyd were taught in the house, by a private tutor—a Mr. Page— a tall, gaunt sapling of a man, who did not speak a dozen words to a slave in a whole year. The overseers' children go off somewhere to school; and they, therefore, bring no foreign or dangerous influence from abroad, to embarrass the natural operation of the slave system of the place. Not even the mechanics—through whom there is an occasional out-burst of honest and telling indignation, at cruelty and wrong on other plantations—are white men, on this plantation. Its whole public is made up of, and divided into, three classes—SLAVE-HOLDERS, SLAVES and OVERSEERS. Its blacksmiths, wheelwrights, shoe-makers, weavers, and coopers, are slaves. Not even commerce, selfish and iron-hearted as it is, and ready, as it ever is, to side with the strong against the weak—the rich against the poor—is trusted or permitted within its secluded precints. Whether with a view of guarding against the escape of its secrets, I know not, but it is a fact, that every leaf and grain of the produce of this plantation, and those of the neighboring farms belonging to Col. Lloyd, are transported to Baltimore in Col. Lloyd's own vessels; every man and boy on board of which—except the captain—are owned by him. In return, everything brought to the plantation, comes through the same channel. Thus, even the glimmering and unsteady light of trade, which sometimes exerts a civilizing influence, is excluded from this "tabooed" spot.

Nearly all the plantations or farms in the vicinity of the "home plantation" of Col. Lloyd, belong to him; and those which do not, are owned by personal friends of his, as deeply interested in maintaining the slave system, in all its rigor, as Col. Lloyd himself. Some of his neighbors are said to be even more stringent than he. The Skinners, the Peakers, the Tilgmans, the Lockermans, and the Gipsons, are in the same boat; being slaveholding neighbors, they may have strengthened each other in their iron rule. They are on intimate terms, and their interests and tastes are identical.

Public opinion in such a quarter, the reader will see, is not likely to be very efficient in protecting the slave from cruelty. On the contrary, it must increase and intensify his wrongs. Public opinion seldom differs very widely from public practice. To be a restraint upon cruelty and vice, public opinion must emanate from a humane and virtuous community. To no such humane and virtuous community, is Col. Lloyd's plantation exposed. That plantation is a little nation of its own, having its own language, its own rules, regulations and customs. The laws and institutions of the state, apparently touch it nowhere. The troubles arising here, are not settled by the civil power of the state. The overseer is generally accuser, judge, jury, advocate and executioner. The criminal is always dumb. The overseer attends to all sides of a case.

There are no conflicting rights of property, for all the people are owned by one man; and they can themselves own no property. Religion and politics are alike excluded. One class of the population is too high to be reached by the preacher; and the other class is too low to be cared for by the preacher. The poor have the gospel preached to them, in this neighborhood only when they are able to pay for it. The slaves, having no money, get no gospel. The politician keeps away, because the people have no votes, and the preacher keeps away, because the people have no money. The rich planter can afford to learn politics in the parlor, and to dispense with religion altogether.

In its isolation, seclusion, and self-reliant independence, Col. Lloyd's plantation resembles what the baronial domains were, during the middle ages in Europe. Grim, cold, and unapproachable by all genial influences from communities without, *there it stands;* full three hundred years behind the age, in all that relates to humanity and morals.

This, however, is not the only view that the place presents. Civilization is shut out, but nature cannot be. Though separated from the rest of the world; though public opinion, as I have said, seldom gets a chance to penetrate its dark domain; though the whole

place is stamped with its own peculiar, iron-like individuality; and
though crimes, high-handed and atrocious, may there be committed,
with almost as much impunity as upon the deck of a pirate ship,—
it is, nevertheless, altogether, to outward seeming, a most strikingly
interesting place, full of life, activity, and spirit; and presents a very
favorable contrast to the indolent monotony and languor of Tuckahoe. Keen as was my regret and great as was my sorrow at leaving the
latter, I was not long in adapting myself to this, my new home. A
man's troubles are always half disposed of, when he finds endurance
his only remedy. I found myself here; there was no getting away;
and what remained for me, but to make the best of it? Here were
plenty of children to play with, and plenty of places of pleasant
resort for boys of my age, and boys older. The little tendrils of
affection, so rudely and treacherously broken from around the darling
objects of my grandmother's hut, gradually began to extend, and to
entwine about the new objects by which I now found myself surrounded.

There was a windmill (always a commanding object to a child's
eye) on Long Point—a tract of land dividing Miles river from the
Wye—a mile or more from my old master's house. There was a
creek to swim in, at the bottom of an open flat space, of twenty
acres or more, called "the Long Green"—a very beautiful playground
for the children.

In the river, a short distance from the shore, lying quietly at
anchor, with her small boat dancing at her stern, was a large sloop—
the Sally Lloyd; called by that name in honor of a favorite daughter
of the colonel. The sloop and the mill were wondrous things, full
of thoughts and ideas. A child cannot well look at such objects without *thinking*.

Then here were a great many houses; human habitations, full of
the mysteries of life at every stage of it. There was the little red
house, up the road, occupied by Mr. Sevier, the overseer. A little
nearer to my old master's stood a very long, rough, low building,
literally alive with slaves, of all ages, conditions and sizes. This was
called "the Long Quarter." Perched upon a hill, across the Long
Green, was a very tall, dilapidated, old brick building—the architec-
tural dimensions of which proclaimed its erection for a different
purpose—now occupied by slaves, in a similar manner to the Long
Quarter. Besides these, there were numerous other slave houses and
huts, scattered around in the neighborhood, every nook and corner
of which was completely occupied. Old master's house, a long, brick

building, plain, but substantial, stood in the center of the plantation life, and constituted one independent establishment on the premises of Col. Lloyd.

Besides these dwellings, there were barns, stables, store-houses, and tobacco-houses; blacksmiths' shops, wheelwrights' shops, coopers' shops—all objects of interest; but, above all, there stood the grandest building my eyes had then ever beheld, called by everyone on the plantation, the "Great House." This was occupied by Col. Lloyd and his family. They occupied it; *I* enjoyed it. The great house was surrounded by numerous and variously shaped out-buildings. There were kitchens, wash-houses, dairies, summer-houses, green-houses, hen-houses, turkey-houses, pigeon-houses, and arbors, of many sizes and devices, all neatly painted, and altogether interspered with grand old trees, ornamental and primitive, which afforded delightful shade in summer, and imparted to the scene a high degree of stately beauty. The great house itself was a large, white, wooden building, with wings on three sides of it. In front, a large portico, extending the entire length of the building, and supported by a long range of columns, gave to the whole establishment an air of solemn grandeur. It was a treat to my young and gradually opening mind, to behold this elaborate exhibition of wealth, power, and vanity. The carriage entrance to the house was a large gate, more than a quarter of a mile distant from it; the intermediate space was a beautiful lawn, very neatly trimmed, and watched with the greatest care. It was dotted thickly over with delightful trees, shrubbery, and flowers. The road, or lane, from the gate to the great house, was richly paved with white pebbles from the beach, and, in its course, formed a complete circle around the beautiful lawn. Carriages going in and retiring from the great house, made the circuit of the lawn, and their passengers were permitted to behold a scene of almost Eden-like beauty. Outside this select inclosure, were parks, where—as about the residences of the English nobility—rabbits, deer, and other wild game, might be seen, peering and playing about, with none to molest them or make them afraid. The tops of the stately poplars were often covered with the red-winged black-birds, making all nature vocal with the joyous life and beauty of their wild, warbling notes. These all belonged to me, as well as to Col. Edward Lloyd, and for a time I greatly enjoyed them.

A short distance from the great house, were the stately mansions of the dead, a place of somber aspect. Vast tombs, embowered beneath the weeping willow and the fir tree, told of the antiquities of the Lloyd family, as well as of their wealth. Superstition was rife among the slaves about this family burying ground. Strange sights had been seen there by some of the older slaves. Shrouded ghosts, riding on great black horses, had been seen to enter; balls of fire had been seen to fly there at midnight, and horrid sounds had been repeatedly heard. Slaves know enough of the rudiments of theology to believe that those go to hell who die slaveholders; and they often fancy such persons wishing themselves back again, to wield the lash. Tales of sights and sounds, strange and terrible, connected with the huge black tombs, were a very great security to the grounds about them, for few of the slaves felt like approaching them even in the day time. It was a dark, gloomy and forbidding place, and it was difficult to feel that the spirits of the sleeping dust there deposited, reigned with the blest in the realms of eternal peace.

The business of twenty or thirty farms was transacted at this, called, by way of eminence, "great house farm." These farms all belonged to Col. Lloyd, as did, also, the slaves upon them. Each farm was under the management of an overseer. As I have said of the overseer of the home plantation, so I may say of the overseers on the smaller ones; they stand between the slave and all civil constitutions—their word is law, and is implicitly obeyed.

The colonel, at this time, was reputed to be, and he apparently was, very rich. His slaves, alone, were an immense fortune. These small and great, could not have been fewer than one thousand in number, and though scarcely a month passed without the sale of one or more lots to the Georgia traders, there was no apparent diminution in the number of his human stock: the home plantation merely groaned at a removal of the young increase, or human crop, then proceeded as lively as ever. Horse-shoeing, cart-mending, plow-repairing, coopering, grinding, and weaving, for all the neighboring farms, were performed here, and slaves were employed in all these branches. "Uncle Tony" was the blacksmith; "Uncle Harry" was the cartwright; "Uncle Abel" was the shoemaker, and all these had hands to assist them in their several departments.

These mechanics were called "uncles" by all the younger slaves, not because they really sustained that relationship to any, but according to plantation *etiquette*, as a mark of respect, due from the younger to the older slaves. Strange, and even ridiculous as it may seem, among a people so uncultivated, and with so many stern trials to look in the face, there is not to be found, among any people, a more rigid enforcement of the law of respect to elders, than they maintain. I set this down as partly constitutional with my race, and partly conventional. There is no better material in the world for making a gentleman, than is furnished in the African. He shows to others, and exacts for himself, all the tokens of respect which he is compelled to manifest toward his master. A young slave must approach the company of the older with hat in hand, and woe betide him, if he fails to acknowledge a favor, of any sort, with the accustomed *"tank'ee,"* &c. So uniformly are good manners enforced among slaves, that I can easily detect a "bogus" fugitive by his manners.

Among other slave notabilities of the plantation, was one called by everybody Uncle Isaac Copper. It is seldom that a slave gets a surname from anybody in Maryland; and so completely has the south shaped the manners of the north, in this respect, that even abolitionists make very little of the surname of a negro. The only improvement on the "Bills," "Jacks," "Jims," and "Neds" of the south, observable here is, that "William," "John," "James," "Edward," are substituted. It goes against the grain to treat and address a negro precisely as they would treat and address a white man. But, once in a while, in slavery as in the free states, by some extraordinary circumstance, the negro has a surname fastened to him, and holds it against all conventionalities. This was the case with Uncle Isaac Copper. When the "uncle" was dropped, he generally had the prefix "doctor," in its stead. He was our doctor of medicine, and doctor of divinity as well. Where he took his degree I am unable to say, for he was not very communicative to inferiors, and I was emphatically such, being but a boy seven or eight years old. He was too well established in his profession to permit questions as to his native skill, or his attainments. One qualification he undoubtedly had—he was a confirmed *cripple;* and he could neither work, nor would he bring anything if offered for sale in the market. The old man, though lame, was no sluggard. He was a man that made his crutches do him good service. He was always on the alert, looking up the sick, and all such as were supposed to need his counsel. His remedial prescriptions embraced four articles. For diseases of the body, *Epsom salts* and *castor oil;* for those of the soul, *the Lord's Prayer,* and *hickory switches!*

I was not long at Col. Lloyd's before I was placed under the care of Doctor Isaac Copper. I was sent to him with twenty or thirty other children, to learn the "Lord's Prayer." I found the old gentleman seated on a huge three-legged oaken stool, armed with several large hickory switches; and, from his position, he could reach—lame as he was—any boy in the room. After standing awhile to learn what was expected of us, the old gentleman, in any other than a devotional tone, commanded us to kneel down. This done, he commenced telling us to say everything he said. "Our Father"—this we repeated after him with promptness and uniformity; "Who art in heaven"—was less promptly and uniformly repeated; and the old gentleman paused in the prayer, to give us a short lecture upon the consequences of inattention, both immediate and future, and especially those more immediate. About these he was absolutely certain, for he held in his right hand the means of bringing all his predictions and warnings to pass. On he proceeded with the prayer; and we with our thick tongues and unskilled ears, followed him to the best of our ability. This, however, was not sufficient to please the old gentleman. Everybody, in the south, wants the privilege of whipping somebody else. Uncle Isaac shared the common passion of his country, and, therefore, seldom found any means of keeping his disciples in order short of flogging. "Say everything I say;" and bang would come the switch on some poor boy's undevotional head. *"What you looking at there"*—*"Stop that pushing"*—and down again would come the lash.

The whip is all in all. It is supposed to secure obedience to the slaveholder, and is held as a sovereign remedy among the slaves themselves, for every form of disobedience, temporal or spiritual. Slaves, as well as slaveholders, use it with an unsparing hand. Our devotions at Uncle Isaac's combined too much of the tragic and comic, to make them very salutary in a spiritual point of view; and it is due to truth to say, I was often a truant when the time for attending the praying and flogging of Doctor Isaac Copper came on.

The windmill under the care of Mr. Kinney, a kind hearted old Englishman, was to me a source of infinite interest and pleasure. The old man always seemed pleased when he saw a troop of darkey little urchins, with their tow-linen shirts fluttering in the breeze, approaching to view and admire the whirling wings of his wondrous machine. From the mill we could see other objects of deep interest. These were, the vessels from St. Michael's, on their way to Baltimore. It was a source of much amusement to view the flowing sails and complicated rigging, as the little crafts dashed by, and to speculate upon Baltimore, as to the kind and quality of the place. With so many sources of interest around me, the reader may be prepared to learn that I began to think very highly of Col. L.'s plantation. It was just a place to my boyish taste. There were fish to be caught in the creek, if one only had a hook and line; and crabs, clams and oysters were to be caught by wading, digging and raking for them. Here was a field for industry and enterprise, strongly inviting; and the reader may be assured that I entered upon it with spirit.

Even the much dreaded old master, whose merciless fiat had brought me from Tuckahoe, gradually, to my mind, parted with his terrors. Strange enough, his reverence seemed to take no particular notice of me, nor of my coming. Instead of leaping out and devouring me, he scarcely seemed conscious of my presence. The fact is, he was occupied with matters more weighty and important than either looking after or vexing me. He probably thought as little of my advent, as he would have thought of the addition of a single pig to his stock!

As the chief butler on Col. Lloyd's plantation, his duties were numerous and perplexing. In almost all important matters he answered in Col. Lloyd's stead. The overseers of all the farms were in some sort under him, and received the law from his mouth. The colonel himself seldom addressed an overseer, or allowed an overseer to address him. Old master carried the keys to all the store houses; measured out the allowance for each slave at the end of every month; superintended the storing of all goods brought to the plantation; dealt out the raw material to all the handicraftsmen; shipped the grain, tobacco, and all saleable produce of the plantation to market, and had the general oversight of the coopers' shop, wheelwrights' shop, blacksmiths' shop, and shoemakers' shop. Besides the care of these, he often had business for the plantation which required him to be absent two and three days.

Thus largely employed, he had little time, and perhaps as little disposition, to interfere with the children individually. What he was to Col. Lloyd, he made Aunt Katy to him. When he had anything to say or do about us, it was said or done in a wholesale manner; disposing of us in classes or sizes, leaving all minor details to Aunt Katy, a person of whom the reader has already received no very favorable impression. Aunt Katy was a woman who never allowed herself to act greatly within the margin of power granted to her, no matter how broad that authority might be. Ambitious, ill-tempered and cruel, she found in her present position an ample field for the exercise of her ill-omened qualities. She had a strong hold on old master—she was considered a first rate cook, and she really was very industrious. She was, therefore, greatly favored by old master, and as one mark of his favor, she was the only mother who was permitted to retain her children around her. Even to these children she was often fiendish in her brutality. She pursued her son Phil, one day, in my presence, with a huge butcher knife, and dealt a blow with its edge which left a shocking gash on his arm, near the wrist. For this, old master did sharply rebuke her, and threatened that if she ever should do the like again, he would take the skin off her back. Cruel, however, as Aunt Katy was to her own children, at times she was not destitute of maternal feling, as I often had occasion to know, in the bitter pinches of hunger I had to endure. Differing from the practice of Col. Lloyd, old master, instead of allowing so much for each slave, committed the allowance for all to the care of Aunt Katy, to be divided after cooking it, amongst us. The allowance, consisting of coarse corn-meal, was not very abundant—indeed, it was very slender; and in passing through Aunt Katy's hands, it was made more slender still, for some of us. William, Phil and Jerry were her children, and it is not to accuse her too severely, to allege that she was often guilty of starving myself and the other children, while she was literally cramming her own. Want of food was my chief trouble the first summer at my old master's. Oysters and clams would do very well, with an occasional supply of bread, but they soon failed in the absence of bread. I speak but the simple truth, when I say, I have often been so pinched with hunger, that I have fought with the dog—"Old Nep"—for the smallest crumbs that fell from the kitchen table, and have been glad when I won a single crumb in the combat. Many times have I followed, with eager step, the waiting-girl when she went out to shake the table cloth, to get the crumbs and small bones flung out for the cats. The water, in which meat had been boiled, was as eagerly sought for by me. It was a great thing to get the privilege of dipping a piece of bread in such water; and the skin taken from rusty bacon, was a positive luxury. Nevertheless, I sometimes got full meals and kind words from sympathizing old slaves, who knew my sufferings, and received the comforting assurance that I should be a man some day. "Never mind, honey—better day comin'," was even then a solace, a cheering consolation to me in my troubles. Nor were all the kind words I received from slaves. I had a friend in the parlor, as well, and one to whom I shall be glad to do justice, before I have finished this part of my story.

I was not long at old master's, before I learned that his surname was Anthony, and that he was generally called "Captain Anthony"— a title which he probably acquired by sailing a craft in the Chesapeake Bay. Col. Lloyd's slaves never called Capt. Anthony "old master," but always Capt. Anthony; and *me* they called "Captain Anthony Fed." There is not, probably, in the whole south, a plantation where the English language is more imperfectly spoken than on Col. Lloyd's. It is a mixture of Guinea and everything else you please. At the time of which I am now writing, there were slaves there who had been brought from the coast of Africa. They never used the "*s*" in indication of the possessive case. "Cap'n Ant'ney Tom," "Lloyd Bill," "Aunt Rose Harry," means "Captain Anthony's Tom," "Lloyd's Bill," &c. "*Oo you dem long to?*" means, "Whom do you belong to?" "*Oo dem got any peachy?*" means, "Have you got any peaches?" I could scarcely understand them when I first went among them, so broken was their speech; and I am persuaded that I could not have been dropped anywhere on the globe, where I could reap less, in the way of knowledge, from my immediate associates, than on this plantation. Even "Mas' Daniel," by his association with his father's slaves, had measurably adopted their dialect and their ideas, so far as they had ideas to be adopted. The equality of nature is strongly asserted in childhood, and childhood requires children for associates. *Color* makes no difference with a child. Are you a child with wants, tastes and pursuits common to children, not put on, but natural? then, were you black as ebony you would be welcome to the child of alabaster whiteness. The law of compensation holds here, as well as elsewhere. Mas' Daniel could not associate with ignorance without sharing its shade; and he could not give his black playmates his company, without giving them his intelligence, as well. Without knowing this, or caring about it, at the time, I, for some cause or other, spent much of my time with Mas' Daniel, in preference to spending it with most of the other boys.

Mas' Daniel was the youngest son of Col. Lloyd; his older brothers were Edward and Murray—both grown up, and fine looking men. Edward was especially esteemed by the children, and by me among the rest; not that he ever said anything to us or for us, which could be called especially kind; it was enough for us, that he never looked nor acted scornfully toward us. There were also three sisters, all married; one to Edward Winder; a second to Edward Nicholson; a third to Mr. Lownes.

The family of old master consisted of two sons, Andrew and Richard; his daughter, Lucretia, and her newly married husband, Capt. Auld. This was the house family. The kitchen family consisted of Aunt Katy, Aunt Esther, and ten or a dozen children, most of them older than myself. Capt. Anthony was not considered a rich slaveholder, but was pretty well off in the world. He owned about thirty "*head*" of slaves, and three farms in Tuckahoe. The most valuable part of his property was his slaves, of whom he could afford to sell one every year. This crop, therefore, brought him seven or eight hundred dollars a year, besides his yearly salary, and other revenue from his farms.

The idea of rank and station was rigidly maintained on Col. Lloyd's plantation. Our family never visited the great house, and the Lloyds never came to our home. Equal non-intercourse was observed between Capt. Anthony's family and that of Mr. Sevier, the overseer.

Such, kind reader, was the community, and such the place, in which my earliest and most lasting impressions of slavery, and of slave-life, were received; of which impressions you will learn more in the coming chapters of this book.

(1855)

Nemesis

At last our proud Republic is overtaken. Our National Sin has found us out. The National Head is bowed down, and our face is mantled with shame and confusion. No foreign arm is made bare for our chastisement. No distant monarch, offended at our freedom and prosperity, has plotted our destruction; no envious tyrant has prepared for our necks his oppressive yoke. Slavery has done it all. Our enemies are those of our own household. It is civil war, the worst of all wars, that has unveiled its savage and wrinkled front amongst us. During the last twenty years and more, we have as a nation been forging a bolt for our own national destruction, collecting and augmenting the fuel that now threatens to wrap the nation in its malignant and furious flames. We have sown the wind, only to reap the whirlwind. Against argument, against all manner of appeal and remonstrances coming up from the warm and merciful heart of humanity, we have gone on like the oppressors of Egypt, hardening our hearts and increasing the burdens of the American slave, and strengthening the arm of his guilty master, till now, in the pride of his giant power, that master is emboldened to lift rebellious arms against the very majesty of the law, and defy the power of the Government itself. In vain have we plunged our souls into new and unfathomed depths of sin, to conciliate the favor and secure the loyalty of the slaveholding class. We have hated and persecuted the Negro; we have scourged him out of the temple of justice by the Dred Scott decision; we have shot and hanged his friends at Harper's Ferry; we have enacted laws for his further degradation, and even to expel him from the borders of some of our States; we have joined in the infernal chase to hunt him down like a beast, and fling him into the hell of slavery; we have repealed and trampled upon laws designed to prevent the spread of slavery, and in a thousand ways given our strength, our moral and political influence to increase the power and ascendency of slavery over all departments of Government; and now, as our reward, this slaveholding power comes with sword, gun and cannon to take the life of the nation and overthrow the great American Government. Verily, they have their reward. The power given to crush the Negro now overwhelms the white man. The Republic has put one end of the chain upon the ankle of the bondman, and the other end about its own neck. They have been planting tyrants, and are now getting a harvest of civil war and anarchy. The land is now to weep and howl, amid ten thousand desolations brought upon it by the sins of two centuries against millions on both sides of eternity. Could we write as with lightning, and speak as with the voice of thunder, we should write and cry to the nation, *Repent, Break Every Yoke, let the Oppressed Go Free for Herein alone is deliverance and safety!* It is not too late. The moment is propitious, and we may even yet escape the complete vengeance of the threatened wrath and fury, whose balls of fire are already dropping to consume us. Now is the time to put an end to the source of all our present national calamities. Now is the time to change the cry of vengeance long sent up from the tasked and toiling bondman, into a grateful prayer for the peace and safety of the Government. Slaveholders have in their madness invited armed abolition to march to the deliverance of the slave. They have furnished the occasion, and bound up the fate of the Republic and that of the slave in the same bundle, and the one and the other must survive or perish together. Any attempt now to separate the freedom of the slave from the victory of the Government over slaveholding rebels and traitors; any attempt to secure peace to the whites while leaving the blacks in chains; any attempt to heal the wounds of the Republic, while the deadly virus of slavery is left to poison the blood, will be labor lost. The American people and the Government at Washington may refuse to recognize it for a time; but the "inexorable logic of events" will force it upon them in the end; that the war now being waged in this land is a war for and against slavery; and that it can never be effectually put down till one or the other of these vital forces is completely destroyed. The irrepressible conflict, long confined to words and votes, is now to be carried by bayonets and bullets, and may God defend the right!

(1861)

Woman Suffrage Movement

The simplest truths often meet the sternest resistance, and are slowest in getting general acceptance. There are none so blind as those who will not see, is an old proverb. Usage and prejudice, like forts built of sand, often defy the power of shot and shell, and play havoc with their besiegers. No simpler proposition, no truth more self-evident or more native to the human soul, was ever presented to human reason or consciousness than was that which formed our late anti-slavery movement. It only affirmed that every man is, and of right ought to be, the owner of his own body; and that no man can rightfully claim another man as his property. And yet what a tempest and whirlwind of human wrath, what clouds of ethical and theological dust, this simple proposition created. Families, churches, societies, parties, and States were riven by it, and at last the sword was called in to decide the questions which it raised. What was true of this simple truth was also true as to the people's right to a voice in their own

Government, and the right of each man to form for himself his own religious opinions. All Europe ran blood before humanity and reason won this sacred right from priestcraft, bigotry, and superstition. What to-day seems simple, obvious, and undeniable, men looking through old customs, usages, and prejudices in other days denied altogether. Our friends of the woman's suffrage movement should bear this fact in mind, and share the patience of truth while they advocate the truth. It is painful to encounter stupidity as well as malice; but such is the fate of all who attempt to reform an abuse, to urge on humanity to nobler heights, and illumine the world with a new truth.

Now we know of no truth more easily made appreciable to human thought than the right of the woman to vote, or, in other words, to have a voice in the Government under which she lives and to which she owes allegiance. The very admission that woman owes allegiance, implies her right to vote. No man or woman who is not consulted can contract an obligation, or have an obligation created for him or her as the case may be. We can owe nothing by the mere act of another. Woman is not a censenting party to this Government. She has never been consulted. Ours is a Government of men, by men, each agreeing with all and all agreeing with each in respect to certain fundamental propositions, and women are wholly excluded. So far as respects its relation to woman, our Government is in its essence, a simple usurpation, a Government of force, and not of reason. We legislate for woman, and protect her, precisely as we legislate for and protect animals, asking the consent of neither.

It is nothing against this conclusion that our legislation has for the most part been eminently just and humane. A despotism is no less a despotism because the reigning despot may be a wise and good man. The principle is unaffected by the character of the man who for the moment may represent it. He may be kind or cruel, benevolent or selfish, in any case he rules according to his own sovereign will—and precisely such is the theoretical relation of our American Government toward woman. It simply takes her money without asking her consent and spends the same without in any wise consulting her wishes. It tells her that there is a code of laws which men have made, and which she must obey or she must suffer the consequences. She is absolutely in the hands of her political masters: and though these may be kind and tender hearted, (the same was true of individual slave masters, as before stated,) this in nowise mitigates the harshness of the principle— and it is against this principle we understand the woman's suffrage movement to be directed. It is intended to claim for woman a place by the side of man, not to rule over him, not to antagonize him, but to rule with him, as an equal subject to the solemn requirements of reason and law.

To ourselves the great truth underlying this woman's movement is just as simple, obvious, and indisputable as either of the great truths referred to at the beginning of this article. It is a part of the same system of truths. Its sources are individuality, rationality, and sense of accountability.

If woman is admitted to be a moral and intellectual being, possessing a sense of good and evil, and a power of choice between them, her case is already half gained. Our natural powers are the foundation of our natural rights; and it is a consciousness of powers which suggests the exercise of rights. Man can only exercise the powers he possesses, and he can only conceive of rights in presence of powers. The fact that woman has the power to say "I choose *this* rather than *that*" is all-sufficient proof that there is no natural reason against the exercise of that power. The power that makes her a moral and an accountable being gives her a natural right to choose the legislators who are to frame the laws under which she is to live, and the requirements of which she is bound to obey. By every fact and by every argument which man can wield in defence of his natural right to participate in government, the right of woman so to participate is equally defended and rendered unassailable.

Thus far all is clear and entirely consistent. Woman's natural abilities and possibilities, not less than man's, constitute the measure of her rights in all directions and relations, including her right to participate in shaping the policy and controlling the action of the Government under which she lives, and to which she is assumed to owe obedience. Unless it can be shown that woman is morally, physically, and intellectually incapable of performing the act of voting, there can be no natural prohibition of such action on her part. Usage, custom, and deeply rooted prejudices are against woman's freedom. They have been against man's freedom, national freedom, religious freedom, but these will all subside in the case of woman as well as elsewhere. The thought has already been conceived; the word has been spoken; the debate has begun; earnest men and women are choosing sides. Error may be safely tolerated while truth is left free to combat it, and nobody need fear the result. The truth can hurt nothing which ought not to be hurt, and it alone can make men and women free.

(1870)

SAMUEL WARD

(1817-1864)

*Samuel Ward, whose parents, escaping from slavery, brought
him as a child of three to New York state, became a leading figure of
the antislavery circuit. Forced to leave New York because of his defiance of the fugitive slave laws, he went to Canada in 1851. From
there he contributed to Frederick Douglass' North Star and wrote
the Autobiography of A Fugitive Slave (1855), which exhibits his
literary powers.*

*Ward was held in high esteem in the antislavery movement, be-
cause of both his courage and his eloquence. His relative isolation in
Canada after 1851 from the direct currents of the struggle undoubtedly diminished the contribution he would have made.*

From *Autobiography of a Fugitive Negro*

CHAPTER I

FAMILY HISTORY

I was born on the 17th October, 1817, in that part of the State of Maryland, U.S., commonly called the Eastern Shore. I regret that I can give no accurate account of the precise location of my birthplace. I may as well state now the reason of my ignorance of this matter. My parents were slaves. I was born a slave. They escaped, and took their then only child with them. I was not then old enough to know anything about my native place; and as I grew up, in the State of New Jersey, where my parents lived till I was nine years old, and in the State of New York subsequently, where we lived for many years, my parents were always in danger of being arrested and re-enslaved. To avoid this, they took every possible caution: among their measures of caution was the keeping of the children quite ignorant of their birthplace, and of their condition, whether free or slave, when born; because children might, by the dropping of a single word, lead to the betrayal of their parents. My brother, however, was born in New Jersey; and my parents, supposing (as is the general presumption) that to be born in a free State is to be born free, readily allowed us to tell where my brother was born; but *my* birthplace I was neither permitted to tell nor to know. Hence, while the secrecy and mystery thrown about the matter led me, most naturally, to suspect that I was born a slave, I never received direct evidence of it, from either of my parents, until I was four-and-twenty years of age; and then my mother informed my wife, in my absence. Generous reader, will you therefore kindly forgive my inability to say exactly where I was born; what gentle stream arose near the humble cottage where I first breathed—how that stream sparkled in the sunlight, as it meandered through green meadows and forests of stately oaks, till it gave its increased self as a contribution to the Chesapeake Bay—if I do not tell you the name of my native town and county, and some interesting details of their geographical, agricultural, geological, and revolutionary history—if I am silent as to just how many miles I was born from Baltimore the metropolis, or Annapolis the capital, of my native State? Fain would I satisfy you in all this; but I cannot, from sheer ignorance. I was born a slave—where? Wherever it was, it was where I dare not be seen or known, lest those who held my parents and ancestors in slavery should make a claim, hereditary or legal, in some form, to the ownership of my body and soul.

My father, from what I can gather, was descended from an African prince. I ask no particular attention to this, as it comes to me simply from tradition—such tradition as poor slaves may maintain. Like the sources of the Nile, my ancestry, I am free to admit, is rather difficult of tracing. My father was a pure-blooded Negro, perfectly black, with wooly hair; but, as is frequently true of the purest Negroes, of small, handsome features. He was about 5 feet 10 inches in height, of good figure, cheerful disposition, bland manners, slow in deciding, firm when once decided, generous and unselfish to a fault; and one of the most consistent, simple-hearted, straightforward Christians, I ever knew. What I have grouped together here concerning him you would see in your first acquaintance with him, and you would see the same throughout his entire life. Had he been educated, free, and admitted to the social privileges in early life for which nature fitted him, and for which even slavery could not, did not, altogether *unfit* him, my poor crushed, outraged people would never have had nor needed a better representation of themselves—a better specimen of the black gentleman. Yes: among the heaviest of my maledictions against slavery is that which it deserves for keeping my poor father— and many like him—in the midnight and dungeon of the grossest ignorance. Cowardly system as it is, it does not dare to allow the slave access to the commonest sources of light and learning.

After his escape, my father learned to read, so that he could enjoy the priceless privilege of searching the Scriptures. Supporting himself by his trade as a house painter, or whatever else offered (as he was a man of untiring industry), he lived in Cumberland County, New

Jersey, from 1820 until 1826; in New York city from that year until 1838; and in the city of Newark, New Jersey, from 1838 until May 1851, when he died, at the age of 68.

In April I was summoned to his bedside, where I found him the victim of paralysis. After spending some few days with him, and leaving him very much better, I went to Pennsylvania on business, and returned in about ten days, when he appeared still very comfortable; I then, for a few days, left him. My mother and I knew that another attack was to be feared—another, we knew too well, would prove fatal; but when it would occur was of course beyond our knowledge; but we hoped for the best. My father and I talked very freely of his death. He had always maintained that a Christian ought to have his preparation for his departure made, and completed in Christ, before death, so as when death should come he should have nothing to do BUT TO DIE. "That," said my father, "is enough to do at once: let repenting, believing, everything else, be sought at a proper time; let dying alone be done at the dying time." In my last conversation with him he not only maintained, but he *felt*, the same. Then, he seemed as if he might live a twelve-month; but eight-and-forty hours from that time, as I sat in the Rev. A. G. Beeman's pulpit, in New Haven, after the opening services, while singing the hymn which immediately preceded the sermon, a telegraphic despatch was handed me, announcing my father's death. I begged Mr. Beeman to preach; his own feelings were such, that he could not, and I was obliged to make the effort. No effort ever cost me so much. Have I trespassed upon your time too much by these details? Forgive the fondness of the filial, the bereaved, the fatherless.

My mother was a widow at the time of her marriage with my father, and was ten years his senior. I know little or nothing of her early life: I think she was not a mother by her first marriage. To my father she bore three children, all boys, of whom I am the second. Tradition is my only authority for my maternal ancestry: that authority saith, that on the paternal side my mother descended from Africa. Her mother, however, was a woman of light complexion; her grandmother, a mulattress; her great-grandmother, the daughter of an Irishman, named Martin, one of the largest slaveholders in Maryland— a man whose slaves were so numerous, that he did not know the number of them. My mother was of dark complexion, but straight silklike hair; she was a person of large frame, as tall as my father, of quick discernment, ready decision, great firmness, strong will, ardent temperament, and of deep, devoted, religious character. Though a woman, she was not of so pleasing a countenance as my father, and I am thought strongly to resemble her. Like my father, she was converted in early life, and was a member of the Methodist denomination (though a lover of all Christian denominations) until her death. This event, one of the most afflictive of my life, occurred on the first day of September, 1853, at New York. Since my father's demise I had not seen her for nearly a year; when, being about to sail for England, at the risk of being apprehended by the United States' authorities for a breach of their execrable republican Fugitive Slave Law, I sought my mother, found her, and told her I was about to sail at three p.m., that day (April 20th, 1853), for England. With a calmness and composure which she could always command when emergencies required it, she simply said, in a quiet tone, "To England, my son!" embraced me, commended me to God, and suffered me to depart without a murmur. It was our last meeting. May it be our last parting! For the kind sympathy shown me, upon my reception of the melancholy news of my mother's decease, by many English friends, I shall ever be grateful: the recollection of that event, and the kindness of which it was the occasion, will dwell together in my heart while reason and memory shall endure.

In the midst of that peculiarly bereaved feeling inseparable from realizing the thought that one is both fatherless and motherless, it was a sort of melancholy satisfaction to know that my dear parents were gone beyond the reach of slavery and the Fugitive Law. Endangered as their liberty always was, in the *free* Northern States of New York and New Jersey—doubly so after the law of 1851—I could but feel a great deal of anxiety concerning them. I knew that there was no living claimant of my parents' bodies and souls; I knew, too, that neither of them would tamely submit to re-enslavement: but I also knew that it was quite possible there should be creditors, or heirs at law; and that there is no State in the American Union wherein there were not free and independent democratic republicans, and *soi-disant* Christians, "ready, aye ready" to aid in overpowering and capturing a runaway, *for pay*. But when God was pleased to take my father in 1851, and my mother in 1853, I felt relief from my greatest earthly anxiety. Slavery had denied them education, property, caste, rights, liberty; but it could not deny them the application of Christ's blood, nor an admittance to the rest prepared for the righteous. They could not be buried in the same part of a common graveyard, with whites, in their native country; but they can rise at the sound of the first trump, in the day of resurrection. Yes, reader: we who are slaveborn derive a comfort and solace from the death of those dearest to us, if they have the sad misfortune to be BLACKS and AMERICANS, that you know not. God forbid that you or yours should ever have occasion to know it!

My eldest brother died before my birth: my youngest brother, Isaiah Harper Ward, was born April 5th, 1822, in Cumberland County, New Jersey; and died at New York, April 16th, 1838, in the triumphs of faith. He was a lad partaking largely of my father's qualities, resembling him exceedingly. Being the youngest of the family, we all sought to fit him for usefulness, and to shield him from the thousand snares and the ten thousand forms of cruelty and injustice which the unspeakably cruel prejudice of the whites visits upon the head and the heart of every black young man, in New York. To that end, we secured to him the advantages of the Free School, for coloured youth, in that city—advantages which, I am happy to say, were neither lost upon him nor unappreciated by him. Upon leaving school he commenced learning the trade of a printer, in the office of Mr. Henry R. Piercy, of New York—a gentleman who, braving the prejudices of his craft and of the community, took the lad upon the same terms as those upon which he took white lads: a fact all the more creditable to Mr. Piercy, as it was in the very teeth of the abominably debased public sentiment of that city (and of the whole country, in fact) on this subject. But ere Isaiah had finished his trade, he suddenly took a severe cold, which resulted in pneumonia, and—in death.

I expressed a doubt, in a preceding page, as to the legal validity of my brother's freedom. True, he was born in the nominally Free State of New Jersey; true, the inhabitants born in Free States are *generally* free. But according to slave law, "the child follows the condition of the mother, during life." My mother being born of a slave woman, and not being legally freed, those who had a legal claim to her had also a legal claim to her offspring, wherever born, of whatever paternity. Besides, at that time New Jersey had not entirely ceased to be a Slave State. Had my mother been legally freed before his birth, then my brother would have been born free, because born of a free woman. As it was, we were all liable at any time to be captured, enslaved, and re-enslaved—first, because we had been robbed of our liberty; then, because our ancestors had been robbed in like manner; and, thirdly and conclusively, in law, because we were black Americans.

I confess I never felt any personal fear of being retaken—

primarily because, as I said before, I knew of no legal claimants; but chiefly because I knew it would be extremely difficult to identify me. I was less than three years old when brought away: to identify me as a man would be no easy matter. Certainly, slaveholders and their more wicked Northern parasites are not very particularly scrupulous about such matters; but still, I never had much fear. My private opinion is, that he who would have enslaved me would have "caught a Tartar": for my peace principles never extended so far as to *either seek or accept peace at the expense of liberty*—if, indeed, a state of slavery can by any possibility be a state of peace.

I beg to conclude this chapter on my family history by adding, that my father had a cousin, in New Jersey, who had escaped from slavery. In the spring of 1826 he was cutting down a tree, which accidentally fell upon him, breaking both thighs. While suffering from this accident his master came and took him back into Maryland. He continued *lame* a very great while, without any *apparent* signs of amendment, until one fine morning he was gone! They never took him again.

Two of my father's nephews, who had escaped to New York, were taken back in the most summary manner, in 1828. I never saw a family thrown into such deep distress by the death of any two of its members, as were our family by the re-enslavement of these two young men. Seven-and-twenty years have past, but we have none of us heard a word concerning them, since their consignment to the living death, the temporal hell, of American slavery.

Some kind persons who may read these pages will accuse me of bitterness towards Americans generally, and slaveholders particularly: indeed, there are many *professional* abolitionists, on both sides of the Atlantic, who have no idea that a black man should feel towards and speak of his tormenters as a white man would concerning his. But suppose the blacks had treated *your* family in the manner the Americans have treated *mine*, for five generations: how would you write about these blacks, and their system of bondage? You would agree with me, that the 109th Psalm, from the 5th to the 21st verses inclusive, was written almost purposely for them.

(1855)

FRANCES HARPER

(1825-1911)

Born free in Baltimore, Maryland, Frances Ellen Watkins Harper was a lifelong reformer. Active in the antislavery movement until emancipation, she then devoted most of her attention to the temperance crusade. As a poet she was widely celebrated, taking her models from the reform poetry of both England and New England. Her poems are those of an eloquent platform reader and may be expected to have been far more impressive in her delivery than in cold print. Particularly would this be true of such poems as are presented here, which treat the theme of the moral degradation of slavery. Poems on Miscellaneous Subjects *(1854) was frequently reprinted and reached a wide public.*

Mrs. Harper also attempted fiction about both biblical and current themes. Examples of the first genre are Moses: A Story of the Nile *(1869) and* Idylls of the Bible *(1901). The second is illustrated by her novel* Iola Leroy, or Shadows Uplifted *(1892), which is probably modelled on Brown's* Clotel, *with its tragic mulatto theme, though Mrs. Harper manages to contrive a happy ending. A full-length study of this remarkable woman is long overdue.*

The Slave Auction

The sale began—young girls were there,
    Defenceless in their wretchedness,
Whose stifled sobs of deep despair
    Revealed their anguish and distress.

And mothers stood with streaming eyes,
    And saw their dearest children sold;
Unheeded rose their bitter cries,
    While tyrants bartered them for gold.

And woman, with her love and truth—
    For these in sable forms may dwell—
Gazed on the husband of her youth,
    With anguish none may paint or tell.

And men, whose sole crime was their hue,
    The impress of their Maker's hand,
And frail and shrieking children, too,
    Were gathered in that mournful band.

Ye who have laid your love to rest,
    And wept above their lifeless clay,
Know not the anguish of that heart,
    Whose loved are rudely torn away.

Ye may not know how desolate
    Are husbands rudely forced to part,
And how a dull and heavy weight
    Will press the life-drops from the heart.

The Slave Mother

Heard you that shriek? It rose
  So wildly in the air,
It seemed as if a burdened heart
Was breaking in despair.

Saw you those hands so sadly clasped—
  The bowed and feeble head—
The shuddering of that fragile form—
  That look of grief and dread?

She is a mother, pale with fear,
  Her boy clings to her side,
And in her kirtle vainly tries
  His trembling form to hide.

He is not hers, although she bore
  For him a mother's pains;
He is not hers, although her blood
  Is coursing through his veins!

He is not hers, for cruel hands
  May rudely tear apart
The only wreath of household love
  That binds her breaking heart.

Bury Me in a Free Land

Make me a grave where'er you will,
In a lowly plain, or a lofty hill;
Make it among earth's humblest graves,
But not in a land where men are slaves.

I could not rest if around my grave
I heard the steps of a trembling slave;
His shadow above my silent tomb
Would make it a place of fearful gloom.

I could not rest if I heard the tread
Of a coffle gang to the shambles led,
And the mother's shriek of wild despair
Rise like a curse on the trembling air.

I could not sleep if I saw the lash
Drinking her blood at each fearful gash,
And I saw her babes torn from her breast,
Like trembling doves torn from their parent nest.

I'd shudder and start if I heard the bay
Of bloodhounds seizing their human prey,
And I heard the captive plead in vain
As they bound afresh his galling chain.

If I saw young girls from their mothers' arms
Bartered and sold for their youthful charms,
My eye would flash with a mournful flame,
My death-paled cheek grow red with shame.

I would sleep, dear friends, where bloated might
Can rob no man of his dearest right;
My rest shall be calm in any grave
Where none can call his brother a slave.

I ask no monument, proud and high,
To arrest the gaze of the passers-by;
All that my yearning spirit craves,
Is bury me not in a land of slaves.

SPIRITUALS

When the text of a spiritual is isolated and treated as a work of purely verbal art, considerable violence is done to its nature, far more so than when a ballad is so treated. In the spiritual, which is a lyric form, the musical elements merge completely with the verbal elements to create a whole that is on a plane different from that of lyric poetry in the usual sense of the term. Nevertheless the spiritual represents a kind of poetry of the people in several ways: It grows out of the experience of slavery shared by millions of black people in the American South; it was transmitted through several generations by the people, or more specifically by those among them with the gifts essential for such transmission. Exact and detailed information on the spiritual is no more available than for most other forms of popular art. Most speculations on the origin and development of the spirituals are merely that and are, in addition, often demonstrably inadmissible.

The spiritual is only one type of "slave song." Consequently, not every antebellum mention of the singing of the slaves necessarily refers to the spiritual. It may indeed be supposed that relatively few whites had occasion to hear the spirituals during their period of active creation, for they seem closely allied in mood and spirit to the prayer services conducted by the slaves for their personal consolation in remote and inaccessible places. The spirituals entered documentary history during the Civil War, when they were heard and commented upon by white commanders of black troops such as Thomas Wentworth Higginson and General Armstrong, later of Hampton Institute. But it was the Civil War which brought to an end the actual conditions which created and nurtured the spiritual. The tradition of singing spirituals in prayer services, of course, continued and may be considered to be yet alive, and an occasional new creation probably took place, but the Civil War marks the terminal point for the main corpus of the spiritual. The secularization of the spiritual by musically sophisticated groups such as the Fisk Jubilee Singers has no direct relation to the consideration of the spiritual as poetry of the people.

Musically the spiritual belongs to that vast matrix of song sprung from African roots and nurtured on American soil. Febrile attempts in the past to derive the spiritual from purely European sources have been made by persons fundamentally ignorant of African music and conveniently oblivious of the fact that the spiritual contains many elements inexplicable in European terms. The procedures of canto-metrics, developed through the researches of Alan Lomax and his associates, demonstrate unquestionably the Africanity of the spiritual. Textually, of course, we have to do with works in English; however, the imagery and syntax in these texts frequently defy the mentality and linguistic drift of the English language.

The group of texts presented here to represent the spiritual demonstrate recurrent themes: oppression, suffering, escape from adversity. The predominance of these themes has led some, including DuBois, to refer to them as sorrow songs, a designation that is misleading, since many spirituals deal with triumph and joy. When the spirituals allude to events, these are overwhelmingly taken from the Old Testament history of the Jews, a history illustrative of oppression and divine chastisement. The songs are less indebted to the New Testament, though it should not be surprising that the Crucifixion is often treated and is the subject of one of the noblest spirituals. Water is indeed the master symbol of the spiritual texts: It signifies cleansing, coolness, release from earthly care. The Christian rite of baptism is closely connected to this symbol, but West African lustration rites and river deities are probably also to be taken into account, as Herskovits has implied.

There are no definitive works on the spirituals from either the musical or textual point of view. For the general reader the essay by Locke reproduced in this anthology will be of great interest. The two collections of music and texts made by James Weldon and J. Rosamond Johnson will interest those with some musical training. A treatment of the texts such as that of Miles Mark Fisher, which finds the spirituals a kind of secret antislavery code, is subject to all the disabilities of a unitary theory, but read critically it throws light on some of the texts it treats. Howard Thurman provides a very different approach with no claim to historical explanation in The Negro Spiritual Speaks of Life and Death.

Sometimes I Feel Like a Motherless Child

Sometimes I feel like a motherless child,
Sometimes I feel like a motherless child,
Sometimes I feel like a motherless child,
A long ways from home;
A long ways from home.

True believer,
A long ways from home,
A long ways from home.

Sometimes I feel like I'm almos' gone,
Sometimes I feel like I'm almos' gone,
Sometimes I feel like I'm almos' gone;
Way up in de heab'nly lan'
Way up in de heab'nly lan'

True believer,
Way up in de heab'nly lan'
Way up in de heab'nly lan'

Sometimes I feel like a motherless child,
Sometimes I feel like a motherless child,
Sometimes I feel like a motherless child,
A long ways from home.

Go Down Moses

Go down, Moses
'Way down in Egypt land,
Tell ole—Pharaoh
To let my people go.

Go down, Moses
'Way down in Egypt land,
Tell ole—Pharaoh,
To let my people go.

When Israel was in Egypt land:
Let my people go,
Oppressed so hard they could not stand,
Let my people go.

Go down, Moses
'Way down in Egypt land,
Tell ole—Pharaoh,
To let my people go.

When spoke the Lord, bold Moses said:
Let my people go
If not I'll smite your first born dead,
Let my people go.

Go down, Moses
'Way down in Egypt land,
Tell ole—Pharaoh,
To let my people go.

Joshua Fit De Battle of Jericho

Joshua fit de battle ob
Jericho, Jericho, Jericho,
Joshua fit de battle ob Jericho,
An' de walls come tumblin' down.

You may talk about yo' king ob Gideon,
You may talk about yo' man ob Saul,
Dere's none like good ole Joshua
At de battle ob Jericho,

Up to de walls ob Jericho.
He marched with spear in han'
"Go blow dem ram horns"
Joshua a cried,
"Kase de battle am in my han."

Den de lam' ram sheep horns begin to blow,
Trumpets begin to soun'
Joshua commanded chillen to shout,
An' de walls come tumblin' down.

Dat mornin' Joshua fit de battle ob Jericho,
Jericho, Jericho,
Joshua fit de battle ob Jericho,
An' de walls come tumblin' down.

Steal Away to Jesus

Steal away,
Steal away,
Steal away to Jesus!

Steal away,
Steal away home,
I ain't got long to stay here.

Steal away,
Steal away,
Steal away to Jesus!

Steal away,
Steal away home,
I ain't got long to stay here.

My Lord, He calls me,
He calls me by the thunder,
The trumpet sounds within a my soul,
I ain't got long to stay here.

Roll, Jordan, Roll

Roll Jordan, roll,
Roll Jordan, roll,
I want to go to heav'n when I die,
To hear ol' Jordan roll.

O, brethren,
Roll Jordan roll,
Roll Jordan roll,
Wanter go to heav'n when I die,
To hear ol' Jordan roll.

Oh, brothers you oughter been dere,
Yes, my Lord
A sittin' up in de kingdom,
To hear ol' Jordan roll.

Sing it ovah,
Oh, roll.
O, Roll Jordan, roll,
Roll Jordan, roll,
I wanter go to heav'n when I die,
To hear ol' Jordan roll.

Crucifixion

They crucified my Lord,
An' He never said a mumbalin' word;
They crucified my Lord,
An' He never said a mumbalin' word,
Not a word, not a word, not a word.

They nailed him to the tree,
An' He never said a mumbalin' word;
They nailed him to the tree,
An' He never said a mumbalin' word.
Not a word, not a word, not a word.

They pierced him in the side,
An' He never said a mumbalin' word,
They pierced Him in the side,
An' He never said a mumbalin' word.
Not a word, not a word, not a word.

The blood came twinklin' down,
An' He never said a mumbalin' word;
The blood came twinklin' down,
An' He never said a mumbalin' word.
Not a word, not a word, not a word.

He bow'd His head an' died,
An' He never said a mumbalin' word,
He bow'd his head an' died,
An' He never said a mumbalin' word;
Not a word, not a word, not a word.

Part II

The Civil War
to World War I

The post-Civil War period in American culture has been aptly named the Gilded Age. Beneath a façade of gentility, Victorian morality, and burgeoning wealth was the dark reality of racism, robber barons, and violence. America's lofty ideals masked the pursuit of wealth and the indifference to humanity. The rich became richer as government gave monopolies full sway; the poor remained poor as social welfare was left to the conscience of the rich. Darwin had proposed the theory of the survival of the fittest; in nineteenth-century America, the fit were unquestionably the rich. Industry boomed, electricity came to the cities, the East and West coasts were linked by the Union Pacific Railroad and eventually the Panama Canal. Meanwhile, America limited immigration for Orientals, and the plight of the poor and the nonwhite continued to worsen as conditions on farm and in factory deteriorated.

American literature reflected the increasing vapidity of the culture. By the last decade of the nineteenth century all the great romantics were dead or silent. In their wake came writers of sentiment and cynicism: The Horatio Alger books, with their theme of rags-to-riches, portrayed the sagacious hero who, through cunning and good fortune, achieves success, that is, wealth. On a more artistic level, Mark Twain was writing cynical books about the evil in mankind; Henry James, Edith Wharton and later William Dean Howells were writing fiction picturing the narrow experience of the affluent. At the end of the century genteel realism merged into the naturalism of Jack London, Stephen Crane, Theodore Dreiser, and Upton Sinclair. In poetry there was the sequestered lyricism of the recluse, Emily Dickinson. A great deal of the literature of the era consisted of sentimental, moralistic preachments, signifying nothing—except perhaps the philosophical emptiness of a materialistic age.

For black Americans, these years were a time of toil and trouble, disillusion and despair. The bright hopes of freedom were soon dimmed by unspeakable conditions which the government not only permitted but often sanctioned. A succession of laws established strict segregation in nearly all areas of life, the Ku Klux Klan began its reign of terror, and the ballot was wrested from the eager hands of the new citizens. Lynchings and race riots occurred with monotonous frequency. The black American was left disfranchised, uneducated, and impoverished.

Meanwhile, black intellectuals struggled to work out a viable philosophy of survival in a hostile land and to implement this philosophy with practical measures. In retrospect, the period seems full of furious activity. Schools for blacks were founded, virtually all with the financial backing of white philanthropists. Fisk University, the Atlanta colleges, Howard University, and many others opened during these years. Black periodicals became the forum for the presentation of varying ideas about what direction to take: T. Thomas Fortune's *New York Age*, William Monroe Trotter's *Boston Guardian*, John H. Murphy's *Afro-American*, the *Washington Bee*, and others. Groups were formed to reach specific goals—Alexander Crummell's American Negro Academy, Booker T. Washington's National Business League, and, later, Carter G. Woodson's Association for the Study of Negro Life and History. Pressure groups were formed and became effective weapons in the struggle for civil rights—for example, T. Thomas Fortune's Afro-American Council and W. E. B. Du Bois' Niagara Movement, which prefigured the NAACP.

The quest for the way to full citizenship was led by the two outstanding figures of the period, Booker T. Washington and W. E. B. Du Bois, who advocated two different methods for reaching the same goal. Booker T. Washington himself was the personification of the Horatio Alger hero. He expressed great faith in middle-class values and based much of his philosophy on these values. An incredibly energetic man with a great deal of practical sagacity, he had clawed his way up from slavery to a pinnacle of power. Washington exercised tremendous control over black thought by manipulating people of influence: He controlled several newspapers and had decision-making power in government and private black-oriented activities. In his public pronouncements he advocated a policy of conciliation and gradualism as the means of obtaining civil rights. He felt that the black man must become educated for voting before he could reasonably demand the vote, must become economically self-sufficient, and must be "morally" acceptable in order to deserve full citizenship. Washington emphasized industrial education for black people at the expense of higher learning: A black youngster studying French while living in poverty was, to him, the height of the absurd.

Du Bois, whose genius always kept him ahead of his time, took a far more militant stand. In fiery editorials and scholarly essays he exposed the brutality of white America and demanded redress. He insisted that the ballot was the means of obtaining economic and educational advance, not vice versa. He stressed the importance of higher education to black youth, especially to the Talented Tenth, that intellectual elite of exceptional people whom he envisioned as the future leaders of the black movement. Whereas Washington saw salvation through material success (an idea perfectly consistent with the ethic of his time), Du Bois saw salvation through intelligent and educated men and women and through forthright demands for immediate civil rights.

The scholars, journalists, and religious leaders of the time argued on one side or the other, sometimes changed sides, or were equivocal. Editor T. Thomas Fortune changed from Du Bois' ideology to that of Washington; James Weldon Johnson changed from Washington to Du Bois; editor William Monroe Taylor remained firmly anti-Washington; Kelly Miller remained at a point midway between the two camps. For nearly twenty years the debate delineated the poles of black thought and formed the backbone of many progressive moves. For a while Washington's ideology dominated. In time, however, the Du Bois views prevailed. By the time of Washington's death in 1915, his influence had diminished considerably.

The literature of the period reflected the peculiarities of the culture. The times were more conducive to mental probing than to artistic creativity. There were few educated blacks to write or to read, few with sufficient respite from toil to become conscious artists, The educated individuals who did write were often plagued by the dilemmas which arose from having to work in an essentially white literary world. As a result, the body of imaginative literature of the age was not only thin, but pale.

By far the major form of literature was the essay. Historical, social, and personal essays, as well as speeches and editorials, record the thoughts of intellectual men seeking solutions to the so-called Negro Problem.

Scholars looked to the past with great interest. Immediately after the Civil War, William Wells Brown reported the black man's part in the conflict in *The Negro in the American Rebellion* (1867). Five years later, William Still published a valuable collection, *The Underground Rail Road: A Record of Facts, Authentic Narratives, Letters* (1872). Other useful historical essays on the war are contained in Joseph T. Wilson's *The Black Phalanx* (1888) and in George Washington Williams' *A History of the Negro Troops in the War of Rebellion* (1888). Additional histories which recorded the progress of the black American are *The Remarkable Achievement of the Afro-American* (1902), by J. W. Gibson and William F. Crogman, and *Fifty Years of Emancipation* (1913), by William Pickens. By far the most distinguished study was W. E. B. Du Bois' *The Suppression of the African Slave Trade to the United States* (1896). This work remains a landmark of scholarship in this area.

More numerous than historical studies were the essays that attempted to analyze the current situation and, often, to offer at least a partial solution. For the most part, though not entirely, these essays took stands in the conciliation versus militancy debate begun by the Washington-Du Bois controversy: The essay which started the controversy was Washington's speech at the Atlanta exposition in 1895, For the next twenty years Washington was reiterating the ideas of that address in other speeches, in articles, and in books like *Working with the Hands* (1904), *Putting the Most into Life* (1906), and *The Man Farthest Down* (1912).

W. E. B. Du Bois' response to Washington is contained in his collection of essays, *The Souls of Black Folk* (1903). This book is the most distinguished work published during the period. In lyrical prose and logical, lucid exposition, Du Bois examines the history, analyzes the present, and enunciates the goals of black people. The book had a profound effect on the intellectuals of his and of later generations; it is still being avidly read. Du Bois' aggressive demand for immediate remediation of wrongs continued in his editorials in the magazine of the NAACP, *The Crisis*, of which he was founder and editor.

Among other prominent thinkers who contributed to the discussion of the "problem" were T. Thomas Fortune, who published *Black and White: Land, Labor, and Politics in the South* (1884) and *The Negro in Politics* (1885), and Alexander Crummell, scholar and influential religious leader, who wrote *The Race Problem in America* (1889), *Incidents of Hope for the Negro Race in America* (1895) and *Civilization: The Primal Need of the Race* (1898).

All of these writers published individual essays and articles in periodicals. One of the most interesting was Kelly Miller's reply to Thomas Dixon's *The Leopard's Spots*. William Pickens wrote a number of sociological articles in leading magazines. The passionate anti-Washington editorials of William Monroe Trotter still make fascinating reading. Washington, Du Bois, and others contributed essays to a collection called *The Negro Problem* (1903). Washington and Du Bois collaborated on *The Negro in the South: His Economic Progress in Relation to His Moral and Religious Development* (1907).

Essays appeared that were not essentially political. The most important of these was Benjamin Brawley's *The Negro in Literature and Art in the United States* (1910). Brawley's careful scholarship gives the book lasting value. An earlier work significant to later generations was Irvine G. Penn's *The Afro-American Press and Its Editors* (1891).

Biography and autobiography, useful before the war as antislavery argument, now became a means of focusing on prominent blacks as a way to prove to black as well as to white readers that blacks really were not "like that." Many interesting works resulted. Elizabeth Keckley, who had worked for Mrs. Abraham Lincoln, published *Behind the Scenes; or, Thirty Years in the White House* (1868). This autobiography is still considered an excellent source of information about Lincoln and his family. Another interesting but less historically accurate work is William Wells Brown's *The Rising Son; or the Antecedents and Advancement of the Colored Race* (1874), which is generally considered autobiography, although it is written in the third person. Other autobiographical works were Henry Ossian Flipper's *The Colored Cadet at West Point* (1878), Bishop Daniel A. Payne's *Recollections of Seventy Years* (1899), John Mercer Langston's *From the Virginia Plantation to the National Capitol* (1894), and William Pickens' *The Heir of Slaves* (1910). By far the most popular autobiography of the time was Booker T. Washington's *Up from Slavery*, first serialized in *Outlook* magazine, and published in book form in 1901. William J. Simmons wrote a significant collective biography, *Men of Mark: Eminent, Progressive and Rising* (1887). Frederick Douglass was the subject of Booker T. Washington's *The Life of Frederick Douglass* (1907) and Williams Pickens' *Frederick Douglass and the Spirit of Freedom* (1912). Pickens published another biography, *Abraham Lincoln, Man and Statesman* (1909). Other white benefactors were the subjects of two biographies by Archibald H. Grimké, one of the intellectual leaders of the period: *William Lloyd Garrison* (1891) and *The Life of Charles Sumner* (1891). Perhaps the most scholarly study was Du Bois' *Life of John Brown* (1909),

There is little poetry or fiction of outstanding artistic value, although what exists provides interesting insights on the black psyche of the period.

The white public's degrading image of black people, superimposed on America's Victorian mediocrity, hovered over the imaginative literature. So dark was its shadow that the writer had few choices if he wanted to publish his work. Some writers combatted the stereotype by creating counterstereotypes. In their poetry and fiction one-dimensional characters muddle their way through hackneyed situations, speaking in stilted, rhetorical diction. Other writers reinforced the white public's stereotyped image, and in their works simple child-like Negroes dance, make love, and weep, talking all the while in plantation dialect. Some authors responded to the stereotype by ignoring the issue entirely and writing sentimental, moralistic works for the uplift of their readers, Of course, the limitations of all these works are obvious: there was very little rendering of the reality of black life, or any life at all, since the characters were generally pasteboard people caught up in unlikely situations.

Some poets, however, achieved a measure of success in their medium. Frances E. W. Harper, who had been a popular poet and lecturer before the war, published several volumes in the later years of the century—*Moses; A Story of the Nile* (1869), *Sketches of Southern Life* (1873), and several new editions of her collected poems. Albery A. Whitman, a minister who had been born a slave, published a long poem, "Not a Man Yet a Man" (1877), revised the next year as *Twasinta's Seminoles: or the Rape of Florida*. In 1901 he published *The Octoroon, An Idyl of the South*. Whitman was one of the scholarly poets later called "mockingbird" poets because their work resembled those of earlier poets in form and technique. Both Whitman and Mrs. Harper were passionate writers with a genuine devotion to poetry. In a different age, they might have excelled.

The star of the age in poetry was, of course, Paul Laurence

Dunbar. Equipped with a talent for writing lyrics, Dunbar followed in the wake of the white Southern local colorists who were so popular at the time. Although he wrote commemorative verses and romantic lyrics in standard English, his dialect poems were the ones that made him famous. Dunbar was an oddity to the white public. In any event, he became the first professional Negro poet, and published many volumes which went through many editions. Though his characters were more sympathetically portrayed than those of sentimentalized white apologists for the plantation system, the dialect poems yielded a sentimental image of black life.

James Edwin Campbell, who published *Echoes from the Cabin and Elsewhere* (1905), wrote in Gullah dialect. Other dialect poets were James David Carruthers and Daniel Webster Davis. Poems in dialect went over well as social recitations, but their range of possibilities was narrow. James Weldon Johnson later stated in the introduction to *God's Trombones* (1927) that dialect poetry was "limited to two stops: pathos and humor."

William Stanley Braithwaite chose a different way to react to the pressures of the white public. He largely ignored the question of race and urged other writers to free themselves from the shackles of racial themes. He himself wrote delicate lyrics on a number of subjects. Braithwaite became a recognized critic and anthologist of American literature. *Lyrics of Love and Life* (1905) and *The House of Falling Leaves* (1908) contain his own poems.

Always the exception to the current trend, W. E. B. Du Bois was writing a different kind of poetry from most others. In periodicals he was publishing individual poems on various aspects of black experience, especially those aspects involving the black man's reaction to oppression. Poems like "The Song of the Smoke" insisted on the strength and beauty of blackness in a manner which anticipated the emphasis on black awareness sixty years later.

In fiction, there was even less talent than in poetry. Frances E. W. Harper published *Iola Leroy* (1892), a novel with a trite plot and wooden characters—the tragic mulatto, the noble black lover. Sutton Griggs wrote novels of beautiful idealized Negroes. Paul Laurence Dunbar wrote short stories and several novels. Three of his novels, *The Uncalled* (1898), *The Love of Landry* (1900), and *The Fanatics* (1901), are about white characters. A fourth, *The Sport of the Gods* (1904), concerning a Negro family who migrate from the South to New York City, does begin to come to grips with social realities. But Dunbar's fiction in general is technically weak and ineffective.

By far the most talented writer of fiction was Charles W. Chesnutt. Chesnutt's "The Goophered Grapevine," which appeared in *The Atlantic Monthly* in 1887, was the first Afro-American story to appear in a major publication. Two volumes of stories appeared later —*The Conjure Woman* (1899) and *The Wife of His Youth* (1899) —and several novels, *The House Behind the Cedars* (1900), *The Marrow of Tradition* (1901), and *The Colonel's Dream* (1906). Chesnutt was a compelling story-teller and creator of characters.

ALEXANDER CRUMMELL
(1819-1898)

*A native of New York, Alexander Crummell became an Episco-
pal priest at the age of twenty-three. A few years later he traveled to
England, where he studied at Queen's College, Cambridge, and received his Bachelor of Arts degree in 1853. From England he traveled
to Liberia, where he remained for twenty years. Crummell was at
that time a militant nationalist in favor of black colonization in Liberia; he felt that the black man had no future in America. Although
he later modified this conviction, Crummell always advocated pride
in the African heritage.*

*In 1878 he relinquished the idea of colonization and returned to
the United States. Crummell's thought reflected social Darwinism in
its projected solution to the "Negro problem." He felt that economic
and social development and cultivation of high moral character would
be more effective than emphasis on the franchise and political agitation. He was convinced, too, of the black man's need for unity and
organization to achieve these ends. He was convinced that black
people primarily needed manual education, and denounced as evil
the overemphasis on higher education. Thus, Crummell anticipated
the ideas advocated by Booker T. Washington, whose thought later
dominated the age.*

*Paradoxically, he also anticipated the ideas of Washington's in-
tellectual adversary, W. E. B. Du Bois. Crummell's thinking broadened
so that he eventually rejected his earlier stand on industrial education
and economic success as the key to the racial problem and asserted*

that the hope of the black man lay in the hands of the college-educated black elite. Thus he enunciated the idea which Du Bois later developed into the theory of leadership of a Talented Tenth. In 1897, only a year before his death, Crummell founded the American Negro Academy, whose objectives included the fostering of intellectual tastes and the publication of scholarly works.

The Attitude of the American Mind
Toward the Negro Intellect

The American mind has refused to foster and to cultivate the Negro intellect. Join to this a kindred fact, of which there is the fullest evidence. Impelled, at times, by pity, a modicum of schooling and training has been given the Negro; but even this almost universally, with reluctance, with cold criticism, with microscopic scrutiny, with icy reservation, and at times, with ludicrous limitations.

Cheapness characterizes almost all the donations of the American people to the Negro:—Cheapness, in all the past, has been the regimen provided for the Negro in every line of his intellectual, as well as his lower life. And so, cheapness is to be the rule in the future, as well for his higher, as for his lower life:—cheap wages and cheap food, cheap and rotten huts; cheap and dilapidated schools; cheap and stinted weeks of schooling; cheap meeting houses for worship; cheap and ignorant ministers; cheap theological training; and now, cheap learning, culture and civilization!

Noble expectations are found in the grand literary circles in which Mr. Howells moves—manifest in his generous editing of our own Paul Dunbar's poems. But this generosity is not general, even in the world of American letters.

You can easily see this in the attempt, now-a-days, to sidetrack the Negro intellect, and to place it under limitations never laid upon any other class.

The elevation of the Negro has been a moot question for a generation past. But even to-day what do we find the general reliance of the American mind in determining this question? Almost universally the resort is to material agencies! The ordinary, and sometimes the *extraordinary* American is unable to see that the struggle of a degraded people for elevation is, in its very nature, a warfare, and that its main weapon is the cultivated and scientific mind.

Ask the great men of the land how this Negro problem is to be solved, and then listen to the answers that come from divers classes of our white fellow-citizens. The merchants and traders of our great cities tell us—"The Negro must be taught to work;" and they will pour out their moneys by thousands to train him to toil. The clergy in large numbers, cry out—"Industrialism is the only hope of the Negro"; for this is the bed-rock, in their opinion, of Negro evangelization! "Send him to Manual Labor Schools," cries out another set of philanthropists. "Hic haec, hoc, is going to prove the ruin of the Negro" says the Rev. Steele, an erudite Southern *Savant*. "You must begin at the bottom with the Negro," says another eminent authority—as though the Negro had been living in the clouds, and had never reached the bottom. Says the Honorable George T. Barnes, of Georgia—"The kind of education the Negro should receive should not be very refined nor classical, but adapted to his present condition:" as though there is to be no future for the Negro.

And so you see that even now, late in the 19th century, in this land of learning and science, the creed is—"Thus far and no farther," *i.e.* for the American black man.

One would suppose from the universal demand for the mere industrialism for this race of ours, that the Negro had been going daily to dinner parties, eating terrapin and indulging in champagne; and returning home at night, sleeping on beds of eiderdown; breakfasting in the morning in his bed, and then having his valet to clothe him daily in purple and fine linen—all these 250 years of his sojourn in this land. And then, just now, the American people, tired of all this Negro luxury, was calling him, for the first time, to blister his hands with the hoe, and to learn to supply his needs by sweatful toil in the cotton fields.

Listen a moment, to the wisdom of a great theologian, and withal as great philanthropist, the Rev. Dr. Wayland, of Philadelphia. Speaking, not long since, of the "Higher Education" of the colored people of the South, he said "that this subject concerned about 8,000,000 of our fellow-citizens, among whom are probably 1,500,000 voters. The education suited to these people is that which should be suited to white people under the same circumstances. These people are bearing the impress, which was left on them by two centuries of slavery and several centuries of barbarism. This education must begin at the bottom. It must first of all produce the power of self-support to assist them to better their condition. It should teach them good citizenship and should build them up morally. It should be, first, a good English education. They should be imbued with the knowledge of the Bible. They should have an industrial education. An industrial education leads to self-support and to the elevation of their condition. Industry is itself largely an education, intellectually and morally, and, above all, an education of character. Thus we should make these people self-dependent. This education will do away with pupils being taught Latin and Greek, while they do not know the rudiments of English."

Just notice the cautious, restrictive, limiting nature of this advice! Observe the lack of largeness, freedom and generosity in it. Dr. Wayland, I am sure, has never specialized just such a regimen for the poor Italians, Hungarians or Irish, who swarm, in lowly degradation, in immigrant ships to our shores. No! for them he wants, all Americans want, the widest, largest culture of the land; the instant opening, not simply of the common schools; and then an easy passage to the bar, the legislature, and even the judgeships of the nation. And they oft times get there.

But how different the policy with the Negro. *He* must have "an education which begins at the bottom." "He should have an industrial education," &c. His education must, first of all, produce the power of self-support &c.

Now, all this thought of Dr. Wayland is all true. But, my friends it is all false, too; and for the simple reason that it is only half truth. Dr. Wayland seems unable to rise above the plane of burden-bearing for the Negro. He seems unable to gauge the idea of the Negro becoming a thinker. He seems to forget that a race of thoughtless toilers are destined to be forever a race of senseless *boys;* for only beings who think are men.

How pitiable it is to see a great good man be-fuddled by a half truth. For to allege "Industrialism" to be the grand agency in the elevation of a race of already degraded labourers, is as much a mere platitude as to say, "they must eat and drink and sleep," for man cannot live without these habits. But they never civilize man; and *civilization* is the objective point in the movement for Negro elevation. Labor, just like eating and drinking, is one of the inevitabilities of life, one of its positive necessities. And the Negro has had it for centuries; but it has never given him manhood. It does not *now,* in wide areas of population, lift him up to moral and social elevation. Hence the need of a new factor in his life. The Negro needs light: . . . the light of civilization.

The Negro Race in this land must repudiate this absurd notion which is stealing on the American mind. The Race must declare that it is not to be put into a single groove; and for the simple reason (1) that *man* was made by his Maker to traverse the whole circle of existence, above as well as below; and that universality is the kernel of all true civilization, of all race elevation. And (2) that the Negro mind, imprisoned for nigh three hundred years, needs breadth and freedom, largeness, altitude, and elasticity; not stint nor rigidity, nor contractedness.

But the "Gradgrinds" are in evidence on all sides, telling us that the colleges and scholarships given us since emancipation, are all a mistake: and that the whole system must be reversed. The conviction is widespread that the Negro has no business in the higher walks of scholarship; that, for instance, Prof. Scarborough has no right to labor in philosophy; Professor Kelly Miller in mathematics; Professor DuBois, in history; Dr. Bowen, in theology; Professor Turner, in science; nor Mr. Tanner in art. There is no repugnance to the Negro buffoon, and the Negro scullion; but so soon as the Negro stands forth as an intellectual being, this toad of American prejudice, as at the touch of Ithuriel's spear, starts up a devil!

It is this attitude, this repellant, this forbidding attitude of the American mind, which forces the Negro in this land, to both recognize and to foster the talent and capacity of his own race, and to strive to put that capacity and talent to use for the race. I have detailed the dark and dreadful attempt to stamp that intellect out of existence. It is not only a past, it is also, modified indeed, a present fact; and out of it springs the need of just such an organization as the Negro Academy.

(1898)

T. THOMAS FORTUNE
(1856-1928)

Born a slave before the Civil War, T. Thomas Fortune eventually became the leading black journalist of his time. He was a vigorous fighter who voiced some of the most militant ideas of the Reconstruction period. Among his accomplishments are the establishment of the New York Age, *the nation's leading black newspaper at the end of the nineteenth century, and the founding of the Afro-American League, a civil rights group which came before Du Bois' Niagara Movement and the NAACP. At the end of his life he edited* The Negro World, *the publication of Marcus Garvey's Universal Negro Improvement Association.*

Fortune's career began early. From age ten he worked in various capacities that acquainted him with the convergent worlds of politics and journalism. From page in the Florida Senate to printer's devil to post-office worker, he gathered knowledge and skills. At twenty he began a two-year period as a student at Howard University. He taught for a year in Florida, then went to New York to work as a compositor for a New York newspaper.

In 1881 Fortune collaborated in founding and editing the New York Globe, *which for two years was a strong voice for the black man. The* Globe *suspended operations when Fortune and his partner disagreed on policy. A week later Fortune began the* New York Freeman, *which later changed its name to* New York Age. *The* Age *became a leading Afro-American organ during the 1880s and 1890s.*

Fortune's early essays were often militant. In 1883, for example, he advocated violent retribution for blacks who suffered indignities at the hands of whites: "One or two murders growing from this intolerable nuisance would break it up." By the 1890s, when many black

124

leaders were becoming disillusioned with the possibilities of any real progress, Fortune became more conservative and supported the ideas of Booker T. Washington. The two were close friends, although the friendship was sometimes troubled.

In his later years Fortune returned to the less conservative attitudes which were probably closer to his natural bent. Earlier he had rejected the idea of Africa as motherland and had regarded it as merely an interesting foreign land. But, as mentioned above, during his final years he was editing The Negro World.

Many of Fortune's essays are available in editorials of the Age, *and in his collections* The Negro in Politics *(1885) and* Black and White: Land, Labor, and Politics in the South *(1884). For much of his career he was regarded as a brilliant firebrand. His more conservative stand may be found in his essay,* "The Negro's Place in American Life at the Present Day," *in* The Negro Problem *(1903). His more radical views may be found in* Black and White, *from which the following essays are taken.*

THE NEGRO AND THE NATION
From *Black and White*

The war of the Rebellion settled only one question: It forever settled the question of chattel slavery in this country. It forever choked the life out of the infamy of the Constitutional right of one man to rob another, by purchase of his person, or of his honest share of the produce of his own labor. But this was the only question permanently and irrevocably settled. Nor was this *the* all-absorbing question involved. The right of a State to secede from the so-called *Union* remains where it was when the treasonable shot upon Fort Sumter aroused the people to all the horrors of internecine war. And the measure of protection which the National government owes the individual members of States, a right imposed upon it by the adoption of the XIVth Amendment to the Constitution, remains still to be affirmed.

It was not sufficient that the Federal government should expend its blood and treasure to unfetter the limbs of four millions of people. There can be a slavery more odious, more galling, than mere chattel slavery. It has been declared to be an act of charity to enforce ignorance upon the slave, since to inform his intelligence would simply be to make his unnatural lot all the more unbearable. Instance the miserable existence of Æsop, the great black moralist. But this is just what the manumission of the black people of this country has accomplished. They are more absolutely under the control of the Southern whites; they are more systematically robbed of their labor; they are more poorly housed, clothed and fed, than under the slave régime; and they enjoy, practically, less of the protection of the laws of the State or of the Federal government. When they appeal to the Federal government they are told by the Supreme Court to go to the State authorities—as if they would have appealed to the one had the other given them that protection to which their sovereign citizenship entitles them!

Practically, there is no law in the United States which extends its protecting arm over the black man and his rights. He is, like the Irishman in Ireland, an alien in his native land. There is no central or auxiliary authority to which he can appeal for protection. Wherever he turns he finds the strong arm of constituted authority powerless to protect him. The farmer and the merchant rob him with absolute immunity, and irresponsible ruffians murder him without fear of punishment, undeterred by the law, or by public opinion —which connives at, if it does not inspire, the deeds of lawless violence. Legislatures of States have framed a code of laws which is more cruel and unjust than any enforced by a former slave State.

The right of franchise has been practically annulled in every one of the former slave States, in not one of which, to-day, can a man vote, think or act as he pleases. He must conform his views to the views of the men who have usurped every function of government— who, at the point of the dagger, and with shotgun, have made themselves masters in defiance of every law or precedent in our history as a government. They have usurped government with the weapons of the coward and assassin, and they maintain themselves in power by the most approved practices of the most odious of tyrants. These men have shed as much innocent blood as the bloody triumvirate of Rome. To-day, red-handed murderers and assassins sit in the high places of power, and bask in the smiles of innocence and beauty.

The newspapers of the country, voicing the sentiments of the people, literally hiss into silence any man who has the courage to protest against the prevailing tendency to lawlessness and bare-faced usurpation; while parties have ceased to deal with the question for other than purposes of political capital. Even this fruitful mine is well-nigh exhausted. A few more years, and the usurper and the man of violence will be left in undisputed possession of his blood-stained inheritance. No man will attempt to deter him from sowing broadcast the seeds of revolution and death. Brave men are powerless to combat this organized brigandage, complaint of which, in derision, has been termed "waving the bloody shirt."

Men organize themselves into society for mutual protection. Government justly derives its just powers from the consent of the governed. But what shall we say of that society which is incapable of extending the protection which is inherent in it? What shall we say of the government which has not power or inclination to insure the exercise of those solemn rights and immunities which it guarantees? To declare a man to be free, and equal with his fellow, and then to refrain from enacting laws powerful to insure him in such freedom and equality, is to trifle with the most sacred of all the functions of sovereignty. Have not the United States done this very thing? Have they not conferred freedom and the ballot, which are necessary the one to the other? And have they not signally failed to make omnipotent the one and practicable the other? The questions hardly require an answer. The measure of freedom the black man enjoys can be gauged by the power he has to vote. He has, practically, no voice in the government under which he lives. His property is taxed and his life is jeopardized, by states on the one hand and inefficient police regulations on the other, and no question is asked or expected of him. When he protests, when he cries out against this flagrant nullification of the very first principles of a republican form of government, the insolent question is asked: "What are you going to do about it?" And here lies the danger.

You may rob and maltreat a slave and ask him what he is going to do about it, and he can make no reply. He is bound hand and foot; he is effectually gagged. Despair is his only refuge. He knows it is useless to appeal from tyranny unto the designers and apologists of tyranny. Ignominious death alone can bring him relief. This was the case of thousands of men doomed by the institution of slavery. *But such is not the case with free men.* You cannot oppress and murder freemen as you would slaves: you cannot so insult them with the question, "What are you going to do about it?" When you ask free men that question you appeal to men who, though sunk to the verge of despair, yet are capable of uprising and ripping hip and thigh those who deemed them incapable of so rising above their condition. The history of mankind is fruitful of such uprisings of races and classes reduced to a condition of absolute despair. The American negro is no better and no worse than the Haytian revolutionists headed by Toussaint l'Overture, Christophe and the bloody Dessalaines.

I do not indulge in the luxury of prophecy when I declare that the American people are fostering in their bosoms a spirit of rebellion which will yet shake the pillars of popular government as they have never before been shaken, unless a wiser policy is inaugurated and honestly enforced. All the indications point to the fulfilment of such declaration.

The Czar of Russia squirms upon his throne, not because he is necessarily a bad man, but because he is the head and center of a condition of things which squeezes the life out of the people. His subjects hurl infernal machines at the tyrant because he represents the system which oppresses them. But the evil is far deeper than the throne, and cannot be remedied by striking the occupant of it—*the throne itself must be rooted out and demolished.* So the Irish question has a more powerful motive to foment agitation and murder than the landlord and landlordism. The landlord simply stands out as the representative of the real grievance. To remove *him* would not remove the evil; agitation would not cease; murder would still stalk abroad at noon-day. *The real grievance is the false system which makes the landlord possible.* The appropriation of the fertile acres of the soil of Ireland, which created and maintains a privileged class, a class that while performing no labor, wrings from the toiler, in the shape of rents, so much of the produce of his labor that he cannot on the residue support himself and those dependent upon him aggravates the situation. It is this system which constitutes the real grievance and makes the landlord an odious loafer with abundant cash and the laborer a constant toiler always upon the verge of starvation. Evidently, therefore, to remove the landlord and leave the system of land monopoly would not remove the evil. Destroy the latter and the former would be compelled to go.

Herein lies the great social wrong which has turned the beautiful roses of freedom into thorns to prick the hands of the black men of the South; which made slavery a blessing, paradoxical as it may appear, and freedom a curse. It is this great wrong which has crowded the cities of the South with an ignorant pauper population, making desolate fields that once bloomed "as fair as a garden of the Lord," where now the towering oak and pine-tree flourish, instead of the corn and cotton which gladdened the heart and filled the purse. It was this gigantic iniquity which created that arrogant class who have exhausted the catalogue of violence to obtain power and the lexicon of sophistry for aruguments to extenuate the exceeding heinousness of crime. How could it be otherwise? To tell a man he is free when he has neither money nor the opportunity to make it, is simply to mock him. To tell him he has no master when he cannot live except by permission of the man who, under favorable conditions, monopolizes all the land, is to deal in the most tantalizing contradiction of terms. But this is just what the United States did for the black man. And yet because he has not grown learned and wealthy in twenty years, because he does not own broad acres and a large bank account, people are not wanting who declare he has no capacity, that he is improvident by nature and mendacious from inclination.

(1884)

BOOKER T. WASHINGTON
(1856-1915)

Undoubtedly the most visible figure in black America at the turn of the century was Booker T. Washington. In an era when the work ethic superseded the Golden Rule, this ex-slave who became the spokesman for the newly freed millions seemed the sable archetype of American ideals. Enthroned at Tuskegee Institute, which he founded, Washington wielded the tremendous power vested in him by the white power structure which had chosen him leader of the blacks. Through wily manipulation of money and influence, Washington fully dominated the activity of black America, or at least the expression of thought by its spokesmen.

Washington was born in a log cabin on a plantation in Virginia. He was never certain of his birthdate. His father was said to be a white man on a neighboring plantation; this alleged white ancestry was sometimes given the credit for Washington's later achievements. His mother and her three children were slaves. After emancipation, when Booker was about seven, his mother and stepfather moved the family to West Virginia. Young Booker's boyhood years were harsh, marked by the back-breaking and often spirit-breaking toil of the ex-slaves. Even then, Washington seemed endowed with unusual drive and energy. From early childhood, he struggled for an education. In his entire life he never acquired the taste for leisure. At age sixteen he set out on foot for Hampton Institute, five hundred miles away, with one dollar and fifty cents in his pocket. He reached his goal, and with some financial aid from wealthy whites, he worked his way through to graduation. After teaching for a while and attending a seminary for a year, Washington returned to Hampton where he supervised the residence hall for young Indian men from the West who were being exposed to the Hampton way. In 1881 he founded Tuskegee Institute. In the years that followed, Washington built up the school, and he himself rose to a position of greater influence than any American black before him had known.

Washington's rise to eminence was greatly accelerated by his Atlanta Exposition Address in 1895. Having been chosen to speak for the black community, he said the things that were comforting to the whites. He praised white leaders for their help to the ignorant black masses. He characterized his race as "the most patient, faithful, law-abiding, and unresentful people the world has seen" and promised their everlasting support to the white South. He urged that blacks remain in the South and learn manual skills; he urged that they wait for citizenship to be awarded rather than demand it. He advocated social separation. In effect he laid responsibility on the black man for much of his own oppressed situation and absolved the white man of a great deal of guilt and responsibility. He disavowed the civil rights goals that were most repugnant to whites.

Following his speech, Washington was acclaimed as the leader of his people—especially by white America, who poured a small fortune into his hands for the construction of his school and for the support of other projects in which he was interested. Government sought his advice on many matters; black projects which did not meet his approval were usually denied aid from Federal and private sources. The mass media published anything he wrote or said, but often rejected the works of those opposed to him. Washington himself gained financial control of several newspapers.

He organized the National Negro Business League, was instrumental in furthering American assistance to Liberia, and participated in numerous projects concerning the educational, economic, and physical benefit of black people.

For a great many years Washington's conciliatory ideas dominated black thought. Many highly intelligent and respected men wrote in his support, and many black children were educated in terms of his ideas. His ideological grip, however, was finally broken by the opposition of W. E. B. Du Bois *and others.*

*Washington was not primarily a creative writer. His works were expository in nature, aimed mainly toward instruction on how to get ahead. Perhaps the subject of his address at the Hampton 1879 commencement was prophetic of his later works—"The Force That Wins." The titles of some of his works clearly reveal the drift of their content—*Sowing and Reaping *(1900),* Working with the Hands

(1904), Putting the Most Into Life *(1906)*, My Larger Education *(1911)*, *and* The Man Farthest Down *(1912)*. *He also wrote a great many speeches and articles. In 1907 he wrote a biography of Frederick Douglass, whose rise from slavery he admired. On many of these works he had the active assistance of his staff at Tuskegee.*

Washington's most popular work was his autobiography, Up From Slavery, *which first appeared serially in* Outlook *magazine and was published in book form in 1901. Interesting as it is in places, the autobiography presents a picture of black life which is highly simplified. Washington constantly minimizes the hard realities of black life. He minimizes, too, the evils of white racism. He describes the Ku Klux Klan as "bands of men who had joined themselves together for the purpose of regulating the behavior of coloured people." Washington ends his account: "I have referred to this unpleasant part of the history of the South simply for the purpose of calling attention to the great change that has taken place since the days of the 'Ku Klux.' To-day there are no such organizations in the South, and the fact that such ever existed is almost forgotten by both races. There are few places in the South now where public sentiment would permit such organizations to exist."*

From *Up from Slavery*

CHAPTER I

A SLAVE AMONG SLAVES

I was born a slave on a plantation in Franklin County, Virginia. I am not quite sure of the exact place or exact date of my birth, but at any rate I suspect I must have been born somewhere and at some time. As nearly as I have been able to learn, I was born near a cross-roads post-office called Hale's Ford, and the year was 1858 or 1859. I do not know the month or the day. The earliest impressions I can now recall are of the plantation and the slave quarters—the latter being the part of the plantation where the slaves had their cabins.

My life had its beginning in the midst of the most miserable, desolate, and discouraging surroundings. This was so, however, not because my owners were especially cruel, for they were not, as compared with many others. I was born in a typical log cabin, about fourteen by sixteen feet square. In this cabin I lived with my mother and a brother and sister till after the Civil War, when we were all declared free.

Of my ancestry I know almost nothing. In the slave quarters, and even later, I heard whispered conversations among the coloured people of the tortures which the slaves, including, no doubt, my ancestors on my mother's side, suffered in the middle passage of the slave ship while being conveyed from Africa to America. I have been unsuccessful in securing any information that would throw any accurate light upon the history of my family beyond my mother. She, I remember, had a half-brother and a half-sister. In the days of slavery not very much attention was given to family history and family records—that is, black family records. My mother, I suppose, attracted the attention of a purchaser who was afterward my owner and hers. Her addition to the slave family attracted about as much attention as the purchase of a new horse or cow. Of my father I know even less than of my mother. I do not even know his name. I have heard reports to the effect that he was a white man who lived on one of the near-by plantations. Whoever he was, I never heard of his taking the least interest in me or providing in any way for my rearing. But I do not find especial fault with him. He was simply another unfortunate victim of the institution which the Nation unhappily had engrafted upon it at that time.

The cabin was not only our living-place, but was also used as the kitchen for the plantation. My mother was the plantation cook. The cabin was without glass windows; it had only openings in the side which let in the light, and also the cold, chilly air of winter. There was a door to the cabin—that is, something that was called a door—but the uncertain hinges by which it was hung, and the large cracks in it, to say nothing of the fact that it was too small, made the room a very uncomfortable one. In addition to these openings there was, in the lower right-hand corner of the room, the "cat-hole,"—a contrivance which almost every mansion or cabin in Virginia possessed during the ante-bellum period. The "cat-hole" was a square opening, about seven by eight inches, provided for the purpose of letting the cat pass in and out of the house at will during the night. In the case of our particular cabin I could never understand the necessity for this convenience, since there were at least a half-dozen other places in the cabin that would have accommodated the cats. There was no wooden floor in our cabin, the naked earth being used as a floor. In the centre of the earthen floor there was a large, deep opening covered with boards, which was used as a place in which to store sweet potatoes during the winter. An impression of this potato-hole is very distinctly engraved upon my memory, because I recall that during the process of putting the potatoes in or taking them out I would often come into possession of one or two, which I roasted and thoroughly enjoyed. There was no cooking-stove on our plantation, and all the cooking for the whites and slaves my mother had to do over an open fireplace, mostly in pots and "skillets." While the poorly built cabin caused us to suffer with cold in the winter, the heat from the open fireplace in summer was equally trying.

The early years of my life, which were spent in the little cabin, were not very different from those of thousands of other slaves. My mother, of course, had little time in which to give attention to the training of her children during the day. She snatched a few moments for our care in the early morning before her work began, and at night after the day's work was done. One of my earliest recollections is that of my mother cooking a chicken late at night, and awakening her children for the purpose of feeding them. How or where she got it I do not know. I presume, however, it was procured from our owner's farm. Some people may call this theft. If such a thing were to happen now, I should condemn it as theft myself. But taking place at the time it did, and for the reason that it did, no one could ever make me believe that my mother was guilty of thieving. She was simply a victim of the system of slavery. I cannot remember having slept in a bed until after our family was declared free by the Emancipation Proclamation. Three children—John, my older brother, Amanda, my sister, and myself—had a pallet on the dirt floor, or, to be more correct, we slept in and on a bundle of filthy rags laid upon the dirt floor.

I was asked not long ago to tell something about the sports and pastimes that I engaged in during my youth. Until that question was asked it had never occurred to me that there was no period of my life that was devoted to play. From the time that I can remember anything, almost every day of my life has been occupied in some kind of labour; though I think I would now be a more useful man if I had had time for sports. During the period that I spent in slavery I was not large enough to be of much service, still I was occupied most of the time in cleaning the yards, carrying water to the men in the fields, or going to the mill, to which I used to take the corn, once a week, to be ground. The mill was about three miles from the plantation. This work I always dreaded. The heavy bag of corn would be thrown across the back of the horse, and the corn divided about evenly on each side; but in some way, almost without exception, on these trips, the corn would shift as to become unbalanced and would fall off the horse, and often I would fall with it. As I was not strong enough to reload the corn upon the horse, I would have to wait, sometimes for many hours, till a chance passer-by came along who would help me out of my trouble. The hours while waiting for some one were usually spent in crying. The time consumed in this way made me late in reaching the mill, and by the time I got my corn ground and reached home it would be far into the night. The road was a lonely one, and often led through dense forests. I was always frightened. The woods were said to be full of soldiers who had deserted from the army, and I had been told that the first thing a deserter did to a Negro boy when he found him alone was to cut off his ears. Besides, when I was late in getting home I knew I would always get a severe scolding or a flogging.

I had no schooling whatever while I was a slave, though I remember on several occasions I went as far as the schoolhouse door with one of my young mistresses to carry her books. The picture of several dozen boys and girls in a schoolroom engaged in study made a deep impression upon me, and I had the feeling that to get into a schoolhouse and study in this way would be about the same as getting into paradise.

So far as I can now recall, the first knowledge that I got of the fact that we were slaves, and that freedom of the slaves was being discussed, was early one morning before day, when I was awakened by my mother kneeling over her children and fervently praying that Lincoln and his armies might be successful, and that one day she and her children might be free. In this connection I have never been able to understand how the slaves throughout the South, completely ignorant as were the masses so far as books or newspapers were concerned, were able to keep themselves so accurately and completely informed about the great National questions that were agitating the country. From the time that Garrison, Lovejoy, and others began to agitate for freedom, the slaves throughout the South kept in close touch with the progress of the movement. Though I was a mere child during the preparation for the Civil War and during the war itself, I now recall the many late-at-night whispered discussions that I heard my mother and the other slaves on the plantation indulge in. These discussions showed that they understood the situation, and that they kept themselves informed of events by what was termed the "grape-vine" telegraph.

During the campaign when Lincoln was first a candidate for the Presidency, the slaves on our far-off plantation, miles from any railroad or large city or daily newspaper, knew what the issues involved were. When war was begun between the North and the South, every slave on our plantation felt and knew that, though other issues were discussed, the primal one was that of slavery. Even the most ignorant members of my race on the remote plantations felt in their hearts, with a certainty that admitted of no doubt, that the freedom of the slaves would be the one great result of the war, if the

Northern armies conquered. Every success of the Federal armies and every defeat of the Confederate forces was watched with the keenest and most intense interest. Often the slaves got knowledge of the results of great battles before the white people received it. This news was usually gotten from the coloured man who was sent to the post-office for the mail. In our case the post-office was about three miles from the plantation and the mail came once or twice a week. The man who was sent to the office would linger about the place long enough to get the drift of the conversation from the group of white people who naturally congregated there, after receiving their mail, to discuss the latest news. The mail-carrier on his way back to our master's house would as naturally retail the news that he had secured among the slaves, and in this way they often heard of important events before the white people at the "big house," as the master's house was called.

I cannot remember a single instance during my childhood or early boyhood when our entire family sat down to the table together, and God's blessing was asked, and the family ate a meal in a civilized manner. On the plantation in Virginia, and even later, meals were gotten by the children very much as dumb animals get theirs. It was a piece of bread here and a scrap of meat there. It was a cup of milk at one time and some potatoes at another. Sometimes a portion of our family would eat out of the skillet or pot, while some one would eat from a tin plate held on the knees, and often using nothing but the hands with which to hold the food. When I had grown to sufficient size, I was required to go to the "big house" at meal-times to fan the flies from the table by means of a large set of paper fans operated by a pulley. Naturally much of the conversation of the white people turned upon the subject of freedom and the war, and I absorbed a good deal of it. I remember that at one time I saw two of my young mistresses and some lady visitors eating ginger-cakes, in the yard. At that time those cakes seemed to me to be absolutely the most tempting and desirable things that I had ever seen; and I then and there resolved that, if I ever got free, the height of my ambition would be reached if I could get to the point where I could secure and eat ginger-cakes in the way that I saw those ladies doing.

Of course as the war was prolonged the white people, in many cases, often found it difficult to secure food for themselves. I think the slaves felt the deprivation less than the white, because the usual diet for the slaves was corn bread and pork, and these could be raised on the plantation; but coffee, tea, sugar, and other articles which the whites had been accustomed to use could not be raised on the plantation, and the conditions brought about by the war frequently made it impossible to secure these things. The whites were often in great straits. Parched corn was used for coffee, and a kind of black molasses was used instead of sugar. Many times nothing was used to sweeten the so-called tea and coffee.

The first pair of shoes that I recall wearing were wooden ones. They had rough leather on the top, but the bottoms, which were about an inch thick, were of wood. When I walked they made a fearful noise, and besides this they were very inconvenient, since there was no yielding to the natural pressure of the foot. In wearing them one presented an exceedingly awkward appearance. The most trying ordeal that I was forced to endure as a slave boy, however, was the wearing of a flax shirt. In the portion of Virginia where I lived it was common to use flax as part of the clothing for the slaves. That part of the flax from which our clothing was made was largely the refuse, which of course was the cheapest and roughest part. I can scarcely imagine any torture, except, perhaps, the pulling of a tooth, that is equal to that caused by putting on a new flax shirt for the first time. It is almost equal to the feeling that one would experience if he had a dozen or more chestnut burrs, or a hundred small pinpoints, in contact with his flesh. Even to this day I can recall accurately the tortures that I underwent when putting on one of these garments. The fact that my flesh was soft and tender added to the pain. But I had no choice. I had to wear the flax shirt or none; and had it been left to me to choose, I should have chosen to wear no covering. In connection with the flax shirt, my brother John, who is several years older than I am, performed one of the most generous acts that I ever heard of one slave relative doing for another. On several occasions when I was being forced to wear a new flax shirt, he generously agreed to put it on in my stead and wear it for several days, till it was "broken in." Until I had grown to be quite a youth this single garment was all that I wore.

One may get the idea from what I have said, that there was bitter feeling toward the white people on the part of my race, because of the fact that most of the white population was away fighting in a war which would result in keeping the Negro in slavery if the South was successful. In the case of the slaves on our place this was not true, and it was not true of any large portion of the slave population in the South where the Negro was treated with anything like decency. During the Civil War one of my young masters was killed, and two were severely wounded. I recall the feeling of sorrow which existed among the slaves when they heard of the death of "Mars' Billy." It was no sham sorrow but real. Some of the slaves had nursed "Mars' Billy"; others had played with him when he was a child. "Mars' Billy" had begged for mercy in the case of others when the overseer or master was thrashing them. The sorrow in the slave quarter was only second to that in the "big house." When the two young masters were brought home wounded, the sympathy of the slaves was shown in many ways. They were just as anxious to assist in the nursing as the family relatives of the wounded. Some of the slaves would even beg for the privilege of sitting up at night to nurse their wounded masters. This tenderness and sympathy on the part of those held in bondage was a result of their kindly and generous nature. In order to defend and protect the women and children who were left on the plantations when the white males went to war, the slaves would have laid down their lives. The slave who was selected to sleep in the "big house" during the absence of the males was considered to have the place of honour. Any one attempting to harm "young Mistress" or "old Mistress" during the night would have had to cross the dead body of the slave to do so. I do not know how many have noticed it, but I think that it will be found to be true that there are few instances, either in slavery or freedom, in which a member of my race has been known to betray a specific trust.

As a rule, not only did the members of my race entertain no feelings of bitterness against the whites before and during the war, but there are many instances of Negroes tenderly caring for their former masters and mistresses who for some reason have become poor and dependent since the war. I know of instances where the former masters of slaves have for years been supplied with money by their former slaves to keep them from suffering. I have known of still other cases in which the former slaves have assisted in the education of the descendants of their former owners. I know of a case on a large plantation in the South in which a young white man, the son of the former owner of the estate, has become so reduced in purse and self-control by reason of drink that he is a pitiable creature; and yet, notwithstanding the poverty of the coloured people themselves on this plantation, they have for years supplied this young white man with the necessities of life. One sends him a little coffee or sugar, another a little meat, and so on. Nothing that the coloured people possess is too good for the son of "old Mars' Tom," who will perhaps never be permitted to suffer while any remain on the place who knew directly or indirectly of "old Mars' Tom."

I have said that there are few instances of a member of my race betraying a specific trust. One of the best illustrations of this which I know of is in the case of an ex-slave from Virginia whom I met not long ago in a little town in the state of Ohio. I found that this man had made a contract with his master, two or three years previous to the Emancipation Proclamation, to the effect that the slave was to be permitted to buy himself, by paying so much per year for his body; and while he was paying for himself, he was to be permitted to labour where and for whom he pleased. Finding that he could secure better wages in Ohio, he went there. When freedom came, he was still in debt to his master some three hundred dollars. Notwithstanding that the Emancipation Proclamation freed him from any obligation to his master, this black man walked the greater portion of the distance back to where his old master lived in Virginia, and placed the last dollar, with interest, in his hands. In talking to me about this, the man told me that he knew that he did not have to pay the debt, but that he had given his word to his master, and his word he had never broken. He felt that he could not enjoy his freedom till he had fulfilled his promise.

From some things that I have said one may get the idea that some of the slaves did not want freedom. This is not true. I have never seen one who did not want to be free, or one who would return to slavery.

I pity from the bottom of my heart any nation or body of people that is so unfortunate as to get entangled in the net of slavery. I have long since ceased to cherish any spirit of bitterness against the Southern white people on account of the enslavement of my race. No one section of our country was wholly responsible for its introduction, and, besides, it was recognized and protected for years by the General Government. Having once got its tentacles fastened on to the economic and social life of the Republic, it was no easy matter for the country to relieve itself of the institution. Then, when we rid ourselves of prejudice, or racial feeling, and look facts in the face, we must acknowledge that, notwithstanding the cruelty and moral wrong of slavery, the ten million Negroes inhabiting this country, who themselves or whose ancestors went through the school of American slavery, are in a stronger and more hopeful condition, materially, intellectually, morally, and religiously, than is true of an equal number of black people in any other portion of the globe. This is so to such an extent that Negroes in this country, who themselves or whose forefathers went through the school of slavery, are constantly returning to Africa as missionaries to enlighten those who remained in the fatherland. This I say, not to justify slavery—on the other hand, I condemn it as an institution, as we all know that in America it was established for selfish and financial reasons, and not from a missionary motive—but to call attention to a fact, and to show how Providence so often uses men and institutions to accomplish a purpose. When persons ask me in these days how, in the midst of what sometimes seem hopelessly discouraging conditions, I can have such faith in the future of my race in this country, I remind them of the wilderness through which and out of which, a good Providence has already led us.

Ever since I have been old enough to think for myself, I have entertained the idea that, notwithstanding the cruel wrongs inflicted upon us, the black man got nearly as much out of slavery as the white man did. The hurtful influences of the institution were not by any means confined to the Negro. This was fully illustrated by the life upon our own plantation. The whole machinery of slavery was so constructed as to cause labour, as a rule, to be looked upon as a badge of degradation, of inferiority. Hence labour was something that both races on the slave plantation sought to escape. The slave system on our place, in a large measure, took the spirit of self-reliance and self-help out of the white people. My old master had many boys and girls, but not one, so far as I know, ever mastered a single trade or special line of productive industry. The girls were not taught to cook, sew or to take care of the house. All of this was left to the slaves. The slaves, of course, had little personal interest in the life of the plantation, and their ignorance prevented them from learning how to do things in the most improved and thorough manner. As a result of the system, fences were out of repair, gates were hanging half off the hinges, doors creaked, window-panes were out, plastering had fallen but was not replaced, weeds grew in the yard. As a rule, there was food for whites and blacks, but inside the house, and on the dining-room table, there was wanting that delicacy and refinement of touch and finish which can make a home the most convenient, comfortable, and attractive place in the world. Withal there was a waste of food and other materials which was sad. When freedom came, the slaves were almost as well fitted to begin life anew as the master, except in the matter of book-learning and ownership of property. The slave owner and his sons had mastered no special industry. They unconsciously had imbibed the feeling that manual labour was not the proper thing for them. On the other hand, the slaves, in many cases, had mastered some handicraft, and none were ashamed, and few unwilling, to labour.

Finally the war closed, and the day of freedom came. It was a momentous and eventful day to all upon our plantation. We had been expecting it. Freedom was in the air, and had been for months. Deserting soldiers returning to their homes were to be seen every day. Others who had been discharged, or whose regiments had been paroled, were constantly passing near our place. The "grape-vine telegraph" was kept busy night and day. The news and mutterings of great events were swiftly carried from one plantation to another. In the fear of "Yankee" invasions, the silverware and other valuables were taken from the "big house," buried in the woods, and guarded by trusted slaves. Woe be to any one who would have attempted to disturb the buried treasure. The slaves would give the Yankee soldiers food, drink, clothing—anything but that which had been specifically intrusted to their care and honour. As the great day grew nearer, there was more singing in the slave quarters than usual. It was bolder, had more ring, and lasted later into the night. Most of the verses of the plantation songs had some reference to freedom. True, they had sung those same verses before, but they had been careful to explain that the "freedom" in these songs referred to the next world, and had no connection with life in this world. Now they gradually threw off the mask; and were not afraid to let it be known that the "freedom" in their songs meant freedom of the body in this world. The night before the eventful day, word was sent to the slave quarters to the effect that something unusual was going to take place at the "big house" the next morning. There was little, if any, sleep that night. All was excitement and expectancy. Early the next morning word was sent to all the slaves, old and young, to gather at the house. In company with my mother, brother, and sister, and a large number of other slaves, I went to the master's house. All of our master's family were either standing or seated on the veranda of the house, where they could see what was to take place and hear what was said. There was a feeling of deep interest, or perhaps sadness, on their faces, but not bitterness. As I now recall the impression they made upon me, they did not at the moment seem to be sad because of the loss of property, but rather because of parting with those whom they had reared and who were in many ways very close to them.

The most distinct thing that I now recall in connection with the scene was that some man who seemed to be a stranger (a United States officer, I presume) made a little speech and then read a rather long paper—the Emancipation Proclamation, I think. After the reading we were told that we were all free, and could go when and where we pleased. My mother, who was standing by my side, leaned over and kissed her children, while tears of joy ran down her cheeks. She explained to us what it all meant, that this was the day for which she had been so long praying, but fearing that she would never live to see.

For some minutes there was great rejoicing, and thanksgiving, and wild scenes of ecstasy. But there was no feeling of bitterness. In fact, there was pity among the slaves for our former owners. The wild rejoicing on the part of the emancipated coloured people lasted but for a brief period, for I noticed that by the time they returned to their cabins there was a change in their feelings. The great responsibility of being free, of having charge of themselves, of having to think and plan for themselves and their children, seemed to take possession of them. It was very much like suddenly turning a youth of ten or twelve years out into the world to provide for himself. In a few hours the great questions with which the Anglo-Saxon race had been grappling for centuries had been thrown upon these people to be solved. These were the questions of a home, a living, the rearing of children, education, citizenship, and the establishment and support of churches. Was it any wonder that within a few hours the wild rejoicing ceased and a feeling of deep gloom seemed to pervade the slave quarters? To some it seemed that, now that they were in actual possession of it, freedom was a more serious thing than they had expected to find it. Some of the slaves were seventy or eighty years old; their best days were gone. They had no strength with which to earn a living in a strange place and among strange people, even if they had been sure where to find a new place of abode. To this class the problem seemed especially hard. Besides, deep down in their hearts there was a strange and peculiar attachment to "old Marster" and "old Missus," and to their children, which they found it hard to think of breaking off. With these they had spent in some cases nearly a half-century, and it was no light thing to think of parting. Gradually, one by one, stealthily at first, the older slaves began to wander from the slave quarters back to the "big house" to have a whispered conversation with their former owners as to the future.

Speech at the Atlanta Exposition

Mr. President and Gentlemen of the Board of Directors and Citizens: One-third of the population of the South is of the Negro race. No enterprise seeking the material, civil, or moral welfare of this section can disregard this element of our population and reach the highest success. I but convey to you, Mr. President and Directors, the sentiment of the masses of my race when I say that in no way have the value and manhood of the American Negro been more fittingly and generously recognized than by the managers of this magnificent Exposition at every stage of its progress. It is a recognition that will do more to cement the friendship of the two races than any occurrence since the dawn of freedom.

Not only this, but the opportunity here afforded will awaken among us a new era of industrial progress. Ignorant and inexperienced, it is not strange that in the first years of our new life we began at the top instead of at the bottom; that a seat in Congress or the State Legislature was more sought than real estate or industrial skill; that the political convention or stump speaking had more attractions than starting a dairy farm or truck garden.

A ship lost at sea for many days suddenly sighted a friendly vessel. From the mast of the unfortunate vessel was seen a signal: "Water, water; we die of thirst!" The answer from the friendly vessel at once came back: "Cast down your bucket where you are." A second time the signal, "Water, water; send us water"; ran up from the distressed vessel, and was answered: "Cast down your bucket where you are." The captain of the distressed vessel, at last heeding the injunction, cast down his bucket, and it came up full of fresh, sparkling water from the mouth of the Amazon River. To those of my race who depend upon bettering their condition in a foreign land, or whom underestimate the importance of cultivating friendly relations with the Southern white man, who is his next door neighbor, I would say: "Cast down your bucket where you are"—cast it down in making friends in every manly way of the people of all races by whom we are surrounded.

Cast it down in agriculture, mechanics, in commerce, in domestic service, and in the professions. And in this connection it is well to bear in mind that whatever other sins the South may be called to bear, when it comes to business, pure and simple, it is in the South that the Negro is given a man's chance in the commercial world, and in nothing is this Exposition more eloquent than in emphasizing this chance. Our greatest danger is, that in the great leap from slavery to freedom we may overlook the fact that the masses of us are to live by the productions of our hands, and fail to keep in mind that we shall prosper in proportion as we learn to draw the line between the superficial and the substantial, the ornamental geegaws of life and the useful. No race can prosper till it learns that there is as much dignity in tilling a field as in writing a poem. It is at the bottom of life we must begin, and not at the top. Nor should we permit our grievances to overshadow our opportunities.

To those of the white race who look to the incoming of those of foreign birth and strange tongue and habits for the prosperity of the South, were I permitted I would repeat what I say to my own race, "Cast down your bucket where you are." Cast it down among the 8,000,000 Negroes whose habits you know, whose fidelity and love you have tested in days when to have proved treacherous mean the ruin of your firesides. Cast down your bucket among these people who have, without strikes and labor wars, tilled your fields, cleared your forests, builded your railroads and cities, and brought forth treasures from the bowels of the earth, and helped make possible this magnificent representation of the progress of the South. Casting down your bucket among my people, helping and encouraging them as you are doing on these grounds, and, with education of head, hand and heart, you will find that they will buy your surplus land, make blossom the waste places in your fields, and run your factories. While doing this, you can be sure in the future, as in the past, that you and your families will be surrounded by the most patient, faithful, law-abiding, and unresentful people that the world has seen. As we have proved our loyalty to you in the past, in nursing your children, watching by the sick bed of your mothers and fathers, and often following them with tear-dimmed eyes to their graves, so in the future, in our humble way, we shall stand by you with a devotion that no foreigner can approach, ready to lay down our lives, if need be, in defense of yours, interlacing our industrial, commercial, civil, and religious life with yours in a way that shall make the interests of both races one. In all things that are purely social we can be as separate as the fingers, yet one as the hand in all things essential to mutual progress.

There is no defense or security for any of us except in the highest intelligence and development of all. If anywhere there are efforts tending to curtail the fullest growth of the Negro, let these efforts be turned into stimulating, encouraging, and making him the most useful and intelligent citizen. Effort or means so invested will pay a thousand per cent interest. These efforts will be twice blessed—blessing him that gives and him that takes.

There is no escape through law of man or God from the inevitable:

> "The laws of changeless justice bind
> Oppressor with oppressed;
> And close as sin and suffering joined
> We march to fate abreast."

Nearly sixteen millions of hands will aid you in pulling the load upwards, or they will pull against you the load downwards. We shall constitute one-third and more of the ignorance and crime of the South, or one-third its intelligence and progress; we shall contribute one-third to the business and industrial prosperity of the South, or we shall prove a veritable body of death, stagnating, depressing, retarding every effort to advance the body politic.

Gentlemen of the Exposition, as we present to you our humble effort at an exhibition of our progress, you must not expect overmuch. Starting thirty years ago with ownership here and there in a few quilts and pumpkins and chickens (gathered from miscellaneous sources), remember the path that has led from these to the invention and production of agricultural implements, buggies, steam engines, newspapers, books, statuary, carving, paintings, the management of drugs stores and banks has not been trodden without contract with thorns and thistles. While we take pride in what we exhibit as a result of our independent efforts, we do not for a moment forget that our part in this exhibition would fall far short of your expectations but for the constant help that has come to our educational life, not only from the Southern States, but especially from Northern philanthropists, who have made their gifts a constant stream of blessing and encouragement.

The wisest among my race understand that the agitation of questions of social equality is the extremest folly, and that progress in the enjoyment of all the privileges that wil come to us must be the result of severe and constant struggle rather than of artificial forcing. No race that has anything to contribute to the markets of the world is long in any degree ostracized. It is important and right that all privileges of the law be ours, but it is vastly more important that we be prepared for the exercise of those privileges. The opportunity to earn a dollar in a factory just now is worth infinitely more than the opportunity to spend a dollar in an opera house.

In conclusion, may I repeat that nothing in thirty years has given us more hope and encouragement, and drawn us so near to you of the white race, as this opportunity offered by the Exposition; and here bending; as it were, over the altar that represents the results of the struggles of your race and mine, both starting practically empty-handed three decades ago, I pledge that, in your effort to work out the great and intricate problem which God has laid at the doors of the South, you shall have at all times the patient, sympathetic help of my race; only let this be constantly in mind that, while from representations in these buildings of the products of field, of forest, of mine, of factory, letters, and art, much good will come, yet far above and beyond material benefits will be the higher good, that let us pray God will come, in a blotting out of sectional differences and racial animosities and suspicions, in a determination to administer absolute justice, in a willing obedience among all classes to the mandates of law. This, coupled with our material prosperity, will bring into our beloved South a new heaven and a new earth.

WILLIAM E. B. DU BOIS
(1868-1963)

W. E. B. Du Bois was not only the most brilliant and prolific black scholar of the early twentieth century, but also the most influential. He lived to be well over ninety; his long career spanned seventy years of writing, speaking, and organizing for human peace, dignity, and justice. His commitment to black Americans broadened to encompass all people descended from Africa, which he called "the Spiritual Frontier of humankind," and eventually to encompass humankind itself in his efforts toward world peace. Because he remained well ahead of his time, his views were often controversial. Because he was an outspoken critic of society, he became increasingly alienated from his native land. He spent his last years as a citizen of Ghana, where he pursued his lifelong project, the Encyclopedia Africana. *Among his accomplishments were the founding of the Niagara Movement, one of the earliest attempts to organize a black pressure group; his part in establishing the NAACP; and four magazines which he founded and edited, including* Phylon, *the Atlanta University journal, and the extremely significant* The Crisis, *official publication of the NAACP. Du Bois wrote nineteen books and hundreds of articles; a complete bibliography would be book-length.*

Du Bois was born in Great Barrington, Massachusetts, a small New England town with few black families. Years of study at Fisk and Harvard Universities and the University of Berlin brought him in contact with some of the most brilliant teachers of two continents. In 1895 he received his doctorate from Harvard. His dissertation, The Suppression of the African Slave Trade to the United States of America, 1638 to 1870, *became the first volume of the Harvard University Series in History.*

For fifteen years after the completion of his formal education, Du Bois was a college professor and researcher. After a year as Professor of Classics at Wilberforce University, he was appointed Assistant Instructor at the University of Pennsylvania, where he conducted sociological research on the condition of Negroes in Philadelphia. In 1899 the results of this study were published in a monograph, The Philadelphia Negro, a Sociological Study, a work of lasting importance. From 1897 to 1910 Du Bois was Professor of History and Economics at Atlanta University. During these years he produced some of his major works. Fifteen volumes of The Atlanta University Publications (1897-1915), edited by Du Bois (the last four with Augustus Dill), remain among the best sources of information about blacks for that time.

The Souls of Black Folk: Essays and Sketches (1903) is a classic in the field of black writing. It triggered the long debate with Booker T. Washington and, in a sense, freed black intellectuals from the incubus of Washington's conciliatory stand. Du Bois' biography John Brown appeared in 1909.

In 1910 Du Bois left Atlanta University to edit The Crisis. For the next twenty-four years he conducted the magazine as a vital weapon of protest, a forum for black opinion, and an important outlet for black writing. Through The Crisis Du Bois became the philosopher-spokesman of black thought. In addition to the militant Crisis, Du Bois founded and edited The Brownies' Book, a magazine for black children, whose purpose was to teach them the beauty of their blackness. Meanwhile, Du Bois was addressing white audiences through articles published in leading white periodicals. During this period Du Bois wrote two novels, The Quest of the Silver Fleece (1911) and Dark Princess (1928). He collected essays and sketches and some poetry in Darkwater (1920), which was followed by The Gift of Black Folk (1924). The Pan-African Congresses also belong to these years.

Du Bois left the NAACP and The Crisis in 1934 after a quarrel over policy and returned to Atlanta University as Professor of Sociology. While at Atlanta University he published two books of history, Black Reconstruction in America, 1860-1880 (1935), Black Folk: Then and Now (1939), an autobiography, Dusk of Dawn (1940), and the prefatory volume of the Encyclopedia of the Negro (1945). Following his involuntary retirement from Atlanta University at the age of seventy-six, he rejoined the NAACP, where he remained until another break four years later.

When he was eighty, Du Bois began another phase of his career. The last fifteen years of his life were spent working vigorously for world peace and African unity. In his last years he became a communist and a citizen of Ghana. Du Bois died in 1963 on the day before the March on Washington.

As a creative writer, Du Bois was probably at his best as essayist. His essays are extant in the Crisis *editorials and in several volumes. The Souls of Black Folk, the first volume of essays, was a landmark in black American literary history. In his introduction to the Fawcett edition, Saunders Redding describes the book as "fixing that moment in history when the American Negro began to reject the idea of the world's belonging to white people only, and think of himself, in concert, as a potential force in the organization of society." In flowing, poetic style, rich in metaphor and musical devices, the essays affirm the strength and dignity of black people, define their aspirations, and remind the nation of their contributions to its culture. The lyricism of the essays is superimposed on the firm mass of Du Bois' historical and sociological observations. The Souls of Black Folk was received with alarm by the white South, but the ideas became firmly implanted in black soil and have since grown to fruition.*

Du Bois wrote comparatively little poetry; however, what he did write is noteworthy. He preferred free verse to the confinement of conventional forms. "A Litany of Atlanta" (1906) is one of the earliest free verse poems by a black author. Du Bois' poetry is extremely passionate and replete with vivid images. Sometimes, as in "A Litany of Atlanta," the long intricate sentences make the poem nearly as much prose as poetry. Du Bois' poetry, like his prose, deals with black themes: the horror of a lynching in "A Litany of Atlanta," black beauty in "The Song of the Smoke," the strength of black women in "The Burden of Black Women," the irony of white American Christianity in "A Christmas Poem."

His novels are not altogether successful. The Quest of the Silver Fleece is essentially a sociological study of the South after the Civil War. Dark Princess bespeaks Du Bois' commitment to Pan-Africanism. In both novels the characters are types rather than people, and the theme in each work is so important that it overshadows the other dimensions of the novel. Toward the end of his life Du Bois wrote a trilogy, The Black Flame. All three novels are heavy with historical data.

In his brilliant articulation of a great cause and in his energetic exploration of many facets of that cause, Du Bois exerted a profound influence on several generations. While his work is a most valuable part of black literature, as important is his encouragement of black writers and his strong influence on the developing black psyche.

There are books on Du Bois by Frederick Broderick (1959) and Elliot Rudwick (1959). Freedomways, *of which Du Bois was a founder, produced a special Du Bois issue in 1965. Many of the articles in this issue reappear in* Du Bois: Black Titan *(1970). His friend and colleague Rayford Logan has edited* W. E. B. Du Bois: A Profile *(1971).*

The Song of the Smoke

I am the smoke king,
I am black.
I am swinging in the sky.
I am ringing worlds on high:
I am the thought of the throbbing mills,
I am the soul of the soul toil kills,
I am the ripple of trading rills,

Up I'm curling from the sod,
I am whirling home to God.
I am the smoke king,
I am black.

I am the smoke king,
I am black.
I am wreathing broken hearts,
I am sheathing devils' darts;
Dark inspiration of iron times,
Wedding the toil of toiling climes
Shedding the blood of bloodless crimes,

Down I lower in the blue,
Up I tower toward the true,
I am the smoke king,
I am black.

I am the smoke king,
I am black.

I am darkening with song,
I am hearkening to wrong;
I will be as black as blackness can,
The blacker the mantle the mightier the man,
My purpl'ing midnights no day dawn may ban.

I am carving God in night,
I am painting hell in white.
I am the smoke king,
I am black.

I am the smoke king,
I am black.

I am cursing ruddy morn,
I am nursing hearts unborn;
Souls unto me are as mists in the night,
I whiten my blackmen, I beckon my white,
What's the hue of a hide to a man in his might!
Hail, then, grilly, grimy hands,

Sweet Christ, pity toiling lands!
Hail to the smoke king,
Hail to the black!

(1899)

A Litany of Atlanta

Done at Atlanta, in the Day of Death, 1906.

O Silent God, Thou whose voice afar in mist and mystery hath left our ears an-hungered in these fearful days—
Hear us, good Lord!

Listen to us, Thy children: our faces dark with doubt are made a mockery in Thy sanctuary. With uplifted hands we front Thy heaven, O God, crying:
We beseech Thee to hear us, good Lord!

We are not better than our fellows, Lord, we are but weak and human men. When our devils do deviltry, curse Thou the doer and the deed: curse them as we curse them, do to them all and more than ever they have done to innocence and weakness, to womanhood and home.
Have mercy upon us, miserable sinners!

And yet whose is the deeper guilt? Who made these devils? Who nursed them in crime and fed them on injustice? Who ravished and debauched their mothers and their grandmothers? Who bought and sold their crime, and waxed fat and rich on public iniquity?
Thou knowest, good God!

Is this Thy justice, O Father, that guile be easier than innocence, and the innocent crucified for the guilt of the untouched guilty?
Justice, O judge of men!

Wherefore de we pray? Is not the God of the fathers dead? Have not seers seen in Heaven's halls Thine hearsed and lifeless form stark amidst the black and rolling smoke of sin, where all along bow bitter forms of endless dead?

Awake, Thou that sleepest!

Thou art not dead, but flown afar, up hills of endless light through blazing corridors of suns, where worlds do swing of good and gentle men, of women strong and free—far from the cozenage, black hypocrisy, and chaste prostitution of this shameful speck of dust!

Turn again, O Lord, leave us not to perish in our sin!

From lust of body and lust of blood,
  Great God, deliver us!

From lust of power and lust of gold,
  Great God, deliver us!

From the leagued lying of despot and of brute,
  Great God, deliver us!

A city lay in travail, God our Lord, and from her loins sprang twin Murder and Black Hate. Red was the midnight; clang, crack and cry of death and fury filled the air and trembled underneath the stars when church spires pointed silently to Thee. And all this was to sate the greed of greedy men who hide behind the veil of vengeance!

Bend us Thine ear, O Lord!

In the pale, still morning we looked upon the deed. We stopped our ears and held our leaping hands, but they—did they not wag their heads and leer and cry with bloody jaws: *Cease from Crime!* The word was mockery, for thus they train a hundred crimes while we do cure one.

Turn again our captivity, O Lord!

Behold this maimed and broken thing; dear God, it was an humble black man who toiled and sweat to save a bit from the pittance paid him. They told him: *Work and Rise.* He worked. Did this man sin? Nay, but some one told how some one said another did—one whom he had never seen nor known. Yet for that man's crime this man lieth maimed and murdered, his wife naked to shame, his children, to poverty and evil.

Hear us, O heavenly Father!

Doth not this justice of hell stink in Thy nostrils, O God? How long shall the mounting flood of innocent blood roar in Thine ears and pound in our hearts for vengeance? Pile the pale frenzy of blood-crazed brutes who do such deeds high on Thine altar, Jehovah Jireh, and burn it in hell forever and forever.

Forgive us, good Lord; we know not what we say!

Bewildered we are, and passion-tost, mad with the madness of a mobbed and mocked and murdered people; straining at the armposts of Thy Throne, we raise our shackled hands and charge Thee, God, by the bones of our stolen fathers, by the tears of our dead mothers, by the very blood of Thy crucified Christ: *What meaneth this?* Tell us the Plan; give us the Sign!

Keep not Thou silence, O God!

Sit no longer blind, Lord God, deaf to our prayer and dumb to our dumb suffering. Surely Thou too art not white, O Lord, a pale, bloodless, heartless thing?

Ah! Christ of all the Pities!

Forgive the thought! Forgive these wild, blasphemous words. Thou art still the God of our black fathers, and in Thy soul's soul sit some soft darkenings of the evening, some shadowings of the velvet night.

But whisper—speak—call, great God, for Thy silence is white terror to our hearts! The way, O God, show us the way and point us the path.

Whither? North is greed and South is blood; within, the coward, and without the liar. Whither? To Death?

Amen! Welcome dark sleep!

Whither? To life? But not this life, dear God, not this. Let the cup pass from us, tempt us not beyond our strength, for there is that clamoring and clawing within, to whose voice we would not listen, yet shudder lest we must,—and it is red, Ah! God! It is a red and awful shape.

Selah!

In yonder East trembles a star.
Vengeance is mine; I will repay, saith the Lord!

Thy will, O Lord, be done!
Kyrie Eleison!

Lord, we have done these pleading, wavering words.
We beseech Thee to hear us, good Lord!

We bow our heads and hearken soft to the sobbing of
women and little children.
We beseech Thee to hear us, good Lord!

Our voices sink in silence and in night.
Hear us, good Lord!

In night, O God of a godless land!
Amen!

In silence, O silent God.
Selah!

Of the Sorrow Songs
From *The Souls of Black Folk*

I walk through the churchyard
  To lay this body down;
I know moon-rise, I know star-rise;
I walk in the moonlight, I walk in the starlight;
I'll lie in the grave and stretch out my arms,
I'll go to judgment in the evening of the day,
And my soul and thy soul shall meet that day,
  When I lay this body down.

NEGRO SONG.

They that walked in darkness sang songs in the olden days—Sorrow Songs—for they were weary at heart. And so before each thought that I have written in this book I have set a phrase, a haunting echo of these weird old songs in which the soul of the black slave spoke to men. Ever since I was a child these songs have stirred me strangely. They came out of the South unknown to me, one by one, and yet at once I knew them as of me and of mine. Then in after years when I came to Nashville I saw the great temple builded of these songs towering over the pale city. To me Jubilee Hall seemed ever made of the songs themselves, and its bricks were red with the blood and dust of toil. Out of them rose for me morning, noon, and night, bursts of wonderful melody, full of the voices of my brothers and sisters, full of the voices of the past.

Little of beauty has America given the world save the rude grandeur God himself stamped on her bosom; the human spirit in this new world has expressed itself in vigor and ingenuity rather than in beauty. And so by fateful chance the Negro folk-song—the rhythmic cry of the slave—stands to-day not simply as the sole American music, but as the most beautiful expression of human experience born this side the seas. It has been neglected, it has been, and is, half despised, and above all it has been persistently mistaken and misunderstood; but notwithstanding, it still remains as the singular spiritual heritage of the nation and the greatest gift of the Negro people.

Away back in the thirties the melody of these slave songs stirred the nation, but the songs were soon half forgotten. Some, like "Near the lake where drooped the willow," passed into current airs and their source was forgotten; others were caricatured on the "minstrel" stage and their memory died away. Then in war-time came the singular Port Royal experiment after the capture of Hilton Head, and perhaps for the first time the North met the Southern slave face to face and heart to heart with no third witness. The Sea Islands of the Carolinas, where they met, were filled with a black folk of primitive type, touched and moulded less by the world about them than any others outside the Black Belt. Their appearance was uncouth, their language funny, but their hearts were human and their singing stirred men with a mighty power. Thomas Wentworth Higginson hastened to tell of these songs, and Miss McKim and others urged upon the world their rare beauty. But the world listened only half credulously until the Fisk Jubilee Singers sang the slave songs so deeply into the world's heart that it can never wholly forget them again.

There was once a blacksmith's son born at Cadiz, New York, who in the changes of time taught school in Ohio and helped defend Cincinnati from Kirby Smith. Then he fought at Chancellorsville and Gettysburg and finally served in the Freedman's Bureau at Nashville. Here he formed a Sunday-school class of black children in 1866, and sang with them and taught them to sing. And then they taught him to sing, and when once the glory of the Jubilee songs passed into the soul of George L. White, he knew his life-work was to let those Negroes sing to the world as they had sung to him. So in 1871 the pilgrimage of the Fisk Jubilee Singers began. North to Cincinnati they rode,—four half-clothed black boys and five girl-women,—led by a man with a cause and a purpose. They stopped at Wilberforce, the oldest of Negro schools, where a black bishop blessed them. Then they went, fighting cold and starvation, shut out of hotels, and cheerfully sneered at, ever northward; and ever the magic of their song kept thrilling hearts, until a burst of applause in the Congregational Council at Oberlin revealed them to the world. They came to New York and Henry Ward Beecher dared to welcome them, even though the metropolitan dailies sneered at his "Nigger Minstrels." So their songs conquered till they sang across the land and across the sea, before Queen and Kaiser, in Scotland and Ireland, Holland and Switzerland. Seven years they sang, and brought back a hundred and fifty thousand dollars to found Fisk University.

Since their day they have been imitated—sometimes well, by the singers of Hampton and Atlanta, sometimes ill, by straggling quartettes. Caricature has sought again to spoil the quaint beauty of the music, and has filled the air with many debased melodies which vulgar ears scarce know from the real. But the true Negro folk-song still lives in the hearts of those who have heard them truly sung and in the hearts of the Negro people.

What are these songs, and what do they mean? I know little of music and can say nothing in technical phrase, but I know something of men, and knowing them, I know that these songs are the articulate message of the slave to the world. They tell us in these eager days that life was joyous to the black slave, careless and happy. I can easily believe this of some, of many. But not all the past South, though it rose from the dead, can gainsay the heart-touching witness of these songs. They are the music of an unhappy people, of the children of disappointment; they tell of death and suffering and unvoiced longing toward a truer world, of misty wanderings and hidden ways.

The songs are indeed the siftings of centuries; the music is far more ancient than the words, and in it we can trace here and there signs of development. My grandfather's grandmother was seized by an evil Dutch trader two centuries ago; and coming to the valleys of the Hudson and Housatonic, black, little, and lithe, she shivered and shrank in the harsh north winds, looked longingly at the hills, and often crooned a heathen melody to the child between her knees. thus:

> Do bana coba gene me, gene me!
> Do bana coba, gene me, gene me!
> Ben d'nuli, nuli, nuli, nuli, bend'le.

The child sang it to his children and they to their children's

162

children, and so two hundred years it has travelled down to us and
we sing it to our children, knowing as little as our fathers what its
words may mean, but knowing well the meaning of its music.

This was primitive African music; it may be seen in larger form
in the strange chant which heralds "The Coming of John":

> "You may bury me in the East,
> You may bury me in the West,
> But I'll hear the trumpet sound in that morning,"

—the voice of exile.

Ten master songs, more or less, one may pluck from this forest
of melody—songs of undoubted Negro origin and wide popular cur-
rency, and songs peculiarly characteristic of the slave. One of these
I have just mentioned. Another whose strains begin this book is
"Nobody knows the trouble I've seen." When, struck with a sudden
poverty, the United States refused to fulfill its promises of land to
the freedmen, a brigadier-general went down to the Sea Islands to
carry the news. An old woman on the outskirts of the throng began
singing this song; all the mass joined with her, swaying. And the
soldier wept.

The third song is the cradle-song of death which all men know,
—"Swing low, sweet chariot,"—whose bars begin the life story of
"Alexander Crummell." Then there is the song of many waters,
"Roll, Jordan, roll," a mighty chorus with minor cadences. There
were many songs of the fugitive like that which opens "The Wings
of Atalanta," and the more familiar "Been a-listening." The seventh
is the song of the End and the Beginning—"My Lord, what a mourning! when the stars begin to fall"; a strain of this is placed before
"The Dawn of Freedom." The song of groping—"My way's cloudy"
—begins "The Meaning of Progress"; the ninth is the song of this
chapter—"Wrestlin' Jacob, the day is a-breaking,"—a pæan of hopeful strife. The last master song is the song of songs—"Steal away,"—
sprung from "The Faith of the Fathers."

There are many others of the Negro folk-songs as striking and
characteristic as these, as, for instance, the three strains in the third,
eighth, and ninth chapters; and others I am sure could easily make
a selection on more scientific principles. There are, too, songs that
seem to be a step removed from the more primitive types: there is the

maze-like medley, "Bright sparkles," one phrase of which heads "The Black Belt"; the Easter carol, "Dust, dust and ashes"; the dirge, "My mother's took her flight and gone home"; and that burst of melody hovering over "The Passing of the First-Born"—"I hope my mother will be there in that beautiful world on high."

These represent a third step in the development of the slave song, of which "You may bury me in the East" is the first, and songs like "March on" (chapter six) and "Steal away" are the second. The first is African music, the second Afro-American, while the third is a blending of Negro music with the music heard in the foster land. The result is still distinctively Negro and the method of blending original, but the elements are both Negro and Caucasian. One might go further and find a fourth step in this development, where the songs of white America have been distinctively influenced by the slave songs or have incorporated whole phrases of Negro melody, as "Swanee River" and "Old Black Joe." Side by side, too, with the growth has gone the debasements and imitations—the Negro "minstrel" songs, many of the "gospel" hymns, and some of the contemporary "coon" songs,—a mass of music in which the novice may easily lose himself and never find the real Negro melodies.

In these songs, I have said, the slave spoke to the world. Such a message is naturally veiled and half articulate. Words and music have lost each other and new and cant phrases of a dimly understood theology have displaced the old sentiment. Once in a while we catch a strange word of an unknown tongue, as the "Mighty Myo," which figures as a river of death; more often slight words or mere doggerel are joined to music of singular sweetness. Purely secular songs are few in number, partly because many of them were turned into hymns by a change of words, partly because the frolics were seldom heard by the stranger, and the music less often caught. Of nearly all the songs, however, the music is distinctly sorrowful. The ten master songs I have mentioned tell in word and music of trouble and exile, of strife and hiding; they grope toward some unseen power and sigh for rest in the End.

The words that are left to us are not without interest, and, cleared of evident dross, they conceal much of real poetry and meaning beneath conventional theology and unmeaning rhapsody. Like all primitive folk, the slave stood near to Nature's heart. Life was a "rough and rolling sea" like the brown Atlantic of the Sea Islands; the "Wilderness" was the home of God, and the "lonesome valley" led to the way of life. "Winter'll soon be over," was the picture of life and death to a tropical imagination. The sudden wild thunder-storms of the South awed and impressed the Negroes,—at times the rumbling seemed to them "mournful," at times imperious:

> "My Lord calls me,
> He calls me by the thunder,
> The trumpet sounds it in my soul."

The monotonous toil and exposure is painted in many words. One sees the ploughmen in the hot, moist furrow, singing:

> "Dere's no rain to wet you,
> Dere's no sun to burn you,
> Oh, push along, believer,
> I want to go home."

The bowed and bent old man cries, with thrice repeated wail:

> "O Lord, keep me from sinking down,"

and he rebukes the devil of doubt who can whisper:

> "Jesus is dead and God's gone away."

Yet the soul-hunger is there, the restlessness of the savage, the wail of the wanderer, and the plaint is put in one little phrase:

> "My soul wants something that's new, that's new."

Over the inner thoughts of the slaves and their relations one with another the shadow of fear ever hung, so that we get but glimpses here and there, and also with them, eloquent omissions and silences. Mother and child are sung, but seldom father; fugitive and weary wanderer call for pity and affection, but there is little of wooing and wedding; the rocks and the mountains are well known, but home is unknown. Strange blending of love and helplessness signs through the refrain:

> "Yonder's my ole mudder,
> Been waggin' at det hill so long;
> 'Bout time she cross over,
> Git home bime-by."

Elsewhere comes the cry of the "motherless" and the "Farewell, farewell, my only child."

Love-songs are scarce and fall into two categories—the frivolous and light, and the sad. Of deep successful love there is omnious silence, and in one of the oldest of these songs there is a depth of history and meaning:

> "Poor Rosy, poor gal;
> Poor Rosy, poor gal;
> Rosy break my poor heart,
> Hear'n shall-a-be my home."

A black woman said of the song, "It can't be sung without a full heart and a troubled sperrit." The same voice sings here that sings in the German folk-song:

> "Jetz Geh i' an's brunele, trink' aber net."

Of death the Negro showed little fear, but talked of it familiarly and even fondly as simply a crossing of the waters, perhaps—who knows?—back to his ancient forests again. Later days transfigured his fatalism, and amid the dust and dirt the toiler sang:

"Dust, dust and ashes, fly over my grave,
But the Lord shall bear my spirit home."

The things evidently borrowed from the surrounding world
undergo characteristic change when they enter the mouth of the
slave. Especially is this true of Bible phrases. "Weep, O captive daughter of Zion," is quaintly turned into "Zion, weep-a-low," and the
wheels of Ezekiel are turned every way in the mystic dreaming of
the slave, till he says:

"There's a little wheel a-turnin' in-a-my heart."

As in olden time, the words of these hymns were improvised by
some leading minstrel of the religious band. The circumstances of the
gathering, however, the rhythm of the songs, and the limitations of
allowable thought, confined the poetry for the most part to single or
double lines, and they seldom were expanded to quatrains or longer
tales, although there are some few examples of sustained efforts,
chiefly paraphrases of the Bible. Three short series of verses have
always attracted me,—the one that heads this chapter, of one line of
which Thomas Wentworth Higginson has fittingly said, "Never, it
seems to me, since man first lived and suffered was his infinite longing
for peace uttered more plaintively." The second and third are descrip-
tions of the Last Judgment,—the one a late improvisation, with some
traces of outside influence:

"Oh, the stars in the elements are falling,
And the moon drips away into blood,
And the ransomed of the Lord are returning unto God,
Blessed be the name of the Lord."

And the other earlier and homelier picture from the low coast lands:

"Michael, haul the boat ashore,
Then you'll hear the horn they blow,
Then you'll hear the trumpet sound,
Trumpet sound the world around,
Trumpet sound for rich and poor,
Trumpet sound the Jubilee,
Trumpet sound for you and me."

Through all the sorrow of the Sorrow Songs there breathes a hope—a faith in the ultimate justice of things. The minor cadences of despair change often to triumph and calm confidence. Sometimes it is faith in life, sometimes a faith in death, sometimes assurance of boundless justice in some fair world beyond. But whichever it is, the meaning is always clear: that sometimes, somewhere, men will judge men by their souls and not by their skins. Is such a hope justified? Do the Sorrow Songs sing true?

The silently growing assumption of this age is that the probation of races is past, and that the backward races of to-day are of proven inefficiency and not worth the saving. Such an assumption is the arrogance of peoples irreverent toward Time and ignorant of the deeds of men. A thousand years ago such an assumption, easily possible, would have made it difficult for the Teuton to prove his right to life. Two thousand years ago such dogmatism, readily welcome, would have scouted the idea of blond races ever leading civilization. So woefully unorganized is sociological knowledge that the meaning of progress, the meaning of "swift" and "slow" in human doing, and the limits of human perfectability, are veiled, unanswered sphinxes on the shores of science. Why should Æschylus have sung two thousand years before Shakespeare was born? Why has civilization flourished in Europe, and flickered, flamed, and died in Africa? So long as the world stands meekly dumb before such questions, shall this nation proclaim its ignorance and unhallowed prejudices by denying freedom of opportunity to those who brought the Sorrow Songs to the Seats of the Mighty?

Your country? How came it yours? Before the Pilgrims landed we were here. Here we have brought our three gifts and mingled them with yours: a gift of story and song—soft, stirring melody in an ill-harmonized and unmelodious land; the gift of sweat and brawn to beat back the wilderness, conquer the soil, and lay the foundations of this vast economic empire two hundred years earlier than your weak hand could have done it; the third, a gift of the Spirit. Around us the history of the land has centred for thrice a hundred years; out of the nation's heart we have called all that was best to throttle and subdue all that was worst; fire and blood, prayer and sacrifice, have billowed over this people, and they have found peace only in the altars of the God of Right. Nor has our gift of the Spirit been merely passive. Actively we have woven ourselves with the very warp and woof of this nation,—we fought their battles, shared their sorrow, mingled our blood with theirs, and generation after generation have pleaded with a headstrong, careless people to despise not Justice, Mercy, and Truth, lest the nation be smitten with a curse. Our song, our toil, our cheer, and warning have been given to this nation in blood-brotherhood. Are not these gifts worth the giving? Is not this work and striving? Would America have been America without her Negro people?

Even so is the hope that sang in the songs of my fathers well sung. If somewhere in this whirl and chaos of things there dwells Eternal Good, pitiful yet masterful, then anon in His good time America shall rend the Veil and the prisoned shall go free. Free, free as the sunshine trickling down the morning into these high windows of mine, free as yonder fresh young voices welling up to me from the caverns of brick and mortar below—swelling with song, instinct with life, tremulous treble and darkening bass. My children, my little children, are singing to the sunshine, and thus they sing:

> Let us cheer the weary traveller,
> Cheer the weary traveller,
> Let us cheer the weary traveller
> Along the heavenly way.

And the traveller girds himself, and sets his face toward the Morning, and goes his way.

(1903)

Crime and Lynching

A favorite argument with shallow thinkers is: Stop crime and lynching will cease. Such a statement is both historically and logically false. Historically, lynching leads to lynching, burning to burning; and lynching for great crimes to lynching for trivial offenses. Moreover, lynching as practised to-day in the United States is not the result of crime—it is a cause of crime, on account of the flagrant, awful injustice it inflicts in so many cases on innocent men . . .

What now must be the feeling of the Negroes . . . ? Are they appalled at their own wickedness? Do they see that the wages of sin is death? Not they. They despise the white man's justice, hate him, and whenever they hear of Negro "crime" in the future they will say: "It's a white man's lie."

Not only this, but these people know how criminals are made and they pity rather than condemn them. Take, for instance, the cries throughout the South against "vagrants." It means the call for the State enslavement of any man who does not work for a white man at the white man's price. The most outrageous laws and arrests are made under the excuse of vagrancy. In Atlanta, on October 15, thirty-seven laborers were arrested at night in their lodging house as "vagrants." In Texas five laborers were arrested as vagrants and proved their hard, steady jobs. "But," remarks the Galveston Tribune chirpily:

"The State chose to prosecute under a different portion of the law, alleging loitering about houses of ill-fame. The court explained, as he has done before, that a person can be a vagrant yet be steadily employed, the law being general in its effect and covering many points upon which a conviction can be had on a charge of vagrancy."

Suppose now a mischievous boy or a loiterer or a laborer out of work is thrown into jail as a vagrant, what happens to him?

From a thousand examples, let us choose but one from a Texas report on a local "chain gang":

"The day's program was invariably this: Up at 4:30 o'clock in the morning, trot two to five miles to the cane fields, work there in squads until noon, when fifteen to twenty minutes would be allowed for the eating of a cold dinner; driven hard during the afternoon and brought back by starlight at night in the same dog trot they went out in the morning. The weak must keep up with the strong in his work or be punished. Convicts slept in their underclothes or naked, as it happened to rain or shine during the day. If it rained they hung up their clothes to dry and slept without. One convict testified that he had frequently taken his clothes from the nail frozen stiff. One man was on a farm a year, and during that time the bedclothes were not washed and were sunned but twice."

Thus desperate criminals are manufactured and turned out day by day.

Can we stop this by lynching? No. The first step toward stopping crime is to stop lynching. The next step is to treat black men like human beings.

(1912)

The Souls of White Folk
From *Darkwater*

. . . I know many souls that toss and whirl and pass, but none there are that intrigue me more than the Souls of White Folk,

Of them I am singularly clairvoyant. I see in and through them. I view them from unusual points of vantage. Not as a foreigner do I come, for I am native, not foreign, bone of their thought and flesh of their language. Mine is not the knowledge of the traveler or the colonial composite of dear memories, words and wonder. Nor yet is my knowledge that which servants have of masters, or mass of class, or capitalist of artisan. Rather I see these souls undressed and from the back and side. I see the working of their entrails. I know their thoughts and they know that I know. This knowledge makes them now embarrassed, now furious! They deny my right to live and be and call me misbirth! My word is to them mere bitterness and my soul, pessimism. And yet as they preach and strut and shout and threaten, crouching as they clutch at rags of facts and fancies to hide their nakedness, they go twisting, flying by my tired eyes and I see them ever stripped—ugly, human.

The discovery of personal whiteness among the world's peoples is a very modern thing—a nineteenth and twentieth century matter, indeed. The ancient world would have laughed at such a distinction. The Middle Age regarded skin color with mild curiosity; and even up into the eighteenth century we were hammering our national manikins into one, great, Universal Man, with fine frenzy which ignored color and race even more than birth. Today we have changed all that, and the world in a sudden, emotional conversion has discovered that it is white and by that token, wonderful!

This assumption that of all the hues of God whiteness alone is inherently and obviously better than brownness or tan leads to curious acts; even the sweeter souls of the dominant world as they discourse with me on weather, weal, and woe are continually playing above their actual words an obligato of tune and tone, saying:

"My poor, un-white thing! Weep not nor rage. I know, too well, that the curse of God lies heavy on you. Why? That is not for me to say, but be brave! Do your work in your lowly sphere, praying the good Lord that into heaven above, where all is love, you may, one day, be born—white!"

I do not laugh. I am quite straight-faced as I ask soberly:

"But what on earth is whiteness that one should so desire it?" Then always, somehow, some way, silently but clearly, I am given to understand that whiteness is the ownership of the earth forever and ever, Amen!

Now what is the effect on a man or a nation when it comes passionately to believe such an extraordinary dictum as this? That nations are coming to believe it is manifest daily. Wave on wave, each with increasing virulence, is dashing this new religion of whiteness on the shores of our time. Its first effects are funny: the strut of the Southerner, the arrogance of the Englishman amuck, the whoop of the hoodlum who vicariously leads your mob. Next it appears dampening generous enthusiasm in what we once counted glorious; to free the slave is discovered to be tolerable only in so far as it freed his master! Do we sense somnolent writhings in black Africa or angry groans in India or triumphant banzais in Japan? "To your tents, O Israel!" These nations are not white!

After the more comic manifestations and the chilling of generous enthusiasm come subtler, darker deeds. Everything considered, the title to the universe claimed by White Folk is faulty. It ought, at least, to look plausible. How easy, then, by emphasis and omission to make children believe that every great soul the world ever saw was a white man's soul; that every great thought the world ever knew was a white man's thought; that every great deed the world ever did was a white man's deed; that every great dream the world ever sang was a white man's dream. In fine, that if from the world were dropped everything that could not fairly be attributed to White Folk, the world would, if anything, be even greater, truer, better than now. And if all this be a lie, is it not a lie in a great cause?

Here it is that the comedy verges to tragedy. The first minor note is struck, all unconsciously, by those worthy souls in whom consciousness of high descent brings burning desire to spread the gift abroad—the obligation of nobility to the ignoble. Such sense of duty assumes two things: a real possession of the heritage and its frank appreciation by the humble-born. So long, then, as humble black folk, voluble with thanks, receive barrels of old clothes from lordly and generous whites, there is much mental peace and moral satisfaction. But when the black man begins to dispute the white man's title to certain alleged bequests of the Fathers in wage and position, authority and training; and when his attitude toward charity is sullen anger rather than humble jollity; when he insists on his human right to swagger and swear and waste—then the spell is suddenly broken and the philanthropist is ready to believe that Negroes are impudent, that the South is right, and that Japan wants to fight America.

After this the descent to Hell is easy. On the pale, white faces which the great billows whirl upward to my tower I see again and again, often and still more often, a writing of human hatred, a deep and passionate hatred, vast by the very vagueness of its expressions. Down through the green waters, on the bottom of the world, where men move to and fro, I have seen a man—an educated gentleman—grow livid with anger because a little, silent, black woman was sitting by herself in a Pullman car. He was a white man. I have seen a great, grown man curse a little child, who had wandered into the wrong waiting-room, searching for its mother: "Here, you damned black—." He was white. In Central Park I have seen the upper lip of a quiet, peaceful man curl back in a tigerish snarl of rage because black folk rode by in a motor car. He was a white man. We have seen, you and I, city after city drunk and furious with ungovernable lust of blood; mad with murder, destroying, killing, and cursing; torturing human victims because somebody accused of crime happened to be of the same color as the mob's innocent victims and because that color was not white! We have seen—Merciful God! in these wild days and in the name of Civilization, Justice, and Motherhood—what have we not seen, right here in America, of orgy, cruelty, barbarism, and murder done to men and women of Negro descent.

Up through the foam of green and weltering waters wells this great mass of hatred, in wilder, fiercer violence, until I look down and know that today to the millions of my people no misfortune could happen—of death and pestilence, failure and defeat—that would not make the hearts of millions of their fellows beat with fierce,

174

vindictive joy! Do you doubt it? Ask your own soul what it would say if the next census were to report that half of black America was dead and the other half dying.

Unfortunate? Unfortunate. But where is the misfortune? Mine? Am I, in my blackness, the sole sufferer? I suffer. And yet, somehow, above the suffering, above the shackled anger that beats the bars, above the hurt that crazes there surges in me a vast pity—pity for a people imprisoned and enthralled, hampered and made miserable for such a cause, for such a phantasy!

Conceive this nation, of all human peoples, engaged in a crusade to make the "World Safe for Democracy"! Can you imagine the United States protesting against Turkish atrocities in Armenia, while the Turks are silent about mobs in Chicago and St. Louis; what is Louvain compared with Memphis, Waco, Washington, Dyersburg, and Estill Springs? In short, what is the black man but America's Belgium, and how could America condemn in Germany that which she commits, just as brutally, within her own borders?

A true and worthy ideal frees and uplifts a people; a false ideal imprisons and lowers. Say to men, earnestly and repeatedly: "Honesty is best, knowledge is power; do unto others as you would be done by." Say this and act it and the nation must move toward it, if not to it. But say to a people: "The one virtue is to be white," and the people rush to the inevitable conclusion, "Kill the 'nigger'!"

Is not this the record of present America? Is not this its headlong progress? Are we not coming more and more, day by day, to making the statement "I am white," the one fundamental tenet of our practical morality? Only when this basic, iron rule is involved is our defense of right nation-wide and prompt. Murder may swagger, theft may rule and prostitution may flourish and the nation gives but spasmodic, intermittent and lukewarm attention. But let the murderer be black or the thief brown or the violator of womanhood have a drop of Negro blood, and the righteousness of the indignation sweeps the world. Nor would this fact make the indignation less justifiable did not we all know that it was blackness that was condemned and not crime.

In the awful cataclysm of World War, where from beating, slandering, and murdering us the white world turned temporarily aside to kill each other, we of the Darker Peoples looked on in mild amaze . . .

Consider our chiefest industry—fighting. Laboriously the Middle Ages built its rules of fairness—equal armament, equal notice, equal conditions. What do we see today? Machine-guns against assegais; conquest sugared with religion; mutilation and rape masquerading as culture—all this, with vast applause at the superiority of white over black soldiers!

War is horrible! This the dark world knows to its awful cost. But has it just become horrible, in these last days, when under essentially equal conditions, equal armament, and equal waste of wealth white men are fighting white men, with surgeons and nurses hovering near? . . .

Behold little Belgium and her pitiable plight, but has the world forgotten Congo? What Belgium now suffers is not half, not even a tenth, of what she has done to black Congo since Stanley's great dream of 1880. . . .

Harris declares that King Leopold's régime meant the death of twelve million natives, "but what we who were behind the scenes felt most keenly was the fact that the real catastrophe in the Congo was desolation and murder in the larger sense. The invasion of family life, the ruthless destruction of every social barrier, the shattering of every tribal law, the introduction of criminal practices which struck the chiefs of the people dumb with horror—in a word, a veritable avalanche of filth and immorality overwhelmed the Congo tribes. . . ."

Here is a civilization that has boasted much. Neither Roman nor Arab, Greek nor Egyptian, Persian nor Mongol ever took himself and his own perfectness with such disconcerting seriousness as the modern white man. We whose shame, humiliation, and deep insult his aggrandizement so often involved were never deceived. We looked at him clearly, with world-old eyes, and saw simply a human thing, weak and pitiable and cruel, even as we are and were.

These super-men and world-mastering demi-gods listened, however, to no low tongues of ours, even when we pointed silently to their feet of clay. Perhaps we, as folk of simpler soul and more primitive type, have been most struck in the welter of recent years by the utter failure of white religion. We have curled our lips in something like content as we have witnessed glib apology and weary explanation. Nothing of the sort deceived us. A nation's religion is its life, and as such white Chistianity is a miserable failure.

Nor would we be unfair in this criticism: We know that we, too, have failed, as you have, and have rejected many a Buddha, even as you have denied Christ; but we acknowledge our human frailty, while you, claiming super-humanity, scoff endlessly at our shortcomings. . . .

Yet the fields of Belgium laughed, the cities were gay, art and science flourished; the groans that helped to nourish this civilization fell on deaf ears because the world round about was doing the same sort of thing elsewhere on its own account.

As we saw the dead dimly through rifts of battlesmoke and heard faintly the cursings and accusations of blood brothers, we darker men said: This is not Europe gone mad; this is not aberration nor insanity; this *is* Europe; this seeming Terrible is the real soul of white culture—back of all culture—stripped and visible today. . . .

Europe has never produced and never will in our day bring forth a single human soul who cannot be matched and over-matched in every line of human endeavor by Asia and Africa. . . .

Why, then, is Europe great? Because of the foundations which the mighty past have furnished her to build upon: the iron trade of ancient, black Africa, the religion and empire-building of yellow Asia, the art and science of the "dago" Mediterranean shore, east, south, and west, as well as north. And where she has builded securely upon this great past and learned from it she has gone forward to greater and more splendid human triumph; but where she has ignored this past and forgotten and sneered at it, she has shown the cloven hoof of poor, crucified humanity—she has played, like other empires gone, the world fool!

If, then, European triumphs in culture have been greater, so, too, may her failures have been greater. How great a failure and a failure in what does the World War betoken? . . . What is that breath of life, thought to be so indispensable to a great European nation? Manifestly it is expansion overseas; it is colonial aggrandizement which explains, and alone adequately explains, the World War. How many of us today fully realize the current theory of colonial expansion, of the relation of Europe which is white, to the world which is black and brown and yellow? Bluntly put, that theory is this: It is the duty of white Europe to divide up the darker world and administer it for Europe's good.

This Europe has largely done. The European world is using black and brown men for all the uses which men know. Slowly but surely white culture is evolving the theory that "darkies" are born beasts of burden for white folk. It were silly to think otherwise, cries the cultured world, with stronger and shriller accord. The supporting arguments grow and twist themselves in the mouths of merchant, scientist, soldier, traveler, writer, and missionary; Darker peoples are dark in mind as well as in body; of dark, uncertain, and imperfect descent; of frailer, cheaper, stuff; they are cowards in the face of mausers and maxims; they have no feelings, aspirations, and loves; they are fools, illogical idiots—"half-devil and half-child."

Such as they are civilization must, naturally, raise them, but soberly and in limited ways. They are not simply dark white men. They are not "men" in the sense that Europeans are men. To the very limited extent of their shallow capacities lift them to be useful to whites, to raise cotton, gather rubber, fetch ivory, dig diamonds—and let them be paid what men think they are worth—white men who know them to be well-nigh worthless.

Such degrading of men by men is as old as mankind and the invention of no one race or people. Ever have men striven to conceive of their victims as different from the victors, endlessly different, in soul and blood, strength and cunning, race and lineage. It has been left, however, to Europe and to modern days to discover the eternal world-wide mark of meanness—color! . . .

This theory of human culture and its aims has worked itself through warp and woof of our daily thought with a thoroughness that few realize. Everything great, good, efficient, fair, and honorable is "white"; everything mean, bad, blundering, cheating, and dishonorable is "yellow"; a bad taste is "brown"; and the devil is "black." The changes of this theme are continually rung in picture and story, in newspaper heading and moving-picture, in sermon anl school book, until, of course, the King can do no wrong—a White Man is always right and a Black Man has no rights which a white man is bound to respect.

There must come the necessary despisings and hatreds of these savage half-men, this unclean *canaille* of the world—these dogs of men. All through the world this gospel is preaching. It has its literature, it has its priests, it has its secret propaganda and above all—it pays!

There's the rub—it pays. Rubber, ivory, and palm-oil; tea, coffee, and cocoa; bananas, oranges, and other fruit; cotton, gold, and copper—they, and a hundred other things which dark and sweating bodies hand up to the white world from their pits of slime, pay and pay well, but of all that the world gets the black world gets only the pittance that the white world throws it disdainfully.

Small wonder, then, that in the practical world of things-that-be there is jealousy and strife for the possession of the labor of dark millions, for the right to bleed and exploit the colonies of the world where this golden stream may be had, not always for the asking, but surely for the whipping and shooting. It was this competition for the labor of yellow, brown, and black folks that was the cause of the World War. Other causes have been glibly given and other contributing causes there doubtless were, but they were subsidiary and subordinate to this vast quest of the dark world's wealth and toil.

Colonies, we call them, these places where "niggers" are cheap and the earth is rich; they are those outlands where like a swarm of hungry locusts white masters may settle to be served as kings, wield the lash of slave-drivers, rape girls and wives, grow as rich as Croesus and send homeward a golden stream. . . .

The cause of war is preparation for war; and of all that Europe has done in a century there is nothing that has equaled in energy, thought, and time her preparation for wholesale murder. The only adequate cause of this preparation was conquest and conquest, not in Europe, but primarily among the darker peoples of Asia and Africa; conquest, not for assimilation and uplift, but for commerce and degradation. For this, and this mainly, did Europe gird herself at frightful cost for war. . . .

Thus the world market most wildly and desperately sought today is the market where labor is cheapest and most helpless and profit is most abundant. This labor is kept cheap and helpless because the white world despises "darkies." If one has the temerity to suggest that these workingmen may walk the way of white workingmen and climb by votes and self-assertion and education to the rank of men, he is howled out of court. They cannot do it and if they could, they shall not, for they are the enemies of the white race and the whites shall rule forever and forever and everywhere. Thus the hatred and despising of human beings from whom Europe wishes to extort her luxuries has led to such jealousy and bickering between European nations that they have fallen afoul of each other and have fought like crazed beasts. Such is the fruit of human hatred.

But what of the darker world that watches? Most men belong to this world. With Negro and Negroid, East Indian, Chinese, and Japanese they form two-thirds of the population of the world. A belief in humanity is a belief in colored men. If the uplift of mankind must be done by men, then the destinies of this world will rest ultimately in the hands of darker nations.

What, then, is this dark world thinking? It is thinking that as wild and awful as this shameful war was, *it is nothing to compare with that fight for freedom which black and brown and yellow men must and will make unless their oppression and humiliation and insult at the hands of the White World cease. The Dark World is going to submit to its present treatment just as long as it must and not one moment longer.*

Let me say this again and emphasize it and leave no room for mistaken meaning: The World War was primarily the jealous and avaricious struggle for the largest share in exploiting darker races. As such it is and must be but the prelude to the armed and indignant protest of these despised and raped peoples. . . .

If Europe hugs this delusion, then this is not the end of world war—it is but the beginning. . . .

For two or more centuries America has marched proudly in the van of human hatred—making bonfires of human flesh and laughing at them hideously, and making the insulting of millions more than a matter of dislike—rather a great religion, a world war-cry: Up white, down black; to your tents, O white folk, and world war with black and parti-colored mongrel beasts!

Instead of standing as a great example of the success of democracy and the possibility of human brotherhood America has taken her place as an awful example of its pitfalls and failures, so far as black and brown and yellow peoples are concerned. . . .

I will not believe that all that was must be, that all the shameful drama of the past must be done again today before the sunlight sweeps the silver seas.

If I cry amid this roar of elemental forces, must my cry be in vain, because it is but a cry—a small and human cry amid Promethean gloom?

Back beyond the world and swept by these wild, white faces of the awful dead, why will this Soul of White Folk—this modern Prometheus—hang bound by his own binding, tethered by a fable of the past? I hear his mighty cry reverberating through the world, "I am white!" Well and good, O Prometheus, divine thief! Is not the world wide enough for two colors, for many little shinings of the sun? Why, then, devour your own vitals if I answer even as proudly, "I am black!"

The Comet
From *Darkwater*

He stood a moment on the steps of the bank, watching the human river that swirled down Broadway. Few noticed him. Few ever noticed him save in a way that stung. He was outside the world— "nothing!" as he said bitterly. Bits of the words of the walkers came to him.

"The comet?"

"The comet—"

Everybody was talking of it. Even the president, as he entered, smiled patronizingly at him, and asked:

"Well, Jim, are you scared?"

"No," said the messenger shortly.

"I thought we'd journeyed through the comet's tail once," broke in the junior clerk affably.

"Oh, that was Halley's," said the president; "this is a new comet, quite a stranger, they say—wonderful, wonderful! I saw it last night. Oh, by the way, Jim," turning again to the messenger, "I want you to go down into the lower vaults today."

The messenger followed the president silently. Of course, they wanted *him* to go down to the lower vaults. It was dangerous for more valuable men. He smiled grimly and listened.

"Everything of value has been moved out since the water began to seep in," said the president; "but we miss two volumes of old records. Suppose you nose around down there,—it isn't very pleasant, I suppose."

"Not very," said the messenger, as he walked out.

"Well, Jim, the tail of the new comet hits us at noon this time," said the vault clerk, as he passed over the keys; but the messenger passed silently down the stairs. Down he went beneath Broadway, where the lim light filtered through the feet of hurrying men; down to the dark basement beneath; down into the blackness and silence beneath that lowest cavern. Here with his dark lantern he groped in the bowels of the earth, under the world.

He drew a long breath as he threw back the last great iron door and stepped into the fetid slime within. Here at last was peace, and he groped moodily forward. A great rat leaped past him and cobwebs crept across his face. He felt carefully around the room, shelf by shelf, on the muddied floor, and in crevice and corner. Nothing. Then he went back to the far end, where somehow the wall felt different. He sounded and pushed and pried. Nothing. He started away. Then something brought him back. He was sounding and working again when suddenly the whole black wall swung as on mighty hinges, and blackness yawned beyond. He peered in; it was evidently a secret vault—some hiding place of the old bank unknown in newer times. He entered hesitatingly. It was a long narrow room with shelves, and at the far end, an old iron chest. On a high shelf lay the two missing volumes of records, and others. He put them carefully aside and stepped to the chest. It was old, strong, and rusty. He looked at the vast and old-fashioned lock and flashed his light on the hinges. They were deeply incrusted with rust. Looking about, he found a bit of iron and began to pry. The rust had eaten a hundred years, and it had gone deep. Slowly, wearily, the old lid lifted, and with a last, low groan lay bare its treasure—and he saw the dull sheen of gold!

"Boom!"

A low, grinding, reverberating crash struck upon his ear. He started up and looked about. All was black and still. He groped for his light and swung it about him. Then he knew! The great stone door had swung to. He forgot the gold and looked death squarely in the face. Then with a sigh he went methodically to work. The cold sweat stood on his forehead; but he searched, pounded, pushed, and worked until after what seemed endless hours his hand struck a cold bit of metal and the great door swung again harshly on its hinges, and then, striking against something soft and heavy, stopped. He had just room to squeeze through. There lay the body of the vault clerk, cold and stiff. He stared at it, and then felt sick and nauseated. The air seemed unaccountably foul, with a strong, peculiar odor. He stepped forward, clutched at the air, and fell fainting across the corpse.

He awoke with a sense of horror, leaped from the body, and groped up the stairs, calling to the guard. The watchman sat as if asleep, with the gate swinging free. With one glance at him the messenger hurried up to the sub-vault. In vain he called to the guards. His voice echoed and re-echoed weirdly. Up into the great basement he rushed. Here another guard lay prostrate on his face, cold and still. A fear arose in the messenger's heart. He dashed up to the cellar floor, up into the bank. The stillness of death lay everywhere and everywhere bowed, bent, and stretched the silent forms of men. The messenger paused and glanced about. He was not a man easily moved; but the sight was appalling! "Robbery and murder," he whispered slowly to himself as he saw the twisted, oozing mouth of the president where he lay half-buried on his desk. Then a new thought seized him: If they found him here alone—with all this money and all these dead men—what would his life be worth? He glanced about, tiptoed cautiously to a side door, and again looked behind. Quietly he turned the latch and stepped out into Wall Street.

How silent the street was! Not a soul was stirring, and yet it was high-noon—Wall Street? Broadway? He glanced almost wildly up and down, then across the street, and as he looked, a sickening horror froze in his limbs. With a choking cry of utter fright he lunged, leaned giddily against the cold building, and stared helplessly at the sight.

In the great stone doorway a hundred men and women and children lay crushed and twisted and jammed, forced into that great, gaping doorway like refuse in a can—as if in one wild, frantic rush to safety, they had crushed and ground themselves to death. Slowly the messenger crept along the walls, wetting his parched mouth and trying to comprehend, stilling the tremor in his limbs and the rising terror in his heart. He met a business man, silk-hatted and frock-coated, who had crept, too, along that smooth wall and stood now stone dead with wonder written on his lips. The messenger turned his eyes hastily away and sought the curb. A woman leaned wearily against the signpost, her head bowed motionless on her lace and silken bosom. Before her stood a street car, silent, and within—but the messenger but glanced and hurried on. A grimy newsboy sat in the gutter with the "last edition" in his uplifted hand: "Danger!" screamed its black headlines. "Warnings wired around the world. The Comet's tail sweeps past us at noon. Deadly gases expected. Close doors and windows. Seek the cellar." The messenger read and staggered on. Far out from a window above, a girl lay with gasping face and sleevelets on her arms. On a store step sat a little, sweet-faced girl looking upward toward the skies, and in the carriage by her lay—but the messenger looked no longer. The cords gave way—the terror burst in his veins, and with one great, gasping cry he sprang desperately forward and ran,—ran as only the frightened run, shrieking and fighting the air until with one last wail of pain he sank on the grass of Madison Square and lay prone and still.

When he arose, he gave no glance at the still and silent forms on the benches, but, going to a fountain, bathed his face; then hiding himself in a corner away from the drama of death, he quietly gripped himself and thought the thing through: The comet had swept the earth and this was the end. Was everybody dead? He must search and see.

He knew that he must steady himself and keep calm, or he would go insane. First he must go to a restaurant. He walked up Fifth Avenue to a famous hostelry and entered its gorgeous, ghost-haunted halls. He beat back the nausea, and, seizing a tray from dead hands, hurried into the street and ate ravenously, hiding to keep out the sights.

"Yesterday, they would not have served me," he whispered, as he forced the food down.

Then he started up the street,—looking, peering, telephoning, ringing alarms; silent, silent all. Was nobody—nobody—he dared not think the thought and hurried on.

Suddenly he stopped still. He had forgotten. My God! How could he have forgotten? He must rush to the subway—then he almost laughed. No—a car; if he could find a Ford. He saw one. Gently he lifted off its burden, and took his place on the seat. He tested the throttle. There was gas. He glided off, shivering, and drove up the street. Everywhere stood, leaned, lounged, and lay the dead, in grim and awful silence. On he ran past an automobile, wrecked and overturned; past another, filled with a gay party whose smiles yet lingered on their death-struck lips; on past crowds and groups of cars, pausing by dead policemen; at 42nd Street he had to detour to Park Avenue to avoid the dead congestion. He came back on Fifth Avenue at 57th and flew past the Plaza and by the park with its hushed babies and silent throng, until as he was rushing past 72nd Street he heard a sharp cry, and saw a living form leaning wildly out an upper window. He gasped. The human voice sounded in his ears like the voice of God.

"Hello—hello—help, in God's name!" wailed the woman. "There's a dead girl in here and a man and—and see yonder dead men lying in the street and dead horses—for the love of God go and bring the officers—" And the words trailed off into hysterical tears.

He wheeled the car in a sudden circle, running over the still body of a child and leaping on the curb. Then he rushed up the steps and tried the door and rang violently. There was a long pause, but at last the heavy door swung back. They stared a moment in silence. She had not noticed before that he was a Negro. He had not thought of her as white. She was a woman of perhaps twenty-five—rarely beautiful and richly gowned, with darkly-golden hair, and jewels. Yesterday, he thought with bitterness, she would scarcely have looked at him twice. He would have been dirt beneath her silken feet. She stared at him. Of all the sorts of men she had pictured as coming to her rescue she had not dreamed of one like him. Not that he was not human, but he dwelt in a world so far from hers, so infinitely far, that he seldom even entered her thought. Yet as she looked at him curiously he seemed quite commonplace and usual. He was a tall, dark workingman of the better class, with a sensitive face trained to stolidity and a poor man's clothes and hands. His face was soft and slow and his manner at once cold and nervous, like fires long banked, but not out.

So a moment each paused and gauged the other; then the thought of the dead world without rushed in and they started toward each other.

"What has happened?" she cried. "Tell me! Nothing stirs. All is silence! I see the dead strewn before my window as winnowed by the breath of God,—and see—" She dragged him through great, silken hangings to where, beneath the sheen of mahogany and silver, a little French maid lay stretched in quiet, everlasting sleep, and near her a butler lay prone in his livery.

The tears streamed down the woman's cheeks and she clung to his arm until the perfume of her breath swept his face and he felt the tremors racing through her body.

"I had been shut up in my dark room developing pictures of the comet which I took last night; when I came out—I saw the dead!

"What has happened?" she cried again.

He answered slowly:

"Something—comet or devil—swept across the earth this morning and—many are dead!"

"Many? Very many?"

"I have searched and I have seen no other living soul but you."
She gasped and they stared at each other.

"My—father!" she whispered.

"Where is he?"

"He started for the office."

"Where is it?"

"In the Metropolitan Tower."

"Leave a note for him here and come."
Then he stopped.

"No," he said firmly—"first, we must go—to Harlem."

"Harlem!" she cried. Then she understood. She tapped her foot at first impatiently. She looked back and shuddered. Then she came resolutely down the steps.

"There's a swifter car in the garage in the court," she said.

"I don't know how to drive it," he said.

"I do," she answered.

In ten minutes they were flying to Harlem on the wind. The Stutz rose and raced like an airplane. They took the turn at 110th Street on two wheels and slipped with a shriek into 135th.

He was gone but a moment. Then he returned, and his face was gray. She did not look, but said:

"You have lost—somebody?"

"I have lost—everybody," he said, simply—"unless—"

He ran back and was gone several minutes—hours they seemed to her.

"Everybody," he said, and he walked slowly back with something film-like in his hand which he stuffed into his pocket.

"I'm afraid I was selfish," he said. But already the car was moving toward the park among the dark and lined dead of Harlem—the brown, still faces, the knotted hands, the homely garments, and the silence—the wild and haunting silence. Out of the park, and down Fifth Avenue they whirled. In and out among the dead they slipped and quivered, needing no sound of bell or horn, until the great, square Metropolitan Tower hove in sight. Gently he laid the dead elevator boy aside; the car shot upward. The door of the office stood open. On the threshold lay the stenographer, and, staring at her, sat the dead clerk. The inner office was empty, but a note lay on the desk, folded and addressed but unsent:

Dear Daughter:

I've gone for a hundred mile spin in Fred's new Mercedes. Shall not be back before dinner. I'll bring Fred with me.

J. B. H.

"Come," she cried nervously. "We must search the city."

Up and down, over and across, back again—on went that ghostly search. Everywhere was silence and death—death and silence! They hunted from Madison Square to Spuyten Duyvel; they rushed across the Williamsburg Bridge; they swept over Brooklyn; from the Battery and Morningside Heights they scanned the river. Silence, silence everywhere, and no human sign. Haggard and bedraggled they puffed a third time slowly down Broadway, under the broiling sun, and at last stopped. He sniffed the air. An odor—a smell—and with the shifting breeze a sickening stench filled their nostrils and brought its awful warning. The girl settled back helplessly in her seat.

"What can we do?" she cried.

It was his turn now to take the lead, and he did it quickly.

"The long distance telephone—the telegraph and the cable—night rockets and then—flight!"

She looked at him now with strength and confidence. He did not look like men, as she had always pictured men; but he acted like one and she was content. In fifteen minutes they were at the central telephone exchange. As they came to the door he stepped quickly before her and pressed her gently back as he closed it. She heard him moving to and fro, and knew his burdens—the poor, little burdens he bore. When she entered, he was alone in the room. The grim switchboard flashed its metallic face in cryptic, sphinx-like immobility. She seated herself on a stool and donned the bright earpiece. She looked at the mouthpiece. She had never looked at one so closely before. It was wide and black, pimpled with usage; inert; dead; almost sarcastic in its unfeeling curves. It looked—she beat back the thought —but it looked,—it persisted in looking like—she turned her head and found herself alone. One moment she was terrified; then she thanked him silently for his delicacy and turned resolutely, with a quick intaking of breath.

"Hello!" she called in low tones. She was calling to the world. The world *must* answer. Would the world *answer?* Was the world—

Silence!

She had spoken too low.

"Hello!" she cried, full-voiced.

She listened. Silence! Her heart beat quickly. She cried in clear, distinct, loud tones: "Hello—hello—hello!"

What was that whirring? Surely—no—was it the click of a receiver?

She bent close, she moved the pegs in the holes, and called and called, until her voice rose almost to a shriek, and her heart hammered. It was as if she had heard the last flicker of creation, and the evil was silence. Her voice dropped to a sob. She sat stupidly staring into the black and sarcastic mouthpiece, and the thought came again. Hope lay dead within her. Yes, the cable and the rockets remained; but the world—she could not frame the thought or say the word. It was too mighty—too terrible! She turned toward the door with a new fear in her heart. For the first time she seemed to realize that she was alone in the world with a stranger, with something more than a stranger,—with a man alien in blood and culture—unknown, perhaps unknowable. It was awful! She must escape—she must fly; he must not see her again. Who knew what awful thoughts—

She gathered her silken skirts deftly about her young, smooth limbs—listened, and glided into a side-hall. A moment she shrank back: the hall lay filled with dead women; then she leaped to the door and tore at it, with bleeding fingers, until it swung wide. She looked out. He was standing at the top of the alley,—silhouetted, tall and black, motionless. Was he looking at her or away? She did not know—she did not care. She simply leaped and ran—ran until she found herself alone amid the dead and the tall ramparts of towering buildings.

She stopped. She was alone. Alone! Alone on the streets—alone in the city—perhaps alone in the world! There crept in upon her the sense of deception—of creeping hands behind her back—of silent, moving things she could not see,—of voices hushed in fearsome conspiracy. She looked behind and sideways, started at strange sounds and heard still stranger, until every nerve within her stood sharp and quivering, stretched to scream at the barest touch. She whirled and flew back, whimpering like a child, until she found that narrow alley again and the dark silent figure silhouetted at the top. She stopped and rested; then she walked silently toward him, looked at him timidly; but he said nothing as he handed her into the car. Her voice caught as she whispered:

"Not—that."

And he answered slowly: "No—not that!"

They climbed into the car. She bent forward on the wheel and sobbed, with great, dry, quivering sobs, as they flew toward the cable office on the east side, leaving the world of wealth and prosperity for the world of poverty and work. In the world behind them were death and silence, grave and grim, almost cynical, but always decent; here it was hideous. It clothed itself in every ghastly form of terror, struggle, hate, and suffering. It lay wreathed in crime and squalor, greed and lust. Only in its dread and awful silence was it like to death everywhere.

Yet as the two, flying and alone, looked upon the horror of the world, slowly, gradually, the sense of all-enveloping death deserted them. They seemed to move in a world silent and asleep,—not dead. They moved in quiet reverence, lest somehow they wake these sleeping forms who had, at last, found peace. They moved in some solemn, world-wide *Friedhof*, above which some mighty arm had waved its magic wand. All nature slept until—until, and quick with the same startling thought, they looked into each other's eyes—he, ashen, and she, crimson, with unspoken thought. To both, the vision of a mighty beauty—of vast, unspoken things, swelled in their souls; but they put it away.

Great, dark coils of wire came up from the earth and down from the sun and entered this low lair of witchery. The gathered lightnings of the world centered here, binding with beams of light the ends of the earth. The doors gaped on the gloom within. He paused on the threshold.

"Do you know the code?" she asked.

"I know the call for help—we used it formerly at the bank."

She hardly heard. She heard the lapping of the waters far below,—the dark and restless waters—the cold and luring waters, as they called. He stepped within. Slowly she walked to the wall, where the water called below, and stood and waited. Long she waited, and he did not come. Then with a start she saw him, too, standing beside the black waters. Slowly he removed his coat and stood there silently. She walked quickly to him and laid her hand on his arm. He did not start or look. The waters lapped on in luring, deadly rhythm. He pointed down to the waters, and said quietly:

"The world lies beneath the waters now—may I go?"

She looked into his stricken, tired face, and a great pity surged within her heart. She answered in a voice clear and calm, "No."

Upward they turned toward life again, and he seized the wheel. The world was darkening to twilight, and a great, gray pall was

falling mercifully and gently on the sleeping dead. The ghastly glare
of reality seemed replaced with the dream of some vast romance.
The girl lay silently back, as the motor whizzed along, and looked
half-consciously for the elf-queen to wave life into this dead world
again. She forgot to wonder at the quickness with which he had
learned to drive her car. It seemed natural. And then as they whirled
and swung into Madison Square and at the door of the Metropolitan
Tower she gave a low cry, and her eyes were great! Perhaps she
had seen the elf-queen?

The man led her to the elevator of the tower and deftly they
ascended. In her father's office they gathered rugs and chairs, and he
wrote a note and laid it on the desk; then they ascended to the roof
and he made her comfortable. For a while she rested and sank to
dreamy somnolence, watching the worlds above and wondering.
Below lay the dark shadows of the city and afar was the shining of
the sea. She glanced at him timidly as he set food before her and
took a shawl and wound her in it, touching her reverently, yet
tenderly. She looked up at him with thankfulness in her eyes, eating
what he served. He watched the city. She watched him. He seemed
very human,—very near now.

"Have you had to work hard?" she asked softly.

"Always," he said.

"I have always been idle," she said. "I was rich."

"I was poor," he almost echoed.

"The rich and the poor are met together," she began, and he
finished:

"The Lord is the Maker of them all."

"Yes," she said slowly; "and how foolish our human distinctions
seem—now," looking down to the great dead city stretched below,
swimming in unlightened shadows.

"Yes—I was not—human, yesterday," he said.

She looked at him. "And your people were not my people,"
she said; "but today—" She paused. He was a man,—no more; but
he was in some larger sense a gentleman,—sensitive, kindly, chival-
rous, everything save his hands and—his face. Yet yesterday—

"Death, the leveler!" he muttered.

"And the revealer," she whispered gently, rising to her feet with
great eyes. He turned away, and after fumbling a moment sent a
rocket into the darkening air. It arose, shrieked, and flew up, a slim
path of light, and, scattering its stars abroad, dropped on the city
below. She scarcely noticed it. A vision of the world had risen

before her. Slowly the mighty prophecy of her destiny overwhelmed her. Above the dead past hovered the Angel of Annunciation. She was no mere woman. She was neither high nor low, white nor black, rich nor poor. She was primal woman; mighty mother of all men to come and Bride of Life. She looked upon the man beside her and forgot all else but his manhood, his strong, vigorous manhood—his sorrow and sacrifice. She saw him glorified. He was no longer a thing apart, a creature below, a strange outcast of another clime and blood, but her Brother Humanity incarnate, Son of God and great All-Father of the race to be.

He did not glimpse the glory in her eyes, but stood looking outward toward the sea and sending rocket after rocket into the unanswering darkness. Dark-purple clouds lay banked and billowed in the west. Behind them and all around, the heavens glowed in dim, weird radiance that suffused the darkening world and made almost a minor music. Suddenly, as though gathered back in some vast hand, the great cloud-curtain fell away. Low on the horizon lay a long, white star—mystic, wonderful! And from it fled upward to the pole, like some wan bridal veil, a pale, wide sheet of flame that lighted all the world and dimmed the stars.

In fascinated silence the man gazed at the heavens and dropped his rockets to the floor. Memories of memories stirred to life in the dead recesses of his mind. The shackles seemed to rattle and fall from his soul. Up from the crass and crushing and cringing of his caste leaped the lone majesty of kings long dead. He arose within the shadows, tall, straight, and stern, with power in his eyes and ghostly scepters hovering to his grasp. It was as though some mighty Pharaoh lived again, or curled Assyrian lord. He turned and looked upon the lady, and found her gazing straight at him.

Silently, immovably, they saw each other face to face—eye to eye. Their souls lay naked to the night. It was not lust; it was not love—it was some vaster, mightier thing that needed neither touch of body nor thrill of soul. It was a thought divine, splendid.

Slowly, noiselessly, they moved toward each other—the heavens above, the seas around, the city grim and dead below. He loomed from out the velvet shadows vast and dark. Pearl-white and slender, she shone beneath the stars. She stretched her jeweled hands abroad. He lighted up his mighty arms, and they cried each to the other, almost with one voice, "The world is dead."

"Long live the—"

"Honk! Honk!" Hoarse and sharp the cry of a motor drifted clearly up from the silence below. They started backward with a cry and gazed upon each other with eyes that faltered and fell, with blood that boiled.

"Honk! Honk! Honk! Honk!" came the mad cry again, and almost from their feet a rocket blazed into the air and scattered its stars upon them. She covered her eyes with her hands, and her shoulders heaved. He dropped and bowed, groped blindly on his knees about the floor. A blue flame spluttered lazily after an age, and she heard the scream of an answering rocket as it flew.

Then they stood still as death, looking to opposite ends of the earth.

"Clang—crash—clang!"

The roar and ring of swift elevators shooting upward from below made the great tower tremble. A murmur and babel of voices swept in upon the night. All over the once dead city the lights blinked, flickered, and flamed; and then with a sudden clanging of doors the entrance to the platform was filled with men, and one with white and flying hair rushed to the girl and lifted her to his breast. "My daughter!" he sobbed.

Behind him hurried a younger, comelier man, carefully clad in motor costume, who bent above the girl with passionate solicitude and gazed into her staring eyes until they narrowed and dropped and her face flushed deeper and deeper crimson.

"Julia," he whispered; "my darling, I thought you were gone forever."

She looked up at him with strange, searching eyes.

"Fred," she murmured, almost vaguely, "is the world—gone?"

"Only New York," he answered; "it is terrible—awful! You know,—but you, how did you escape—how have you endured this horror? Are you well? Unharmed?"

"Unharmed!" she said.

"And this man here?" he asked, encircling her drooping form with one arm and turning toward the Negro. Suddenly he stiffened anl his hand flew to his hip. "Why!" he snarled. "It's—a—nigger—Julia! Has he—has he dared—"

She lifted her head and looked at her late companion curiously and then dropped her eyes with a sigh.

"He has dared—all, to rescue me," she said quietly, "and I—thank him—much." But she did not look at him again. As the couple turned away, the father drew a roll of bills from his pockets.

"Here, my good fellow," he said, thrusting the money into the man's hands, "take that,—what's your name?"

"Jim Davis," came the answer, hollow-voiced.

"Well, Jim, I thank you. I've always liked your people. If you ever want a job, call on me." And they were gone.

The crowd poured up and out of the elevators, talking and whispering.

"Who was it?"

"Are they alive?"

"How many?"

"Two!"

"Who was saved?"

"A white girl and a nigger—there she goes."

"A nigger? Where is he? Let's lynch the damned—"

"Shut up—he's all right—he saved her."

"Saved hell! He had no business—"

"Here he comes."

Into the glare of the electric lights the colored man moved slowly, with the eyes of those that walk and sleep.

"Well, what do you think of that?" cried a bystander; "of all New York, just a white girl and a nigger!"

The colored man heard nothing. He stood silently beneath the glare of the light, gazing at the money in his hand and shrinking as he gazed; slowly he put his other hand into his pocket and brought out a baby's filmy cap, and gazed again. A woman mounted to the platform and looked about, shading her eyes. She was brown, small, and toil-worn, and in one arm lay the corpse of a dark baby. The crowd parted and her eyes fell on the colored man; with a cry she tottered toward him.

"Jim!"

He whirled and, with a sob of joy, caught her in his arms.

WILLIAM MONROE TROTTER
(1872-1934)

One of the most colorful individuals of the early days of the twentieth century was William Monroe Trotter, fiery editor of the Boston Guardian. *His uncompromising stand on the civil and human rights of black people was prophetic of our times.*

Trotter was a Bostonian, who was graduated from Harvard in 1895. He became a real estate broker, but in 1901 he realized his ambition to become a newspaperman by establishing, with George Washington Forbes, the Boston Guardian. *By no coincidence the newspaper plant was located in the same building in which William Lloyd Garrison had published* The Liberator *and in which Harriet Beecher Stowe's* Uncle Tom's Cabin *had been printed.*

In a time when Negro newspapers were generally conservative and heavily influenced by the Booker T. Washington policy of accommodation, the Guardian *was outspoken in its demands for full equality and became the most insistent voice against Washington. Trotter pushed the battle beyond the walls of his newspaper office. In 1903 Trotter and Forbes attended the meeting of the Afro-American Council, where Washington spoke. They tried to get the attention of the chairman, T. Thomas Fortune, but were never recognized. Later that year when Washington spoke at Columbus Avenue African Zion Church in Boston, Trotter and several friends disrupted his speech to protest Washington's alleged control over communication media. Trotter and his friends were arrested.*

Partly as a result of this incident, W. E. B. Du Bois, Trotter, and others organized the Niagara Movement, a pressure group to work for black people's civil rights. When that group later merged with the newly formed NAACP, Trotter refused to join because he did not approve of white leadership in the organization.

Trotter responded to many challenges. In 1910 he demonstrated against the anti-Negro play The Clansman, *based on Thomas Dixon's novel, and had a tumultuous interview with Woodrow Wilson over discrimination in government employment. In 1919, denied a passport, Trotter obtained a job as second cook on a transatlantic ship and appeared in Paris as a delegate from the National Equal Rights League to the Peace Conference.*

Trotter eventually lost many followers, who considered him too passionate and impulsive. Nevertheless, he never retreated in his fight for the black man's human rights.

A study of Trotter by Stephen R. Fox is The Guardian of Boston: William Monroe Trotter *(1970).*

Why Be Silent?

Under the caption, "Principal Washington Defines His Position," the Tuskegee Student, the official organ of Tuskegee, prints the institute letter in which Mr. Washington said: "We cannot elevate and make useful a race of people unless there is held out to them the hope of reward for right living. Every revised constitution throughout the southern states has put a premium upon intelligence, ownership of property, thrift and character." This little sheet begins by saying that the letter "appeared in all of the important papers of the country on Nov. 28. It has been unstintingly praised from one section of the country to the other for its clarity and forcefulness of statement, and for its ringing note of sincerity." Although such words are to be expected from the employes of the school they are for the most part only too true. It is true that, although the letter was sent to the Age Herald of Birmingham, Alabama, it appeared simultaneously "in all the important papers of the country." Then its effect must be admitted to have been greater than if any other Negro had written it, for admittedly no other Negro's letter could have obtained such wide publicity. If it had in it aught that was injurious to the Negro's welfare or to his manhood rights, therefore, such worked far more damage than if any other Negro or any other man, save the president himself, had written the words.

What man is there among us, whether friend or foe of the author of the letter, who was not astounded at the reference to the disfranchising constitutions quoted above. "Every revised constitution throughout the southern states has put a premium upon intelligence, ownership of property, thrift and character," and all the more so because Mr. Washington had not been accused by even the southerners of opposing these disfranchising constitutions. . . . If the statement is false, if it is misleading, if it is injurious to the Negro, all the more blamable and guilty is the author because the statement was gratuitous on his part.

Is it the truth? Do these constitutions encourage Negroes to be thrifty, to be better and more intelligent? For this sort of argument is the most effective in favor of them. . . . Where is the Negro who says the law was or is ever intended to be fairly applied? . . . If so, then every reputable Negro orator and writer, from Hon. A. H. Grimke on, have been mistaken. If so, every Negro clergyman of standing, who has spoken on the subject . . . have been misinformed. We happen to know of an undertaker who has an enormous establishment in Virginia, who now can't vote. Is that encouraging thrift? Two letter carriers, who have passed the civil service examinations, are now sueing because disfranchised. Is that encouraging intelligence? . . . Even a Republican candidate for governor in Virginia recently said Negro domination was to be feared if 10 Negroes could vote because they could have the balance of power. Mr. Washington's statement is shamefully false and deliberately so.

But even were it true, what man is a worse enemy to a race than a leader who looks with equanimity on the disfranchisement of his race in a country where other races have universal suffrage by constitutions that make one rule for his race and another for the dominant race, by constitutions made by conventions to which his race is not allowed to send its representatives, by constitutions that his race although endowed with the franchise by law are not allowed to vote upon, and are, therefore, doubly illegal, by constitutions in violation to the national constitution, because, forsooth, he thinks such disfranchising laws will benefit the moral character of his people. Let our spiritual advisers condemn this idea of reducing a people to serfdom to make them good.

But what was the effect of Mr. Washington's letter on the northern white people? . . .

No thinking Negro can fail to see that, with the influence Mr. Washington wields in the North and the confidence reposed in him by the white people on account of his school, a fatal blow has been given to the Negro's political rights and liberty by his statement. The benevolence idea makes it all the more deadly in its effect. It comes very opportunely for the Negro, too, just when Roosevelt declares the Negro shall hold office, . . . when Congress is being asked to enforce the Negro's constitutional rights, when these laws are being carried to the Supreme Court. And here Mr. Washington, having gained sufficient influence through his doctrines, his school and his elevation by the President, makes all these efforts sure of failure by killing public sentiment against the disfranchising constitutions.

And Mr. Washington's word is the more effective for, discreditable as it may seem, not five Negro papers even mention a statement that belies all their editorials and that would have set aflame the entire Negro press of the country, if a less wealthy and less powerful Negro had made it. Nor will Negro orators nor Negro preachers dare now to pick up the gauntlet thrown down by the great "educator." Instead of being universally repudiated by the Negro race his statement will be practically universally endorsed by its silence because Washington said it, though it sounds the death-knell of our liberty. The lips of our leading politicians are sealed, because, before he said it, Mr. Washington, through the President, put them under obligation to himself. Nor is there that heroic quality now in our race that would lead men to throw off the shackles of fear, of obligation, of policy and denounce a traitor though he be a friend, or even a brother. It occurs to none that silence is tantamount to being virtually an accomplice in the treasonable act of this Benedict Arnold of the Negro race.

O, for a black Patrick Henry to save his people from this stigma of cowardice; to rouse them from their lethargy to a sense of danger; to score the tyrant and to inspire his people with the spirit of those immortal words: "Give Me Liberty or Give Me Death."

(1902)

CHARLES W. CHESNUTT

(1858-1932)

Charles Waddell Chesnutt was the first Afro-American to gain
stature as a writer of fiction. Although his stories and novels may now
be outdated in terms of their image of black realities, Chesnutt is
respected as a literary groundbreaker. His works reflect considerable
talent and attain artistic power that is surprising when one considers
the severe stresses imposed upon black artists at the turn of the
century.

Chesnutt was born in Cleveland, Ohio, two years before the
Civil War. A year after the war ended, the Chesnutt family moved
to North Carolina, the birthplace of his parents. It was here, during
the days of his youth, that he absorbed the folk culture that would
later become the basis of his first successful stories. At the age of
sixteen, Chesnutt was teaching in North Carolina; at twenty-three he
was a school principal. Two years later he left the South, worked as
a newspaperman and stenographer in New York, then finally settled
down in his birthplace, Cleveland, where he became a member of the
bar. Between stenography and the practice of law, he supported
himself while he began his career as a writer of fiction.

"The Goophered Grapevine," Chesnutt's first published story,
appeared in the Atlantic Monthly in 1887. It was based upon the folk
culture which had become so familiar to Chesnutt in North Carolina.
Other stories in this vein followed; these were collected in 1899 in
The Conjure Woman and Other Tales.

For a decade, while these stories were appearing in the Atlantic
Monthly, Chesnutt's public did not suspect that he was not white.
Indeed, there was nothing in these stories to testify to the author's
color. Like white local colorists Joel Chandler Harris and Thomas

Nelson Page, Chesnutt created an elderly black Uncle who tells plantation tales in dialect. The voice of the author, however, speaks in the clipped Northern accents of the wealthy white landowner to whom Uncle Julius and his stories are interpreted through white perceptions to a white audience.

Still, the Conjure Woman stories bear certain signs of blackness. Uncle Julius is not the garrulous old darky weaving romantic tales of the good old days of slavery. Rather, he is a wily old man, wise in the necessities of survival, who by appearing ingenuous and childlike actually manipulates his white folks into doing things advantageous to himself. Also, the tales are rooted in genuine black folk material. An occasional dash of irony in the Conjure Woman pieces reveals the black face beneath the white mask. Saunders Redding, in his critical volume To Make a Poet Black, says of these early stories, "Nearly all the stories of this first collection are tragic with the fatal consequences of human actions and prejudices. It is not the weak pseudo-tragedy of propaganda, it is not pathos and tears in which Chesnutt deals—it is fundamental stuff of life translated into the folk terms of a people who knew true tragedy."

Chesnutt's second collection of stories, also published in 1899, was The Wife of His Youth and Other Stories of the Color Line. These stories dealt with the theme particularly poignant to Chesnutt: the problems of the Afro-American of mixed blood, who belonged neither to the black world nor to the white. With compassion and irony, Chesnutt probes the absurdity of the mulatto's situation. Working sometimes with satire, as in "A Matter of Principle," sometimes with bitter irony, as in "The Sheriff's Children," Chesnutt examines the isolation of the blue-veined people with an interest not often shown by black authors.

Some of Chesnutt's stories do not deal with black people at all. Of these, "Baxter's Procrustes," published in the Atlantic Monthly, June, 1904, is probably the best. Here Chesnutt writes in a Jamesian fashion of brilliant, cultured people, about as far from goophered grapevines as one can get.

Chesnutt wrote three novels, but they were never as successful as his stories. The objectivity of the stories was lost; the novels seldom rose above propaganda. The first novel, The House Behind the Cedars (1900), is probably the best. Chesnutt's craftsmanship is excellent, and there is fervor in his delivery. The other two novels, The Marrow of Tradition (1901) and The Colonel's Dream (1905), contain more anger than order.

Chesnutt also wrote a biography of Frederick Douglass, and several essays and speeches. After 1905 Chesnutt fell silent. In 1928 he was awarded the Spingarn Medal "for pioneer work as a literary artist depicting the life and struggle of Americans of Negro descent."

In spite of his early reluctance to reveal his race, a reluctance which was imposed on him by white racism, Chesnutt was essentially an honest writer, writing from his own knowledge and experience. Speaking especially of Chesnutt's early works, Saunders Redding says in To Make a Poet Black, *"He worked with dangerous, habit-ridden material with passive calm and fearlessness. Considering more than the emotional factors that lay behind the American race problem, he exposed the Negro to critical analysis . . . He is the most solid representative of prose fiction that the Negro could boast before the 1920's."*

There is a biography of Chesnutt by Helen Chesnutt, his daughter. Sylvia Render has written a study of Chesnutt.

The Goophered Grapevine

We alighted from the buggy, walked about the yard for a while, and then wandered off into the adjoining vineyard. Upon Annie's complaining of weariness I led the way back to the yard, where a pine log lying under the spreading elm afforded a shady though somewhat hard seat. One end of the log was already occupied by a venerable-looking colored man. He held on his knees a hat full of grapes, over which he was smacking his lips with great gusto; and a pile of grapeskins near him indicated that the performance was no new thing. We approached him at an angle from the rear, and were close to him before he perceived us. He respectfully rose as we drew near, and was moving away, when I begged him to keep his seat.

"Don't let us disturb you," I said. "There is plenty of room for us all."

He resumed his seat with some embarrassment. While he had been standing, I had observed that he was a tall man, and though slightly bowed by the weight of years, apparently quite vigorous. He was not entirely black, and this fact, together with the quality of his hair, which was about six inches long and very bushy, except on the top of his head, where he was quite bald, suggested a slight strain of other than Negro blood. There was a shrewdness in his eyes, too, which was not altogether African, and which, as we afterwards learned from experience, was indicative of a corresponding shrewdness in his character. He went on eating his grapes, but did not seem to enjoy himself quite so well as he had apparently done before he became aware of our presence.

"Do you live around here?" I asked, anxious to put him at his ease.

"Yas, suh. I lives des ober yander, behine de nex' san'hill, on de Lumberton plank-road."

"Do you know anything about the time when this vineyard was cultivated?"

"Lawd bless you, suh, I knows all about it. Dey ain' na'er a man in dis settlement w'at won' tell you ole Julius McAdoo 'uz bawn en raise' on dis yer same plantation. Is you de Norv'n gemman w'at's gwine ter buy de ole vimya'd?"

"I am looking at it," I replied; "but I don't know that I shall care to buy unless I can be reasonably sure of making something out of it."

"Well, suh, you is a stranger ter me, en I is a stranger to you, en we is bofe strangers ter one anudder, but 'f I 'uz in yo' place, I wouldn't buy dis vimya'd."

"Why not?" I asked.

"Well, I dunno whe'r you b'lieves in conj'in' er not—some er de w'ite folks don't, er says dey don't—but de truf er de matter is dat dis yer ole vimya'd is goophered."

"Is what?" I asked, not grasping the meaning of this unfamiliar word.

"Is goophered—cunju'd, bewitch'."

He imparted this information with such solemn earnestness and with such an air of confidential mystery that I felt somewhat interested, while Annie was evidently much impressed, and drew closer to me.

"How do you know it is bewitched?" I asked.

"I wouldn' spec' fer you ter b'lieve me 'less you know all 'bout de fac's. But ef you en young miss dere doan' min' lis'nin' ter a ole nigger run on a minute er two w'ile you er restin', I kin 'spain to you how it all happen'."

We assured him that we would be glad to hear how it all happened, and he began to tell us. At first the current of his memory—or imagination—seemed somewhat sluggish; but as his embarrassment wore off, his language flowed more freely, and the story acquired perspective and coherence. As he became more and more absorbed in the narrative, his eyes assumed a dreamy expression, and he seemed to lose sight of his auditors, and to be living over again in monologue his life on the old plantation.

"Ole Mars Dugal' McAdoo," he began, "bought dis place long many years befo' de wah, en I 'member well we'en he sot out all dis yer part er de plantation in scuppernon's. De vimes growed monst'us fas', en Mars Dugal' made a thousan' gallon er scuppernon' wine eve'y year.

"Now, ef dey's an'thing a nigger lub, nex' ter 'possum, en chick'n, en watermillyums, it's scuppernon's. Dey ain' nuffin dat kin stan' up side'n de scuppernon' fer sweetness; sugar ain't a suckumstance ter scuppernon'. W'en de season is nigh 'bout ober, en de grapes begin ter swivel up des a little wid de wrinkles er ole age—we'n de skin git sof' en brown—den de scuppernon' make you smack yo' lip en roll yo' eye en wush fer mo'; so I reckon it ain' very 'stonishin' dat niggers lub scuppernon'.

"Dey wuz a sight er niggers in de naberhood er de vimya'd. Dere wuz ole Mars Henry Brayboy's niggers, en ole Mars Jeems McLean's niggers, en Mars Dugal's own niggers; den dey wuz a settlement er free niggers en po' buckrahs down by de Wim'l'ton Road, en Mars Dugal' had de only vimya'd in de naberhood. I reckon it ain' so much so nowadays, but befo' de wah, in slab'ry times, a nigger didn' mine going' fi' er ten mile in a night w'en dey wuz sump'n good ter eat at de yuther een'.

"So atter a w'ile Mars Dugal' begin ter miss his scuppernon's. Co'se he 'cuse' de niggers er it, but dey all 'nied it ter de las'. Mars Dugal' sot spring guns en steel traps, en he en de obseah sot up nights once't or twice't, tel one night Mars Dugal'—he 'uz a monst'us keerless man—got his leg shot full er cow-peas. But somehow er nudder dey couldn' nebber ketch none er de niggers. I dunner how it happen, but it happen des like I tell you, en de grapes kep' on a-goin' des de same.

"But bimeby ole Mars Dugal' fix' up a plan ter stop it. Dey wuz a cunjuh 'oman livin' down 'mongs' de free niggers on de Wim'l'ton Road, en all de darkies fum Rockfish ter Beaver Crick wuz feared er her. She could wuk de mos' powerfulles' kin' er goopher—could make people hab fits, er rheumatiz', er mak 'em des dwinel away en die; en dey say she went out ridin' de niggers at night, fer she wuz a witch 'sides bein' a cunjuh 'oman. Mars Dugal' hearn 'bout Aun' Peggy's doin's, en begun ter 'flect whe'r er no he couldn' git her ter he'p him keep de niggers off'n de grapevimes. One day in de spring er de year, ole miss pack' up a basket er chick'n en poun'cake, en a bottle er scuppernon' wine, en Mars Dugal' tuk it in his buggy en driv over ter Aun' Peggy's cabin. He tuk de basket in, en had a long talk wid Aun' Peggy.

"De nex' day Aun' Peggy come up ter de vimya'd. De niggers seed her slippin' 'round, en dey soon foun' out what she 'uz doin' dere. Mars Dugal' had hi'ed her ter goopher de grapevimes. She sa'ntered 'roun' 'mongs' de vimes, en tuk a leaf fum dis one, en a grape-hull fum dat one, en den a little twig fum here, en a little pinch er dirt fum dere—en put it all in a big black bottle, wid a snake's toof en a speckle hen's gall en some ha'rs fum a black cat's tail, en den fill' de bottle wid scuppernon' wine. W'en she got de goopher all ready en fix', she tuk 'n went out in de woods en buried it under do root uv a red oak tree, en den come back en tole one er de niggers she done goopher de grapevimes, en ae'r a nigger w'at eat dem grapes 'ud be sho ter die inside'n twel' mont's.

"Atter dat de niggers let de scuppernon's 'lone, en Mars Dugal' didn' hab no' casion ter fine no mo' fault; en de season wuz mos' gone, w'en a strange gemman stop at de plantation one night ter see Mars Dugal' on some business; en his coachman, seein' de scuppernon's growin' so nice en sweet, slip 'roun' behine de smoke-house en et all de scuppernon's he could hole. Nobody didn' notice it at de time, but dat night, on de way home, de gemman's hoss runned away en kill' de coachman. W'en we hearn de noos, Aun' Lucy, de cook, she up'n say she seed de strange nigger eat'n' er de scuppernon's behine de smoke-house; en den we knowed de goopher had be'en er wukkin'. Den one er de nigger chilluns runned away from de quarters one day, en got in de scuppernon's, en died de nex' week. White folks say he die' er de fevuh, but de niggers knowed it wuz de goopher. So you k'n be sho de darkies didn' hab much ter do wid dem scuppernon' vimes.

"W'en de scuppernon' season 'uz ober fer dat year, Mars Dugal' foun' he had made fifteen hund'ed gallon er wine; en one er de niggers hearn him laffin' wid de obserseah fit ter kill, en sayin' dem fifteen hund'ed gallon er wine wuz monst'us good intrus' on de ten dollars he laid out on de vimya'd. So I 'low ez he paid Aun' Peggy ten dollars fer to goopher de grapevimes.

"De goopher didn' wuk no mo' tel de nex summer, w'en 'long to'ds de middle er de season one er de fiel' han's died; en ez dat lef' Mars Dugal' sho't er han's, he went off ter town fer ter buy anudder. He fotch de noo nigger home wid 'im. He wuz er ole nigger, er de color er a gingy-cake, en ball ez a hossaple on de top er his head. He wuz a peart ole nigger, do', en could do a big day's wuk.

"Now it happen dat one er de niggers on de nex' plantation, one er ole Mars Henry Brayboy's niggers, had runned away de day befo', en tuk ter de swamp, en ole Mars Dugal' en some er de yuther nabor w'ite folks had gone out wid dere guns en dere dogs fer ter he'p 'em hunt fer de nigger; en de han's on our own plantation wuz all so flusterated dat we fuhgot ter tell de noo han' 'bout de goopher on de scuppernon' vimes. Co'se he smell de grapes en see de vimes, an atter dahk de fus' thing he done wuz ter slip off ter de grapevimes 'dout sayin' nuffin ter nobody. Nex' mawnin' he tole some er de niggers 'bout de fine bait er scuppernon' he et de night befo'.

"W'en dey tole 'im 'bout de goopher on de grapevines, he 'uz dat tarrified dat he turn pale, en look des like he gwine ter die right in his tracks. De obserseah come up en axed w'at 'uz de matter; en w'en dey tole 'im Henry been eaten' er de scuppernon's, en got de goopher on 'im, he gin Henry a big drink er w'iskey, en 'low dat de nex' rainy day he take 'im ober ter Aun' Peggy's, en see ef she wouldn' take de goopher off'n him, seein' ez he didn't know nuffin' erbout it tel he done et de grapes.

"Sho nuff, it rain de nex' day, en de obserseah went ober ter Aun' Peggy's wid Henry. En Aun' Peggy say dat bein' ez Henry didn' know 'bout de goopher, en et de grapes in ign'ance er de conseq'ences, she reckon she mought be able ter take de goopher off'n him. So she fotch out er bottle wid some cunjuh medicine in it, en po'd some out in a go'd fer Henry ter drink. He manage ter git it down; he say it tas'e like w'iskey wid sump'n bitter in it. She 'lowed dat 'ud keep de goopher off'n him tel de spring; but w'en de sap begin ter rise in de grapevimes he ha' ter come en see her ag'in, en she tell him w'at he's ter do.

"Nex' spring, w'en de sap commence' ter rise in de scuppernon' vime, Henry tuk a ham one night. Whar'd he git de ham? I doan know; dey wa'n't no hams on de plantation 'cep'n' w'at 'uz in de smokehouse, but I never see Henry 'bout de smokehouse. But ez I wuz a-sayin', he tuk de ham ober ter Aun' Peggy's; en Aun' Peggy tole 'im dat w'en Mars Dugal' begin ter prune de grapevimes, he must go en take 'n scrape off de sap what it ooze out'n de cut een's er de vimes, en 'n'int his ball head wid it; en ef he do dat once't a year de goopher wouldn't wuk agin 'im long ez he done it. En bein' ez he fotch her de ham, she fix' it so he kin eat all de scuppernon' he want.

"So Henry 'n'int his head wid de sap out'n de big grapevime des ha'f way 'twix de quarters en de big house, en de goopher nebber wuk agin him dat summer. But the beatenes' thing you eber see happen ter Henry. Up ter dat time he wuz ez ball ez a sweeten' 'tater, but des ez soon ez de young leaves begun ter come out on de grapevimes, de ha'r begun ter grow out on Henry's head, en by de middle er de summer he had de bigges' head er ha'r on de plantation. Befo' dat, Henry had tol'able good ha'r 'roun' de aidges, but soon ez de young grapes begun ter come, Henry's ha'r begun to quirl all up in little balls, des like dis yer reg'lar grapy ha'r, en by de time de grapes got ripe his head look des like a bunch er grapes. Combin' it didn' do no good; he wuk at it ha'f de night wid er Jim Crow, en think he git it straighten' out, but in de mawnin' de grapes 'ud be dere des de same. So he gin it up, en tried ter keep de grapes down by havin' his ha'r cut sho't.

"But dat wa'n't de quares' thing 'bout de goopher. When Henry come ter de plantation, he wuz gittin' a little ole and stiff in de j'ints. But dat summer he got des ez spry en libely ez any young nigger on de plantation; fac', he got so biggity dat Mars Jackson, de oberseah, ha' ter th'eaten ter whip 'im ef he didn' stop cuttin' up his didos en behave hisse'f. But de mos' cur'ouses' thing happen' in de fall, when de sap begin ter go down in de grapevimes. Fus, when de grapes 'uz gethered, de knots begun ter straighten out'n Henry's ha'r; en w'en de leaves begin ter fall, Henry's ha'r commence' ter drap out; en when de vimes 'uz bar', Henry's head wuz baller'n it wuz in de spring, en he begin ter git ole en stiff in de j'ints ag'in, en paid no mo' 'tention ter de gals dyoin' er de whole winter. En nex' spring, w'en he rub de sap on ag'in, he got young ag'in, en so soopl en libely dat none er de young niggers on de plantation couldn' jump, ner dance, ner hoe ez much cotton ez Henry. But in de fall er de year his grapes 'mence' ter straighten out, en his j'ints ter git stiff, en his ha'r drap off, en de rheumatiz begin ter wrastle wid 'im.

"Now, ef you'd 'a' knowed ole Mars Dugal' McAdoo, you'd 'a' knowed dat it ha' ter be a mighty rainy day when he couldn' fine sump'n fer his niggers ter do, en it ha' ter be a mighty little hole he couldn' crawl thoo, en ha'ter be a monst'us cloudy night when a dollar git by him in de dahkness; en w'en he see how Henry git young in de spring en ole in de fall, he 'lowed ter hisse'f ez how he could make mo' money out'n Henry dan by wukkin' him in de cotton-fiel'. 'Long de nex' spring, atter de sap 'mence' ter rise, en Henry 'n'int 'is head en sta'ted fer ter git young en soopl, Mars Dugal' up'n tuk Henry ter town, en sole 'im for fifteen hunder' dollars. Co'se de man w'at bought Henry didn' know nuffin 'bout de goopher, en Mars Dugal' didn't see no 'casion fer ter tell 'im. Long to'ds de fall, w'en de sap went down, Henry begin ter git ole ag'in same ez yuzhal, en his noo marster begin ter git skeered les'n he gwine ter lose his fifteen-hunder'-dollar nigger. He sent fer a mighty fine doctor, but de med'cine didn' 'pear ter do no good; de goopher had a good holt. Henry tole de doctor 'bout de goopher, but de doctor des laff at 'im.

"One day in de winter Mars Dugal' went ter town, en wuz

santerin' 'long de Main Street, w'en who should he meet but Henry's noo master. Dey said 'Hoddy,' en Mars Dugal' ax 'im ter hab a seegyar; en atter dey run on awhile 'bout de craps en de weather, Mars Dugal' ax 'im, sorter keerless, like ez ef he des thought of it—

" 'How you like de nigger I sole you las' spring?'

"Henry's marster shuck his head en knock de ashes off'n his seegyar.

" 'Spec' I made a bad bahgin when I bought dat nigger. Henry done good wuk all de summer, but sence de fall set in he 'pears ter be sorter pinin' away. Dey ain' nuffin pertickler de matter wid 'im—leastways de doctor say so—'cep'n' a tech er de rheumatiz; but his ha'r is all fell out, en ef he don't pick up his strenk mighty soon, I spec' I'm gwine ter lose 'im.'

"Dey smoked on awhile, en bimeby ole mars say, 'Well, a bahgin's a bahgin, but you en me is good fren's, en I doan wan' ter see you lose all de money you paid fer dat nigger; en ef w'at you say is so, en I ain't 'sputin' it, he ain't wuf much now. I spec's you wukked him too ha'd dis summer, er e'se de swamps down here don't agree wid de san'-hill nigger. So you des lemme know, en ef he gits any wusser, I'll be willin' ter gib yer five hund'ed dollars for 'im, en take my chances on his livin'.'

"Sho' nuff, when Henry begun ter draw up wid de rheumatiz en it look like he gwine ter die fer sho, his noo marster sen' fer Mars Dugal', en Mars Dugal' gin him what he promus, en brung Henry home ag'in. He tuk good keer uv 'im dyoin' er de winter—give 'im w'iskey ter rub his rheumatiz, en terbaker ter smoke, en all he want ter eat—'caze a nigger w'at he could make a thousan' dollars a year off'n didn' grow on eve'y huckleberry bush.

"Nex' spring, w'en de sap rise en Henry's ha'r commence' ter sprout, Mars Dugal' sole 'im ag'in, down in Robeson County dis time; en he kep' dat sellin' business up fer five year er mo'. Henry nebber say nuffin 'bout de goopher ter his noo marsters, 'caze he know he gwine ter be tuk good keer uv de nex' winter, w'en Mars Dugal' buy him back. En Mars Dugal' made 'nuff money off'n Henry ter buy anudder plantation ober on Beaver Crick.

"But 'long 'bout de een 'er dat five year dey come a stranger ter stop at de plantation. De fus' day he 'uz dere he went out wid Mars Dugal' en spent all de mawnin' lookin' ober de vimya'd, en atter dinner dey spent all de evenin' playin' kya'ds. De niggers soon 'skivver' dat he wuz a Yankee, en dat he come down ter Norf C'lina fer ter l'arn de w'ite folks how to raise grapes en make wine. He promus Mars Dugal' he c'd make de grapevimes b'ar twice't ez many grapes, en dat de noo winepress he wuz a-sellin' would make mo' d'n twice't ez many gallons er wine. En ole Mars Dugal' des drunk it all in, des 'peared ter be bewitch' wit dat Yankee. W'en de darkies see dat Yankee runnin' 'roun' de vimya'd en diggin' under de grape-vimes, dey shuk dere heads, en 'lowed dat dey feared Mars Dugal' losin' his min'. Mars Dugal' had all de dirt dug away fum under de roots er all de scuppernon' vimes, an' let 'em stan' dat away fer a week er mo'. Den dat Yankee made de niggers fix up a mixtry er lime en ashes en manyo, en po' it 'roun' de roots er de grapevimes. Den he 'vise Mars Dugal' fer ter trim de vimes close't, en Mars Dugal' tuck 'n done eve'ything de Yankee tole him ter do. Dyoin' all er dis time, mine yer, dis yer Yankee wuz libbin' off'n de fat er de lan', at de big house, en playin' kya'ds wid Mars Dugal' eve'y night; en dey say Mars Dugal' los' mo'n a thousan' dollars dyoin' er de week dat Yankee wuz a-ruinin' de grapevimes.

"W'en de sap ris nex' spring, ole Henry 'n'inted his head ez yuzhal, en his ha'r 'mence' ter grow des de same ez it done eve'y year. De scuppernon' vimes growed monst's fas', en de leaves wuz greener en thicker dan dey eber be'n dyoin' my rememb'ance; en Henry's ha'r growed out thicker dan eber, en he 'peared ter git younger 'n younger, en soopler; en seein' ez he wuz sho't er han's dat spring, havin' tuk in consid'able noo groun', Mars Dugal 'git de crap in en de cotton chop'. Se he kep' Henry on de plantation.

"But 'long 'bout time fer de grapes ter come on de scuppernon' vimes, dey 'peared ter come a change ober 'em; de leaves witherd en swivel' up, en de young grapes turn' yaller, n bimeby eve'ybody on de plantation could see dat de whole vimya'd wuz dyin'. Mars Dugal' tuk'n water de vimes en done all he could, but 't wa'n no use; dat Yankee had done bus' de watermillyum. One time de vimes picked up a bit, en Mars Dugal' 'lowed dey wuz gwine ter come out ag'in; but dat Yankee done dug too close under de roots, en prune de branches too close ter de vime, en all dat lime en ashes done burn de life out'm de vimes, en dey des kep' a-with'in' en a-swivelin'.

"All dis time de goopher wuz a-wukkin'. When de vimes sta'ted ter wither, Henry 'mence' ter complain er his rheumatiz; en when de leaves begin ter dry up, his ha'r 'mence' ter drap out. When de vimes fresh' up a bit, Henry'd git peart ag'in, en when de vimes wither' ag'in, Henry'd git ole ag'in, en des kep' gittin' mo' fitten fer nuffin; he des pined away, en pined away, en fin'ly tuk ter his cabin; en when de big vime whar he got de sap ter 'n'int his head withered en turned yaller en died, Henry died too—des went out sorter like a cannel. Dey didn't 'pear ter be nuffin de matter wid 'im, 'cep'n de rheumatiz, but his strenk des dwinel' away 'tel he didn' hab ernuff lef' ter draw his bref. De goopher had got de under holt, en th'owed Henry dat time fer good en all.

"Mars Dugal' tuk on might'ly 'bout losin' his vimes en his nigger in de same year; en he swo' dat ef he could git holt er dat Yankee he'd wear 'im ter a frazzle, en den chaw up de frazzle; en he'd done it, too, for Mars Dugal' 'uz a monst'us brash man w'en he once git started. He sot de vimy'd out ober ag'in, but it wuz th'ee er fo' year befo' de vimes got ter b'arin' any scuppernon's.

"W'en de wah broke out, Mars Dugal' raise' a comp'ny, en went off ter fight de Yankees. He say he wuz mighty glad wah come, en he des want ter kill a Yankee fer eve'y dollar he los' 'long er dat grape-raisin' Yankee. En I 'spec' he would 'a' done it, too, ef de Yankees hadn' 's'picioned sump'en en killed him fus'. Atter de s'render, ole Miss move' ter town, de niggers all scattered 'way fum de planta-tion, en de vimya'd ain' be'n cultervated sence."

"Is that story true?" asked Annie doubtfully, but seriously, as the old man concluded his narrative.

"It's des ez true ez I'm a-settin' here, miss. Dey's a easy way ter prove it: I kin lead de way right ter Henry's grave ober yonder in de plantation buryin'-groun'. En I tell yer w'at, marster, I wouldn' 'vise you to buy dis yer ole vimya'd, 'caze de goopher's on it yit, en dey ain' no tellin' w'en it's gwine ter crap out."

"But I thought you said all the old vines died."

"Dey did 'pear ter die, but a few un 'em come out ag'in, en is mixed in 'mongs' de yuthers. I ain' skeered ter eat de grapes 'caze I knows de old vimes fum de noo ones, but wid strangers dey ain 'no tellin' w'at mought happen. I wouldn' 'vise yer ter buy dis vimya'd."

I bought the vineyard, nevertheless, and it has been for a long time in a thriving condition, and is often referred to by the local press as a striking illustration of the opportunities open to Northern capital in the development of Southern industries. The luscious scup-pernong holds first rank among our grapes, though we cultivate a great many other varieties; and our income from grapes packed and shipped to the Northern markets is quite considerable. I have not noticed any developments of the goopher in the vineyard, although I have a mild suspicion that our colored assistants do not suffer from want of grapes during the season.

I found, when I bought the vineyard, that Uncle Julius had occupied a cabin on the place for many years, and derived a respectable revenue from the product of the neglected grapevines. This, doubtless, accounted for his advice to me not to buy the vineyard, though whether it inspired the goopher story I am unable to state. I believe, however, that the wages I paid him for his services as coachman, for I gave him employment in that capacity, were more than an equivalent for anything he lost by the sale of the vineyard.

PAUL LAURENCE DUNBAR
(1872-1906)

Paul Laurence Dunbar, the son of ex-slaves, rose from an elevator boy composing verses to an internationally known poet. Like other black writers in the turbulent days following the Civil War, Dunbar was artistically inhibited by the distorted image of black people which was comfortable for the white book-buying public. Nevertheless, Dunbar was a lyricist of considerable ability, who proved to the literary public (who discounted the magnificent folk culture then extant) that a black man could be an artist.

Dunbar was born in Dayton, Ohio, in 1872. From youth he was a black prodigy in a white world. The only black student in his high school class, he was tremendously popular because of what Benjamin Brawley calls "his modest and yet magnetic personality." Notwithstanding this modesty and magnetism, after high school Dunbar had to work at one of the few jobs open to black youngsters—that of elevator boy.

Dunbar's first volume of poems was Oak and Ivy, *privately published in 1893. It was followed two years later by a second collection,* Majors and Minors. *Dunbar had to sell these books himself. He began to give readings of his poems and soon built up a following. The poems came to the attention of William Dean Howells, who reviewed them in* Harper's Weekly.

In 1896 Dunbar published the volume which made him famous, Lyrics of Lowly Life. *Howells wrote his widely known introduction to this work, praising the dialect poems:*

[The *precious difference in temperament*] *between the*

*races is best preserved and most charmingly suggested by Dun-
bar in those pieces of his where he studies the moods and traits
of his race in its own accents of our English . . . They are
really not dialect so much as personal attempts and failures for
the written and spoken language . . . pieces which . . . described the range between appetite and emotion, with certain
lifts far beyond it and above it . . . He reveals in these a finely
ironical perception of the Negro's limitations, with a tenderness
for them which I think so very rare as to be almost quite new.
I should say, perhaps, that it was this humorous quality Mr.
Dunbar has added to our literature, and it would be this which
would most distinguish him, now and hereafter."*

Read in the light of today's perceptions, the introduction reveals
the white critic's clouded vision of black realities. Although Howells
undoubtedly felt that he was praising Dunbar to the highest, he was
actually putting the kiss of death on any possibility of Dunbar's acceptance as a serious artist.

However, fame and some fortune followed the publication of
Lyrics of Lowly Life. Dunbar gave readings in England in 1897, and
in the same year began a short period as an aide in the Library of
Congress. In 1899 he went South for the first time to give readings.
Meanwhile, he wrote many articles and stories, and four novels, in
addition to more poems. Numerous collections of his works appeared.

In spite of his popular success, Dunbar was restless and dissatis-
fied. He was haunted by a feeling of failure because the dialect poems,
not the standard poems, were considered the more important. He was
haunted, too, by the spectre of early death, and, in fact, succumbed
to tuberculosis in 1906 at the age of thirty-three.

Assessments of Dunbar's work vary from Vernon Loggins' pronouncement that the publication of Lyrics of Lowly Life is "the
"greatest single event in the history of American Literature" to the
feeling among some current black writers that Dunbar was an Uncle
Tom. Several certainties emerge, however: that Dunbar was a highly
talented lyricist; that his writing took on the configuration imposed
upon it by the necessity to survive in a white literary world; and
that he himself valued his standard English poems more highly than
the popular dialect pieces.

One must come to grips with these dialect pieces. Dunbar wrote
them to gain an audience, knowing the fad exploited by Thomas Nel-

son Page, Joel Chandler Harris, and other white apologists for slavery. Dialect was not natural to Dunbar, who never even traveled South until after most of the dialect pieces had been written. From the folk speech he heard in his native Ohio, Dunbar constructed a patch-work dialect which is much like a Northern white's idea of "darky" talk. The form of the dialect poems is conventional literary form, and does not in any way resemble that of folk poetry. By substituting "funny spelling" for standard English, Dunbar produced graceful, quaint poems. The subject matter of the dialect poems is the simple pleasures and sorrows of a childlike people who could be comical or pathetic—seldom anything else. The poems were sympathetic to black people; but a comparison of any Dunbar dialect poem with a spiritual or with folk blues will reveal that the Dunbar poem is about, but not from, black life.

Dunbar speaks more truly in his standard English poems. In conventional forms Dunbar lauds notable people, finds nature a sympathetic companion, enjoys attractive women, and otherwise sings of things which through the ages have inspired poets. However, several obviously personal poems deal effectively with themes that vitally concerned Dunbar: his sense of impending death; his reactions to the damage inflicted upon the black man by American racism; his feelings of failure; his bitter disappointment that his dialect poems were so highly favoured while the standard English poems in which he expressed his powerful emotions were less popular.

Dunbar's stories were generally weak, although a few attained some degree of interest. Three of the novels concern white characters—The Uncalled (1898), The Love of Landry (1900), and The Fanatics (1901), The white public's image of the black man would not permit serious portrayal of black characters. The first novel is particularly revealing in that the leading character is Dunbar's own alter ego, facing a conflict Dunbar himself faced—but in the novel he is white. A fourth novel, The Sport of the Gods (1902), concerns black characters, but is technically weak.

Obviously Dunbar's scope was severely limited by the pressures of the times. Yet his contribution to black literature is considerable. He proved that a black writer could be a popular success—could, indeed, support himself with his pen. He broke the ground for poets to come. In the current upsurge of poetry which reflects black life, black rhythms, black language, we can perhaps detect the spectre of Dunbar.

An Antebellum Sermon

We is gathahed hyeah, my brothahs,
    In dis howlin' wildaness,
Fu' to speak some words of comfo't
    To each othah in distress.
An' we chooses fu' ouah subjic'
    Dis—we'll 'splain it by an' by;
"An' de Lawd said, 'Moses, Moses,'
    An' de man said, 'Hyeah am I.' "

Now ole Pher'oh, down in Egypt,
    Was de wuss man evah bo'n,
An' he had de Hebrew chillun
    Down dah wukin' in his co'n;
'T well de Lawd got tiahed o' his foolin',
    An' sez he: "I'll let him know—
Look hyeah, Moses, go tell Pher'oh
    Fu' to let dem chillun go."

"An' ef he refuse to do it,
    I will make him rue de houah,
Fu' I'll empty down on Egypt
    All de vials of my powah."
Yes, he did—an' Pher'oh's ahmy
    Was n't wuth a ha'f a dime;
Fu' de Lawd will he'p his chillun,
    You kin trust him evah time.

An' yo' enemies may 'sail you
    In de back an' in de front;
But de Lawd is all aroun' you,
    Fu' to ba' de battle's brunt.
Dey kin fo'ge yo' chains an' shackles
    F'om de mountains to de sea;
But de Lawd will sen' some Moses
    Fu' to set his chillun free.

An' de lan' shall hyeah his thundah,
    Lak a blas' f'om Gab'el's ho'n,
Fu' de Lawd of hosts is mighty
    When he girds his ahmor on.
But fu' feah some one mistakes me,
    I will pause right hyeah to say,
Dat I'm still a-preachin' ancient,
    I ain't talkin' 'bout to-day.

But I tell you, felah christuns,
    Things 'll happen mighty strange;
Now, de Lawd done dis fu' Isrul,
    An' his ways don't nevah change,
An' de love he showed to Isrul
    Was n't all on Isrul spent;
Now don't run an' tell yo' mastahs
    Dat I's preachin' discontent.

'Cause I is n't; I'se a-judgin'
    Bible people by deir ac's;
I'se a-givin' you de Scriptuah,
    I'se a-handin' you de fac's.
Cose ole Pher'oh b'lieved in slav'ry
    But de Lawd he let him see,
Dat de people he put bref in,—
    Evah mothah's son was free.

An' dahs othahs thinks lak Pher'oh,
    But dey calls de Scriptuah liar,
Fu' de Bible says "a servant
    Is a-worthy of his hire."
An' you cain't git roun' nor thoo dat,
    An' you cain't git ovah it,
Fu' whatevah place you git in,
    Dis hyeah Bible too 'll fit.

So you see de Lawd's intention,
    Evah sence de worl' began,
Was dat His almighty freedom
    Should belong to evah man,
But I think it would be bettah,
    Ef I'd pause agin to say,
Dat I'm talkin' 'bout ouah freedom
    In a Bibleistic way.

But de Moses is a-comin',
    An' he's comin', suah and fas'
We kin hyeah his feet a-trompin',
    We kin hyeah his trumpit blas'.
But I want to wa'n you people,
    Don't you git too brigity;
An' don't you git to braggin'
    'Bout dese things, you wait an' see.

But when Moses wif his powah
    Comes an' sets us chillun free,
We will praise de gracious Mastah
    Dat has gin us liberty;
An' we'll shout ouah halleluyahs,
    On dat mighty reck'nin' day,
When we'se reco'nised ez citiz'—
    Huh uh! Chillun, let us pray!

We Wear the Mask

We wear the mask that grins and lies,
It hides our cheeks and shades our eyes,—
This debt we pay to human guile;
With torn and bleeding hearts we smile,
And mouth with myriad subtleties.

Why should the world be over-wise,
In counting all our tears and sighs?
Nay, let them only see us, while
    We wear the mask.

We smile, but, O great Christ, our cries
To thee from tortured souls arise.
We sing, but oh the clay is vile
Beneath our feet, and long the mile;
But let the world dream otherwise,
    We wear the mask.

The Poet

He sang of life, serenely sweet.
    With, now and then, a deeper note.
    From some high peak, nigh yet remote,
He voiced the world's absorbing beat.

He sang of love when earth was young,
    And Love, itself, was in his lays.
    But ah, the world, it turned to praise
A jingle in a broken tongue.

Ere Sleep Comes Down to Soothe the Weary Eyes

Ere sleep comes down to soothe the weary eyes,
Which all the day with ceaseless care have sought
The magic gold which from the seeker flies;
Ere dreams put on the gown and cap of thought,
And make the waking world a world of lies,—
Of lies most palpable, uncouth, forlorn,
That say life's full of aches and tears and sighs,—
Oh, how with more than dreams the soul is torn,
Ere sleep comes down to soothe the weary eyes.

Ere sleep comes down to soothe the weary eyes,
How all the griefs and heartaches we have known
Come up like pois'nous vapors that arise
From some base witch's caldron, when the crone,
To work some potent spell, her magic plies.
The past which held its share of bitter pain,
Whose ghost we prayed that Time might exorcise,
Comes up, is lived and suffered o'er again,
Ere sleep comes down to soothe the weary eyes.

Ere sleep comes down to soothe the weary eyes,
What phantoms fill the dimly lighted room;
What ghostly shades in awe-creating guise
Are bodied forth within the teeming gloom.
What echoes faint of sad and soul-sick cries,
And pangs of vague inexplicable pain
That pay the spirit's ceaseless enterprise,
Come thronging through the chambers of the brain,
Ere sleep comes down to soothe the weary eyes.

Ere sleep comes down to soothe the weary eyes,
Where ranges forth the spirit far and free?
Through what strange realms and unfamiliar skies
Tends her far course to lands of mystery?
To lands unspeakable—beyond surmise,
Where shapes unknowable to being spring,
Till, faint of wing, the Fancy fails and dies
Much wearied with the spirit's journeying,
Ere sleep comes down to soothe the weary eyes.

Ere sleep comes down to soothe the weary eyes,
How questioneth the soul that other soul,—
The inner sense which neither cheats nor lies,
But self exposes unto self, a scroll
Full writ with all life's acts unwise or wise,
In characters indelible and known;
So, trembling with the shock of sad surprise,
The soul doth view its awful self alone,
Ere sleep comes down to soothe the weary eyes.

Ere sleep comes down to soothe the weary eyes,
The last dear sleep whose soft embrace is balm,
And whom sad sorrow teaches us to prize
For kissing all our passions into calm,
Ah, then, no more we heed the sad world's cries,
Or seek to probe th' eternal mystery,
Or fret our souls at long-withheld replies,
At glooms through which our visions cannot see,
Ere sleep comes down to soothe the weary eyes.

The Lynching of Jube Benson

Gordon Fairfax's library held but three men, but the air was dense with clouds of smoke. The talk had drifted from one topic to another much as the smoke wreaths had puffed, floated, and thinned away. Then Handon Gay, who was an ambitious young reporter, spoke of a lynching story in a recent magazine, and the matter of punishment without trial put new life into the conversation.

"I should like to see a real lynching," said Gay rather callously.

"Well, I should hardly express it that way," said Fairfax, "but if a real, live lynching were to come my way, I should not avoid it."

"I should," spoke the other from the depths of his chair, where he had been puffing in moody silence. Judged by his hair, which was freely sprinkled with gray, the speaker might have been a man of forty-five or fifty, but his face, though lined and serious, was youthful, the face of a man hardly past thirty.

"What! you, Dr. Melville? Why, I thought that you physicians wouldn't weaken at anything."

"I have seen one such affair," said the doctor gravely; "in fact, I took a prominent part in it."

"Tell us about it," said the reporter, feeling for his pencil and notebook, which he was, nevertheless, careful to hide from the speaker.

The men drew their chairs eagerly up to the doctor's, but for a minute he did not seem to see them, but sat gazing abstractedly into the fire; then he took a long draw upon his cigar and began:

"I can see it all very vividly now. It was in the summertime and about seven years ago. I was practicing at the time down in the little town of Bradford. It was a small and primitive place, just the location for an impecunious medical man, recently out of college.

"In lieu of a regular office, I attended to business in the first of two rooms which I rented from Hiram Daly, one of the more prosperous of the townsmen. Here I boarded and here also came my patients—white and black—whites from every section, and blacks from 'nigger town,' as the west portion of the place was called.

"The people about me were most of them coarse and rough, but they were simple and generous, and as time passed on I had about abandoned my intention of seeking distinction in wider fields and determined to settle into the place of a modest country doctor. This was rather a strange conclusion for a young man to arrive at, and I will not deny that the presence in the house of my host's beautiful young daughter, Annie, had something to do with my decision. She was a girl of seventeen or eighteen, and very far superior to her surroundings. She had a native grace and a pleasing way about her that made everybody that came under her spell her abject slave. White and black who knew her loved her, and none, I thought, more deeply and respectfully than Jube Benson, the black man of all work about the place.

"He was a fellow whom everybody trusted—an apparently steady-going, grinning sort, as we used to call him. Well, he was completely under Miss Annie's thumb, and as soon as he saw that I began to care for Annie, and anybody could see that, he transferred some of his allegiance to me and became my faithful servitor also. Never did a man have a more devoted adherent in his wooing than did I, and many a one of Annie's tasks which he volunteered to do gave her an extra hour with me. You can imagine that I liked the boy, and you need not wonder any more that, as both wooing and my practice waxed apace, I was content to give up my great ambitions and stay just where I was.

"It wasn't a very pleasant thing, then, to have an epidemic of typhoid break out in the town that kept me going so that I hardly had time for the courting that a fellow wants to carry on with his sweetheart while he is still young enough to call her his girl. I fumed, but duty was duty, and I kept to my work night and day. It was now that Jube proved how invaluable he was as coadjutor. He not only took messages to Annie, but brought sometimes little ones from her to me, and he would tell me little secret things that he had overheard her say that made me throb with joy and swear at him for repeating his mistress's conversation. But, best of all, Jube was a perfect Cerberus, and no one on earth could have been more effective in keeping away or deluding the other young fellows who visited the

Dalys. He would tell me of it afterwards, chuckling softly to himself, 'An,' Doctah, I say to Mistah Hemp Stevens, " 'Scuse us, Mistah Stevens, but Miss Annie, she des gone out," an' den he go outer de gate lookin' moughty lonesome. When Sam Elkins come, I say, "Sh, Mistah Elkins, Miss Annie, she done tuk down," an' he say, "What, Jube, you don' reckon hit de—" Den he stop an' look skeert, an' I say, "I feared hit is, Mistah Elkins," an' sheks my haid ez solemn. He goes outer de gate lookin' lak his bes' frien' done daid, an' all de time Miss Annie behine de cu'tain ovah de po'ch des a-laffin' fit to kill.'

"Jube was a most admirable liar, but what could I do? He knew that I was a young fool of a hypocrite, and when I would rebuke him for these deceptions, he would give way and roll on the floor in an excess of delighted laughter until from very contagion I had to join him—and, well, there was no need of my preaching when there had been no beginning to his repentance and when there must ensue a continuance of his wrong-doing.

"This thing went on for over three months, and then, pouf! I was down like a shot. My patients were nearly all up, but the reaction from overwork made me an easy victim of the lurking germs. Then Jube loomed up as a nurse. He put everyone else aside, and with the doctor, a friend of mine from a neighboring town, took entire charge of me. Even Annie herself was put aside, and I was cared for as tenderly as a baby. Tom, that was my physician and friend, told me all about it afterward with tears in his eyes. Only he was a big, blunt man, and his expressions did not convey all that he meant. He told me how Jube had nursed me as if I were a sick kitten and he my mother. Of how fiercely he guarded his right to be the sole one to 'do' for me, as he called it, and how, when the crisis came, he hovered, weeping but hopeful, at my bedside until it was safely passed, when they drove him, weak and exhausted, from the room. As for me, I knew little about it at the time, and cared less. I was too busy in my fight with death. To my chimerical vision there was only a black but gentle demon that came and went, alternating with a white fairy, who would insist on coming in on her head, growing larger and larger and then dissolving. But the pathos and devotion in the story lost nothing in my blunt friend's telling.

"It was during the period of a long convalescence, however, that I came to know my humble ally as he really was, devoted to the point of abjectness. There were times when, for very shame at his goodness to me, I would beg him to go away, to do something else. He would go, but before I had time to realize that I was not being ministered to, he would be back at my side, grinning and puttering just the same. He manufactured duties for the joy of performing them. He pretended to see desires in me that I never had, because he liked to pander to them, and when I became entirely exasperated and ripped out a good round oath, he chuckled with the remark, 'Dah, now, you sholy is gittin' well. Nevah did hyeah a man anywhaih nigh Jo'dan's sho' cuss lak dat.'

"Why, I grew to love him, love him, oh, yes, I loved him as well—oh, what am I saying? All human love and gratitude are damned poor things; excuse me, gentlemen, this isn't a pleasant story. The truth is usually a nasty thing to stand.

"It was not six months after that that my friendship to Jube, which he had been at such great pains to win, was put to too severe a test.

"It was in the summertime again, and, as business was slack, I had ridden over to see my friend, Dr. Tom. I had spent a good part of the day there, and it was past four o'clock when I rode leisurely into Bradford. I was in a particularly joyous mood and no premonition of the impending catastrophe oppressed me. No sense of sorrow, present or to come, forced itself upon me, even when I saw men hurrying through the almost deserted streets. When I got within sight of my home and saw a crowd surrounding it, I was only interested sufficiently to spur my horse into a jog trot, which brought me up to the throng, when something in the sullen, settled horror in the men's faces gave me a sudden, sick thrill. They whispered a word to me, and without a thought save for Annie, the girl who had been so surely growing into my heart, I leaped from the saddle and tore my way through the people to the house.

"It was Annie, poor girl, bruised and bleeding, her face and dress torn from struggling. They were gathered round her with white faces, and oh! with what terrible patience they were trying to gain from her fluttering lips the name of her murderer. They made way for me and I knelt at her side. She was beyond my skill, and my will merged with theirs. One thought was in our minds.

" 'Who?' I asked.

"Her eyes half opened. 'That black—' She fell back into my arms dead.

"We turned and looked at each other. The mother had broken down and was weeping, but the face of the father was like iron.

" 'It is enough,' he said; 'Jube has disappeared.' He went to the door and said to the expectant crowd, 'She is dead.'

"I heard the angry roar without swelling up like the noise of a flood, and then I heard the sudden movement of many feet as the men separated into searching parties, and laying the dead girl back upon her couch, I took my rifle and went out to join them.

"As if by intuition the knowledge had passed among the men that Jube Benson had disappeared, and he, by comment consent, was to be the object of our search. Fully a dozen of the citizens had seen him hastening toward the woods and noted his skulking air, but as he had grinned in his old good-natured way, they had, at the time, thought nothing of it. Now, however, the diabolical reason of his slyness was apparent. He had been shrewd enough to disarm suspicion, and by now was far away. Even Mrs. Daly, who was visiting with a neighbor, had seen him stepping out by a back way, and had said with a laugh, 'I reckon that black rascal's a-running off somewhere.' Oh, if she had only known!

" 'To the woods! To the woods!' that was the cry; and away we went, each with the determination not to shoot, but to bring the culprit alive into town, and then to deal with him as his crime deserved.

"I cannot describe the feelings I experienced as I went out that night to beat the woods for this human tiger. My heart smoldered within me like a coal, and I went forward under the impulse of a will that was half my own, half some more malignant power's. My throat throbbed drily, but water or whisky would not have quenched my thirst. The thought has come to me since, that now I could interpret the panther's desire for blood and sympathize with it, but then I thought nothing. I simply went forward and watched, watched with burning eyes for a familiar form that I had looked for as often before with such different emotions.

"Luck or ill-luck, which you will, was with our party, and just as dawn was graying the sky, we came upon our quarry crouched in the corner of a fence. It was only half light, and we might have passed, but my eyes caught sight of him, and I raised the cry. We leveled our guns and he rose and came toward us.

" 'I t'ought you wa'n't gwine see me,' he said sullenly; 'I didn't mean no harm.'

" 'Harm!'

"Some of the men took the word up with oaths, others were ominously silent.

"We gathered around him like hungry beasts, and I began to see terror dawning in his eyes. He turned to me, 'I's moughty glad you's hyeah, Doc,' he said; 'you ain't gwine let 'em whup me.'

" 'Whip you, you hound,' I said, 'I'm going to see you hanged,' and in the excess of my passion I struck him full on the mouth. He made a motion as if to resent the blow against such great odds, but controlled himself.

"'W'y, Doctah,' he exclaimed in the saddest voice I have ever heard, 'w'y, Doctah! I ain't stole nuffin' o' yo'n, an' I was comin' back. I only run off to see my gal, Lucy, ovah to de Centah.

"'You lie!' I said, and my hands were busy helping others bind him upon a horse. Why did I do it? I don't know. A false education, I reckon, one false from the beginning. I saw his black face glooming there in the half light, and I could only think of him as a monster. It's tradition. At first I was told that the black man would catch me, and when I got over that, they taught me that the devil was black, and when I recovered from the sickness of that belief, here were Jube and his fellows with faces of menacing blackness. There was only one conclusion: This black man stood for all the powers of evil, the result of whose machinations had been gathering in my mind from childhood up. But this has nothing to do with what happened.

"After firing a few shots to announce our capture, we rode back into town with Jube. The ingathering parties from all directions met us as we made our way up to the house. All was very quiet and orderly. There was no doubt that it was, as the papers would have said, a gathering of the best citizens. It was a gathering of stern, determined men, bent on a terrible vengeance.

"We took Jube into the house, into the room where the corpse lay. At the sight of it he gave a scream like an animal's, and his face went the color of storm-blown water. This was enough to condemn him. We divined rather than heard his cry of 'Miss Ann, Miss Ann; oh, my God! Doc, you don't t'ink I done it?'

"Hungry hands were ready. We hurried him out into the yard. A rope was ready. A tree was at hand. Well, that part was the least of it, save that Hiram Daly stepped aside to let me be the first to pull upon the rope. It was lax at first. Then it tightened, and I felt the quivering soft weight resist my muscles. Other hands joined and Jube swung off his feet.

"No one was masked. We knew each other. Not even the culprit's face was covered, and the last I remember of him as he went into the air was a look of sad reproach that will remain with me until I meet him face to face again.

"We were tying the end of the rope to a tree, where the dead man might hang as a warning to his fellows, when a terrible cry chilled us to the marrow.

"'Cut 'im down, cut 'im down; he ain't guilty. We got de one. Cut him down, fu' Gawd's sake. Here's de man; we foun' him hidin' in de barn!'

"Jube's brother, Ben, and another Negro came rushing toward us, half dragging, half carrying a miserable-looking wretch between them. Someone cut the rope and Jube dropped lifeless to the ground.

"'Oh, my Gawd, he's daid, he's daid!' wailed the brother, but with blazing eyes he brought his captive into the center of the group, and we saw in the full light the scratched face of Tom Skinner, the worst white ruffian in town; but the face we saw was not as we were accustomed to see it, merely smeared with dirt. It was blackened to imitate a Negro's.

"God forgive me; I could not wait to try to resuscitate Jube. I knew he was already past help; so I rushed into the house and to the dead girl's side. In the excitement they had not yet washed or laid her out. Carefully, carefully, I searched underneath her broken fingernails. There was skin there. I took it out, the little curled pieces, and went with it into my office.

"There, determinedly, I examined it under a powerful glass, and read my own doom. It was the skin of a white man, and in it were embedded strands of short brown hair or beard.

"How I went out to tell the waiting crowd I do not know, for something kept crying in my ears, 'Blood guilty! Blood guilty!'

"The men went away stricken into silence and awe. The new prisoner attempted neither denial nor plea. When they were gone, I would have helped Ben carry his brother in, but he waved me away fiercely. 'You he'ped murder my brothah, you dat was his frien'; go 'way, go 'way! I'll tek him home myse'f.' I could only respect his wish, and he and his comrade took up the dead man and between them bore him up the street on which the sun was now shining full.

"I saw the few men who had not skulked indoors uncover as they passed, and I—I—stood there between the two murdered ones, while all the while something in my ears kept crying 'Blood guilty! Blood guilty!'"

The doctor's head dropped into his hands and he sat for some time in silence, which was broken by neither of the men; then he rose, saying, "Gentlemen, that was my last lynching."

JAMES E. CAMPBELL

(c. 1860-c. 1905)

James Edwin Campbell was probably the first black poet to write in dialect.

Little is known about Campbell's early life except that he was born in Pomeroy, Ohio, and that he attended Miami College for a while. In his late twenties and early thirties Campbell wrote for various newspapers in Chicago. He was also co-editor of a literary magazine, The Four O'Clock, *which appeared for several years.*

Campbell's poetry differs from Dunbar's in that Campbell is free from the plantation tradition, that is, free from the romantic view of slavery propagated by the white Southern writers who apparently influenced Dunbar. Campbell wrote in Gullah dialect, which is closer to the language of Claude McKay's Songs of Jamaica *than to Dunbar's poetry. Also, whereas Dunbar projected the white image of the humorous or pathetic black, Campbell's work closely approximates genuine folk material. Apparently neither poet influenced the other.*

De Cunjah Man

O chillen run, de Cunjah man,
Him mouf ez beeg ez fryin' pan,
Him yurs am small, him eyes am raid,
Him hab no toof een him ol' haid,
Him hab him roots, him wu'k him trick,
Him roll him eye, him mek you sick—
    De Cunjah man, de Cunjah man,
    O chillen run, de Cunjah man!

Him hab ur ball ob raid, raid ha'r,
Him hide it un' de kitchen sta'r,
Mam Jude huh pars urlong dat way,
An' now huh hab ur snaik, dey say.
Him wrop ur roun' huh buddy tight,
Huh eyes pop out, ur orful sight—
    De Cunjah man, de Cunjah man,
    O chillen run, de Cunjah man!

Miss Jane, huh dribe him f'un huh do',
An' now huh hens woan' lay no mo';
De Jussey cow huh done fall sick,
Hit all done by de cunjah trick.
Him put ur root un' 'Lijah's baid,
An' now de man he sho' am daid—
    De Cunjah man, de Cunjah man,
    O chillen run, de Cunjah man!

Me see him stand' de yudder night
Right een de road een white moon-light;
Him toss him arms, him whirl him 'roun;
Him stamp him foot urpon de groun';
De snaiks come crawlin', one by one,
Me hyuh um hiss, me break an' run.
    De Cunjah man, de Cunjah man,
    O chillen run, de Cunjah man!

Ol' Doc' Hyar

Ur ol' Hyar lib in ur house on de hill,
He hunner yurs ol' an' nebber wuz ill;
He yurs dee so long an' he eyes so beeg,
An' he laigs so spry dat he dawnce ur jeeg;
He lib so long dat he know ebbry tings
'Bout de beas'ses dat walks an' de bu'ds dat sings—
    Dis Ol' Doc' Hyar,
    Whar lib up dar
Een ur mighty find house on ur mighty high hill.

He doctah fur all de beas'ses an' bu'ds—
He put on he specs an' he use beeg wu'ds,
He feel dee pu's' den he look mighty wise,
He pull out he watch an' he shet bofe eyes;
He grab up he hat an' grab up he cane,
Den—"blam!" go de do'—he gone lak de train,
    Dis Ol' Doc' Hyar,
    Whar lib up dar
Een ur mighty fine house on ur mighty high hill.

Mistah Ba'r fall sick—dee sont fur Doc' Hyar,
"Oh, Doctah, come queeck, an' see Mr. B'ar;
He mighty nigh daid des sho'ez you b'on!"
"Too much ur young peeg, too much ur green co'n,"
Ez he put on he hat, said Ol' Doc' Hyar;
"I'll tek 'long meh lawnce, an' lawnce Mistah B'ar,"
          Said Ol' Doc' Hyar,
            Whar lib up dar
Een ur mighty fine house on ur mighty fine hill.

Mistah B'ar he groaned, Mistah B'ar he growled,
W'ile de ol' Mis' B'ar an' de chillen howled:
Doctah Hyar tuk out he sha'p li'l lawnce,
An' pyu'ced Mistah B'ar twel he med him prawnce
Den grab up he hat an' grab up he cane
"Blam!" go de do' an' he gone lak de train,
          Dis Ol' Doc' Hyar,
            Whar lib up dar
Een ur mighty fine house on ur mighty fine hill.

But de vay naix day Mistah B'ar he daid;
Wen dee tell Doc' Hyar, he des scratch he haid:
"Ef pashons git well ur pashons git wu's,
Money got ter come een de Ol' Hyar's pu's;
Not wut folkses does, but fur wut dee know
Does de folkses git paid"—an' Hyar larfed low,
          Dis sma't Ol' Hyar,
            Whar lib up dar
Een de mighty fine house on the mighty high hill!

'Sciplinin' Sister Brown

Shet up dat noise, you chillen! Dar's some one at de do'.
Dribe out dem dogs; you 'Rastus, tek Linkum off de flo'!

Des ma'ch yo'se'f right in sah! (Jane, tek dem ashes out!
Dis house look lak ur hog-pen; you M'randy, jump erbout!)

W'y bress my soul, hit's Ef'um—w'y, Ef'um, how you do?
An' Tempie an' de chillen? I hopes dey's all well too.

Hyuh, M'randy, bresh dat stool off, now, Ef'um, des set down.
Wut's de news f'um off de Ridge an' wut's de news in town?

Now doan' you t'ink dem niggahs hed Susan 'fo de chu'ch
'Bout dawncin' at de pa'ty—dey call dat sinnin' much.

Dey up an' call ur meetin' ter 'scipline Sistah Brown,
But de night dey hol' de meetin' she tuk herse'f to town.

Dey sont de Bo'd ob Deacons, de pahstah at de head,
Ter wait urpon de sistah an' pray wid her, dey said,

But Susan mighty stubbo'n, an' wen dey lif' ur pra'r
She up an' tell de deacons she des wawn' kwine ter cyar.

An' wen de Reb'ren' Pa'son prayed 'bout ur "sheep wuz los'."
An' 'bout de "po bac'slidah," she gin her head ur toss!

I seed de debbil raisin' in de white ob Susan's eyes—
Fyeah she blow dat deacon-bo'd ter "mansions in de skies,"

I des tuk down my bawnjer an' den I 'gins an' plays;
"Come dy fount ob ebbry blessin', chune my ha't ter sing dy praise."

De pa'son an' de deacons dey jined me pooty soon;
Lawd! Dat bawnjer shuk itse'f ur-playin' ob de chune!

An' wen dey mos' wuz shoutin', I tightened up er string,
Drapped right inter "Money Musk" an' gin de chune full swing.

De "Debbil's Dream" come arter—de debbil wuz ter pay,
Dem niggahs fell ter pattin'—I larf mos' ebbry day!

Deacon Jones got on his feet, de pa'son pulled him down;
I played ur little fastah, an' sho's my name am Brown,

De pa'son an' de deacons jined han's right on dis flo',
Su'cled right and su'cled lef'—it sutny wiz er show.

Dey 'naded up an' down de flo' an' w'en hit come ter swing,
De pa'son gin hisse'f a flirt an' cut de pidgin-wing!

An' we'n urfo' de meetin' dat 'mittee med its 'po't
'Bout Sistah Susan's dawncin', dey cut it mighty sho't.

De Chyuhsman, Mr. Pa'son, said in tones so mil' an' sweet:
"Sistah Brown wa'n't guilty, caze—SHE NEBBER CROSSED HER
    FEET!"

GEORGE McCLELLAN

(1860-1934)

George Marion McClellan was one of the scholar-poets of the turn of the century who attempted to counteract the negative image of blacks by writing decorous poetry in the English tradition.

He was born into a relatively affluent family in Belfast, Tennessee, and was very well educated. He earned a bachelor's and a master's degree from Fisk University and a divinity degree from the Hartford Theological Seminary. Subsequently he spent an extremely active life as minister and educator. He traveled frequently on fund-raising ventures for Fisk University and for various charities organized to alleviate the condition of black people.

McClellan's poetry hardly reflected the down-to-earth activities of his busy life. He wrote lyrics that would seem to issue from the ivory tower—scholarly works, formal in language, style, and structure, well-controlled in emotion. He produced a number of volumes: Poems *(1895),* Book of Poems and Short Stories *(1895),* Old Greenbottom Inn *(1896),* Songs of a Southerner *(1896), and* Path of Dreams *(1916). His themes were generally romantic (sometimes sentimental), taken from nature: flowers, the seasons, love, death. Rarely did he write of blackness.*

For a while McClellan's poetry was popular among intellectual readers. If it did not literally reflect the experience of the black masses, it did provide some insight into the thinking of educated men seeking to reconcile their blackness with a devotion to art.

Eternity

Rock me to sleep, ye waves, and drift my boat
With undulations soft far out to sea;
Perchance where sky and wave wear one blue coat,
My heart shall find some hidden rest remote.
My spirit swoons, and all my senses cry
For Ocean's breast and covering of the sky.
Rock me to sleep, ye waves, and outward bound,
Just let me drift far out from toil and care,
Where lapping of the waves shall be the sound,
Which mingled with the winds that gently bear
Me on between a peaceful sea and sky,
To make my soothing slumberous lullaby;
Thus drifting on and on upon thy breast,
My heart shall go to sleep and rest and rest.

The April of Alabama

Fair Alabama, "Here we rest," thy name—
And in this stretch of oak and spotted ash,
Well said that long past swarthy tribe who came
Here, "Alabama," in these glamour wilds.
To-day thy April woods have had for me
A thousand charms, elusive loveliness,
That melt in shimmering views which flash
From leaves and buds in half-grown daintiness
From every tree and living thing there smiles
A touch of summer's glory yet to be.
Already overhead the sky resumes
Its summer softness, and a hand of light
All through the woods has beckoned with its blooms
Oh honey suckle wild and dogwood white
As bridal robes—
                    With bashful azure eyes
All full of dew-born laughing falling tears
The violets more blue than summer skies
Are rioting in vagrancy around
Beneath old oaks, old pines and sending out
Like prodigals their sweets to spicy airs.
And as to-day this loveliness for years
Unknown has come and gone. To-day it wears
Its pageantry of youth with sylvan sound
Of many forest tribes which fairly shout
Their ecstacies. But soon with summer smiles
Will such a gorgeousness of flaming hues
Bedeck those Alabama glamour wilds
As ever burst to life by rain and dews.

A Decoration Day

The reign of death was there,
Where swept the winter winds with
    pipes and moans,
And, stretched in silence bare,
A colonnade of gray sepulchral stones.

But then it was May
And all the fields were bright and gay
    With tune
That Decoration Day,
And blossoms wore their hues and breath
    Of June.

A motley crowd that came,
But who more fit than they that once
    were slaves,
Despised, unknown to fame,
With love should decorate the
    soldiers' graves?

Black feet trod cheerily
From out the town in crowds or
    straggling bands,
And flowers waved and flaunted merrily
    From little Negro hands.

And far, far away
From home and love, deep in a silent bed,
Beneath the sky of May,
Was sleeping there, in solitude, the dead.

But for the hearts that day
Who in the distant North was sore and sighed,
Black hands, with sweets of May,
Made green the graves of those who for them died.

KELLY MILLER

(1863-1939)

During the first years of the new century, when the debate be-tween Booker T. Washington and W. E. B. Du Bois delineated the poles of black thinking on many issues, Kelly Miller represented the view of a great many intellectuals who favored adopting a middle ground. A leading educator and essayist of his time, he was influential in molding opinions of black leaders for the first quarter of the century.

Kelly Miller was born in Winnsboro, South Carolina, during the Civil War. His boyhood years saw the abridgement of black people's civil rights and the tides of racial hatred and violence that took place South and North during Reconstruction and the years that followed. Miller was educated at Howard University and Johns Hopkins, then became a teacher of mathematics and eventually a dean at Howard University. He was active in many of the attempts to resolve the "Negro problem," and was a well-known lecturer and writer of ar-ticles, essays, and pamphlets.

Miller agreed with Booker T. Washington that industrial educa-tion was desirable for black people, but he insisted that in order for the race to rise economically and politically it was also necessary for a large number of young people to receive higher education. Miller felt that the solution to the race problem lay in racial unity and in political and economic independence. As he grew older he tended more to the side of the protesters than to that of the accommodaters.

As an essayist Miller wrote in a clear, straightforward style. His emotion is restrained but clearly evident, especially in the later essays. He makes effective use of time-honored rhetorical devices such as analogy, contrast, and exemplification. His works are deliberate and scholarly but not pedantic. His tone is moderate, for he is attempting to harmonize divergent views in search of the racial solidarity he espoused. In general, Miller's views are outdated in terms of today's conditions and attitudes. His works are worthy of study because of their statement of the problem and their demonstration of the thinking of many Negro leaders.

Miller's essays are collected in several volumes. The first, Race Adjustment *(1908), expresses his early, more conservative views. The essays in* Out of the House of Bondage *(1914) present his views on education, politics, crime, and other aspects of Afro-America fifty years after emancipation.* An Appeal to Conscience *(1918) reflects Miller's increased militancy after World War I. The element of protest is presented with moderation, but also with firmness and logic. Other works by Miller are the* History of the World War and the Important Part taken by the Negroes *(1919) and* The Everlasting Stain *(1924).*

An Open Letter to Thomas Dixon, Jr.

September, 1905.

Mr. Thomas Dixon, Jr.
Dear Sir:—
I am writing you this letter to express the attitude and feeling of ten millions of your fellow citizens toward the evil propagandism of race animosity to which you have lent your great literary powers. Through the widespread influence of your writings you have become the chief priest of those who worship at the shrine of race hatred and wrath. This one spirit runs through all your books and published utterances, like the recurrent theme of an opera. As the general trend of your doctrine is clearly epitomized and put forth in your contribution to the *Saturday Evening Post* of August 19, I beg to consider chiefly the issues therein raised. You are a white man born in the midst of the civil war, I am a Negro born during the same stirring epoch. You were born with a silver spoon in your mouth, I was born with an iron hoe in my hand. Your race has inflicted accumulated injury and wrong upon mine, mine has borne yours only service and good will. You express your views with the most scathing frankness; I am sure, you will welcome an equally candid expression from me.

Permit me to acknowledge the personal consideration which you have shown me. You will doubtless recall that when I addressed The Congregational Ministers, of New York City, some year or more ago, you asked permission to be present and listened attentively to what I had to say, although as might have been expected, you beat a precipitous retreat when luncheon was announced. In your article in the *Post* you make several references to me and to other colored men with entire personal courtesy. So far as I know you have never varied from this rule in your personal dealings with members of my race. You are merciless, however, in excoriating the race as a whole, thus keenly wounding the sensibilities of every individual of that blood. I assure you that this courtesy of personal treatment will be reciprocated in this letter, however sharply I may be compelled to take issue with the views you set forth and to deplore your attitude. I shall endeavor to indulge in no bitter word against your race nor against the South, whose exponent and special pleader you assume to be.

I fear that you have mistaken personal manners, the inevitable varnish of any gentleman of your antecedents and rearing, for friendship to a race which you hold in despite. You tell us that you are kind and considerate to your personal servants. It is somewhat strange that you should deem such assurance necessary, any more than it is necessary for us to assure us that you are kind to and fond of your horse or your dog. But when you write yourself down as "one of their best friends," you need not be surprised if we retort the refrain of the ritual: "From all such proffers of friendship, good Lord deliver us."

Your fundamental thesis is that "no amount of education of any kind, industrial, classical or religious, can make a Negro a white man or bridge the chasm of the centuries which separates him from the white man in the evolution of human history." This doctrine is as old as human oppression. Calhoun made it the arch stone in the defense of Negro slavery—and lost.

This is but a recrudescence of the doctrine which was exploited and exploded during the antislavery struggle. Do you recall the school of proslavery scientists who demonstrated beyond doubt that the Negro's skull was too thick to comprehend the substance of Aryan knowledge? Have you not read in the discredited scientific books of that period, with what triumphant acclaim it was shown that the Negro's shape and size of skull, facial angle, and cephalic configuration rendered him forever impervious to the white man's civilization? But all enlightened minds are now as ashamed of that doctrine as they are of the onetime dogma that the Negro had no soul. We become aware of mind through its manifestations. Within forty years of only partial opportunity, while playing as it were in the back yard of civilization, the American Negro has cut down his illiteracy by over fifty per cent; has produced a professional class, some fifty thousand strong, including ministers, teachers, doctors, lawyers, editors, authors, architects, engineers and all higher lines of listed pursuits in which white men are engaged; some three thousand Negroes have taken collegiate degrees, over three hundred being from the best institutions in the North and West established for the most favored white youth; there is scarcely a first-class institution in America, excepting some three or four in the South, that is without colored students who pursue their studies generally with success, and sometimes with distinction; Negro inventors have taken out four hundred patents as a contribution to the mechanical genius of America; there are scores of Negroes who, for conceded ability and achievements, take respectable rank in the company of distinguished Americans.

It devolves upon you, Mr. Dixon, to point out some standard, either of intelligence, character, or conduct to which the Negro can not conform. Will you please tell a waiting world just what is the psychological difference between the races? No reputable authority, either of the old or the new school of psychology, has yet pointed out any sharp psychic discriminant. There is not a single intellectual, moral, or spiritual excellence attained by the white race to which the Negro does not yield an appreciative response. If you could show that the Negro was incapable of mastering the intricacies of Aryan speech, that he could not comprehend the intellectual basis of European culture, or apply the apparatus of practical knowledge, that he could not be made amenable to the white man's ethical code or appreciate his spiritual motive, then your case would be proved. But in default of such demonstration, we must relegate your eloquent pronouncement to the realm of generalization and prophecy, an easy and agreeable exercise of the mind in which the romancer is ever prone to indulge.

The inherent, essential, and unchangeable inferiority of the Negro to the white man lies at the basis of your social philosophy. You disdain to examine the validity of your fondly cherished hope. You follow closely in the wake of Tom Watson, in the June number of his homonymous magazine. You both hurl your thesis of innate racial inferiority at the head of Booker T. Washington. You use the same illustrations, the same arguments, set forth in the same order of recital, and for the most part in identical language. This seems to be an instance of great minds, or at least of minds of the same grade, running in the same channel.

These are your words: "What contribution to human progress have the millions of Africa who inhabit this planet made during the past four thousand years? Absolutely nothing." These are the words of Thomas Watson spoken some two months previous: "What does civilization owe to the Negro race? Nothing! Nothing!! Nothing!!!" You answer the query with the most emphatic negative noun and the strongest qualifying adjective in the language. Mr. Watson, of a more ecstatic temperament, replies with the same noun and six exclamation points. One rarely meets, outside of yellow journalism, with such lavishness of language, wasted upon a hoary dogma. A discredited dictum that has been bandied about the world from the time of Canaan to Calhoun, is revamped and set forth with as much ardor and fervency of feeling as if discovered for the first time and proclaimed for the illumination of a waiting world.

But neither boastful asseveration on your part nor indignant denial on mine will affect the facts of the case. That Negroes in the average are not equal in developed capacity to the white race, is a proposition which it would be as simple to affirm as it is silly to deny. The Negro represents a backward race which has not yet taken a commanding part in the progressive movement of the world. In the great cosmic scheme of things, some races reach the limelight of civilization ahead of others. But that temporary forwardness does not argue inherent superiority is as evident as any fact of history. An unfriendly environment may hinder and impede the one, while fortunate circumstances may quicken and spur the other. Relative superiority is only a transient phase of human development. You tell us that "The Jew had achieved a civilization—had his poets, prophets, priests, and kings, when our Germanic ancestors were still in the woods cracking cocoanuts and hickory-nuts with the monkeys." Fancy some learned Jew at that day citing your query about the contribution of the Germanic races to the culture of the human spirit, during the thousands of years of their existence! Does the progress of history not prove that races may lie dormant and fallow for ages and then break suddenly into prestige and power? Fifty years ago you doubtless would have ranked Japan among the benighted nations and hurled at their heathen heads some derogatory query as to their contribution to civilization. But since the happenings at Mukden and Port Arthur, and Portsmouth, I suppose that you are ready to change your mind. Or maybe since the Jap has proved himself "a first-class fighting man," able to cope on equal terms with the best breeds in Europe, you will claim him as belonging to the white race, notwithstanding his pig eye and yellow pigment.

The Negro enters into the inheritance of all the ages on equal terms with the rest, and who can say that he will not contribute his quota of genius to enrich the blood of the world?

The line of argument of every writer who undertakes to belittle the Negro is a well-beaten path. Liberia and Haiti are bound to come in for their share of ridicule and contemptuous handling. Mr. Watson calls these experiments freshly to mind, lest we forget. We are told all about the incapacity of the black race for self-government, the relapse into barbarism and much more of which we have heard before; and yet when we take all the circumstances into account, Haiti presents to the world one of the most remarkable achievements in the annals of human history. The panegyric of Wendell Phillips on Toussaint L'Ouverture is more than an outburst of rhetorical fancy; it is a just measure of his achievements in terms of his humble environment and the limited instrumentalities at his command. Where else in the course of history has a slave, with the aid of slaves, expelled a powerfully intrenched master class, and set up a government patterned after civilized models and which without external assistance or reinforcement from a parent civilization, has endured for a hundred years in face of a frowning world? When we consider the difficulties that confront a weak government, without military or naval means to cope with its more powerful rivals, and where commercial adventurers are ever and anon stirring up internal strife, thus provoking the intervention of stronger governments, the marvel is that the republic of Haiti still endures, the only self-governing state of the Antilles. To expect as effective and proficient government to prevail in Haiti as at Washington would be expecting more of the black men in Haiti than we find in the white men of South America. And yet, I suspect that the million Negroes in Haiti are as well governed as the corresponding number of blacks in Georgia, where only yesterday eight men were taken from the custody of the law and lynched without judge or jury. It is often charged that these people have not maintained the pace set by the old master class, that the plantations are in ruin and that the whole island wears the aspect of dilapidation. Wherever a lower people overrun the civilization of a higher, there is an inevitable lapse toward the level of the lower. When barbarians and semi-civilized hordes of northern Europe overran the southern peninsulas, the civilization of the world was wrapped in a thousand years of darkness. Relapse inevitably precedes the rebound. Is there anything in the history of Haiti contrary to the law of human development?

You ask: "Can you change the color of the Negro's skin, the kink of his hair, the bulge of his lip, or the beat of his heart, with a spelling book or a machine?" This rhetorical outburst does great credit to your literary skill, and is calculated to delight the simple; but analysis fails to reveal in it any pregnant meaning. Since civilization is not an attribute of the color of skin, or curl of hair, or curve of lip, there is no necessity for changing such physical peculiarities, and if there was, the spelling book and the machine would be very unlikely instruments for its accomplishment. But why, may I ask, would you desire to change the Negro's heart throb, which already beats at a normal human pace? You need not be so frantic about the superiority of your race. Whatever superiority it may possess, inherent or acquired, will take care of itself without such rabid support. Has it ever occurred to you that the people of New England blood, who have done and are doing most to make the white race great and glorious in this land, are the most reticent about extravagant claims to everlasting superiority? You protest too much. Your loud pretensions, backed up by such exclamatory outbursts of passion, make upon the reflecting mind the impression that you entertain a sneaking suspicion of their validity.

Your position as to the work and worth of Booker T. Washington is pitiably anomalous. You recite the story of his upward struggle with uncontrolled admiration: "The story of this little ragged, barefooted pickaninny, who lifted his eyes from a cabin in the hills of Virginia, saw a vision and followed it, until at last he presides over the richest and most powerful institution in the South, and sits down with crowned heads and presidents, has no parallel even in the Tales of the Arabian Nights." You say that his story appeals to the universal heart of humanity. And yet in a recent letter to the *Columbia States*, you regard it as an unspeakable outrage that Mr. Robert C. Ogden should walk arm in arm with this wonderful man who "appeals to the heart of universal humanity," and introduce him to the lady clerks in a dry goods store. Your passionate devotion to a narrow dogma has seriously impaired your sense of humor. The subject of your next great novel has been announced as "The Fall of Tuskegee." In one breath you commend the work of this great institution, while in another you condemn it because it does not fit into your preconceived scheme in the solution of the race problem. The Tuskegee ideal: "to make Negroes producers, lovers of labor, independent, honest, and good" is one which you say that only a fool or a knave can find fault with, because, in your own words, "it rests squarely upon the eternal verities." Over against this you add with all the condemnatory emphasis of italics and exclamation point: *"Tuskegee is not a servant training school!"* And further: "Mr. Washington is not training Negroes to take their places in the industries of the South in which white men direct and control them. He is not training students to be servants and come at the beck and call of any man. He is training them to be masters of men, to be independent, to own and operate their own industries, plant their own field, buy and sell their own goods." All of which you condemn by imperative inference ten times stronger than your faint and forced verbal approval. It is a heedless man who wilfully flaunts his little philosophy in the face of "the eternal verities." When the wise man finds that his prejudices are running against fixed principles in God's cosmic plan, he speedily readjusts them in harmony therewith. Has it never occurred to you to reexamine the foundation of the faith, as well as the feeling, that is in you, since you admit that it runs afoul of the "eternal verities?"

Mr. Washington's motto, in his own words, is that "the Negro has been worked; but now he must learn to work." The man who works for himself is of more service to any community than the man whose labor is exploited by others. You bring forward the traditional bias of the slave regime to modern conditions, viz.: that the Negro did not exist in his own right and for his own sake, but for the benefit of the white man. This principle is as false in nature as it is in morals. The naturalists tell us that throughout all the range of animal creation, there is found no creature which exists for the sake of any other, but each is striving after its own best welfare. Do you fear that the Negro's welfare is incompatible with that of the white man? I commend to you a careful perusal of the words of Mr. E. Gardner Murphy who, like yourself, is a devoted Southerner, and is equally zealous to promote the highest interest of that section: "Have properity, peace and happiness ever been successfully or permanently based upon indolence, inefficiency, and hopelessness? Since time began, has any human thing that God has made taken damage to itself or brought damage to the world through knowledge, truth, hope, and honest toil?" Read these words of your fellow Southerner, Mr. Dixon, meditate upon them; they will do you good as the truth doeth the upright heart.

You quote me as being in favor of the amalgamation of the races. A more careful reading of the article referred to would have convinced you that I was arguing against it as a probable solution of the race problem. I merely stated the intellectual conviction that two races cannot live indefinitely side by side, under the same general regime without ultimately fusing. This was merely the expression of a belief, and not the utterance of a preference nor the formulation of a policy. I know of no colored man who advocates amalgamation as a feasible policy of solution. You are mistaken. The Negro does not "hope and dream of amalgamation." This would be self-stultification with a vengeance. If such a policy were allowed to dominate the imagination of the race, its women would give themselves over to the unrestrained passion of white men, in quest of tawny offspring, which would give rise to a state of indescribable moral debauchery. At the same time you would hardly expect the Negro, in derogation of his common human qualities, to proclaim that he is so diverse from God's other human creatures as to make the blending of the races contrary to the law of nature. The Negro refuses to become excited or share in your frenzy on this subject. The amalgamation of the races is an ultimate possibility, though not an immediate probability. But what have you and I to do with ultimate questions, anyway? Our concern is with duty, not destiny.

But do you know, Mr. Dixon, that you are probably the foremost promoter of amalgamation between the two races? Wherever you narrow the scope of the Negro by preaching the doctrine of hate, you drive thousands of persons of lighter hue over to the white race carrying more or less Negro blood in their train. The blending of the races is less likely to take place if the self-respect and manly opportunity of the Negro are respected and encouraged, than if he is to be forever crushed beneath the level of his faculties for dread of the fancied result. Hundreds of the composite progeny are daily crossing the color line and carrying as much of the despised blood as an albicant skin can conceal without betrayal. I believe that it was Congressman Tillman, brother of the more famous Senator of that name, who stated on the floor of the constitutional convention of South Carolina, that he knew of four hundred white families in that State who had a taint of Negro blood in their veins. I personally know, or know of, fifty cases of transition in the city of Washington. It is a momentous thing for one to change his caste. The man or woman who affects to deny, ignore, or scorn the class with whom he previously associated is usually deemed deficient in the nobler qualities of human nature. It is not conceivable that persons of this class would undergo the self-degradation and humiliation of soul necessary to cross the great "social divide" unless it be to escape for themselves and their descendants an odious and despised status. Your oft expressed and passionately avowed belief that the progressive development of the Negro would hasten amalgamation is not borne out by the facts of observation. The refined and cultivated class among colored people are as much disinclined to such unions as the whites themselves. I am sorry that you saw fit to characterize Frederick Douglass as "a bombastic vituperator." You thereby gave poignant offense to ten millions of his race who regard him as the best embodiment of their possibilities. Besides millions of your race rate him among the foremost and best beloved of Americans. How would you feel if some one should stigmatize Jefferson Davis or Robert E. Lee in such language, these beau ideals of your Southern heart? But I will not undertake to defend Frederick Douglass against your calumniations. I am frank to confess that I do not feel that he needs it. The point I have in mind to make about Mr. Douglass is that he has a hold upon the affection of his race, not on account of his second marriage, but in spite of it. He seriously affected his standing with his people by that marriage.

It seems to me, Mr. Dixon, that this frantic abhorrence of amalgamation is a little late in its appearance. Whence comes this stream of white blood, which flows with more or less spissitude, in the veins of some six out of ten million Negroes? The Afro-American is hardly a Negro at all, except constructively; but a new creature. Who brought about this present approachment between the races? Do you not appreciate the inconsistency in the attitude and the action on the part of many of the loudmouthed advocates of race purity? It is said that old Father Chronos devoured his offspring in order to forestall future complications. Bue we do not learn that he put a bridle upon his passion as the surest means of security. The most effective service you can render to check the evil of amalgamation is to do missionary work among the males of your own race. This strenuous advocacy of race purity in face of proved proneness for miscegenation affords a striking reminder of the lines of Hudibras:—

> The self-same thing they will abhor,
> One way, and long another for.

Again, you say that "we have spent about $800,000,000 on Negro education since the war." This statement is so very wide of the mark, that I was disposed to regard it as a misprint, if you had not reinforced it with an application implying a like amount. In the report of the Bureau of Education for 1901, the estimated expenditure for Negro education in all the former slave States since the Civil War was put down at $121,184,568. The amount contributed by Northern philanthropy during that interval is variously estimated from fifty to seventy-five millions. Your estimate is four times too large. It would be interesting and informing to the world if you would reveal the source of your information. These misstatements of fact are not of so much importance in themselves, as that they serve to warn the reader against the accuracy and value of your general judgments. It would seem that your derive your figures of arithmetic from the same source from which you fashion your figures of speech. You will not blame the reader for not paying much heed to your sweeping generalizations, when you are at such little pains as to the accuracy of easily ascertainable data.

Your proposed solution of the race problem by colonizing the Negroes in Liberia reaches the climax of absurdity. It is difficult to see how such a proposition could emanate from a man of your reputation. Did you consult Cram's Atlas about Liberia? Please do so. You will find that it has an area of 48,000 square miles and a population of 1,500,000, natives and immigrants. The area and population are about the same as those of North Carolina, which, I believe, is your native State. When you tell us that this restricted area, without commerce, without manufacture, without any system of organized industry, can support every Negro in America, in addition to its present population, I beg mildly to suggest that you recall your plan for revision before submitting it to the judgment of a critical world. Your absolute indifference to and heedlessness of the facts, circumstances, and conditions involved in the scheme of colonization well befit the absurdity of the general proposition.

The solution of the race problem in America is indeed a grave and serious matter. It is one that calls for statesmanlike breadth of view, philanthropic tolerance of spirit, and exact social knowledge. The whole spirit of your propaganda is to add to its intensity and aggravation. You stir the slumbering fires of race wrath into an uncontrollable flame. I have read somewhere that Max Nordau, on reading *The Leopard's Spots,* wrote to you suggesting the awful responsibility you had assumed in stirring up enmity between race and race. Your teachings subvert the foundations of law and established order. You are the high priest of lawlessness, the prophet of anarchy. Rudyard Kipling places this sentiment in the mouth of the reckless stealer of seals in the Northern Sea: "There's never a law of God nor man runs north of fifty-three." This description exactly fits the brand of literature with which you are flooding the public. You openly urge your fellow citizens to override all law, human and divine. Are you aware of the force and effect of these words? "Could fatuity reach a sublimer height than the idea that the white man will stand idly by and see the performance? What will he do when put to the test? He will do exactly what his white neighbor in the North does when the Negro threatens his bread—kill him!" These words breathe out hatred and slaughter and suggest the murder of innocent men whose only crime is quest for the God-given right to work. You poison the mind and pollute the imagination through the subtle influence of letters. Are you aware of the force and effect of evil suggestion when the passions of men are in a state of unstable equilibrium? A heterogeneous population, where the elements are, on any account, easily distinguishable, is an easy prey for the promotor of wrath. The fuse is already prepared for the spark. The soul of the mob is stirred by suggestion of hatred and slaughter, as a famished beast at the smell of blood. The rabble responds so much more readily to an appeal to passion than to reason. To wantonly stir up the fires of race antipathy is as execrable a deed as flaunting a red rag in the face of a bull at a summer's picnic, or raising a false cry of "fire" in a crowded house. Human society could not exist one hour except on the basis of law, which holds the baser passions of men in restraint.

In our complex situation it is only the rigid observance of law re-enforced by higher moral restraint that can keep these passions in bound. You speak about giving the Negro a "square deal." Even among gamblers, a "square deal" means to play according to the rules of the game. The rules which all civilized States have set for themselves are found in the Ten Commandments, the Golden Rule, the Sermon on the Mount, and the organic law of the land. You acknowledge no such restraints when the Negro is involved, but waive them all aside with frenzied defiance. You preside at every crossroad lynching of a helpless victim; wherever the midnight murderer rides with rope and torch, in quest of the blood of his black brother, you ride by his side; wherever the cries of the crucified victim go up to God from the crackling flame, behold you are there; when women and children, drunk with ghoulish glee, dance around the funeral pyre and mock the death groans of their fellow man and fight for ghastly souvenirs, you have your part in the inspiration of it all. When guilefully guided workmen in mine and shop and factory, goaded by a real or imaginary sense of wrong, begin the plunder and pillage of property and murder of rival men, your suggestion is justifier of the dastardly doings. Lawlessness is gnawing at the very vitals of our institutions. It is the surpreme duty of every enlightened mind to allay rather than spur on this spirit. You are hastening the time when there is to be a positive and emphatic show of hands—not of white hands against black hands, God forbid; not of Northern hands against Southern hands, heaven forfend; but a determined show of those who believe in law and God and constituted order, against those who would undermine and destroy the organic basis of society, involving all in a common ruin. No wonder Max Nordau exclaimed: "God, man, are you aware of your responsibility!"

But do not think, Mr. Dixon, that when you evoke the evil spirit, you can exorcise him at will. The Negro in the end will be the least of his victims. Those who become inoculated with the virus of race hatred are more unfortunate than the victims of it. Voltaire tells us that it is more difficult and more meritorious to wean men of their prejudices than it is to civilize the barbarian. Race hatred is the most malignant poison that can afflict the mind. It freezes up the fount of inspiration and chills the higher faculties of the soul. You are a greater enemy to your own race than you are to mine.

I have written you thus fully in order that you may clearly understand how the case lies in the Negro's mind. If any show of feeling or bitterness of spirit crops out in the treatment or between the lines, it is wholly without vindictive intent; but is the inevitable outcome of dealing with issues that verge upon the deepest human passion.

Yours truly,
KELLY MILLER.

WILLIAM PICKENS

(1881-1954)

William Pickens was born in Anderson County, South Carolina, the child of former slaves. His autobiography, The Heir of Slaves (1910), describes the deprivations of his childhood, his parents' efforts against terrible odds to educate their children, and his own dogged determination to succeed. Pickens finished Talladega College and Yale University with honors, and he earned a Master of Arts degree from Fisk University.

Equipped with the education he had struggled to achieve, Pickens embarked upon his teaching career. From 1904 to 1914 he taught languages at Talladega. After a year of teaching Greek and sociology at Wiley College, Pickens became dean of Morgan College in Baltimore. From 1920 to 1941 he was Field Secretary and Director of Branches of the NAACP. During World War II he became an official of the U. S. Treasury Department.

In addition to his 1910 autobiography, Pickens' works include two biographies, Abraham Lincoln, Man and Statesman (1909) and Frederick Douglass and the Spirit of Freedom (1912). Other works are Fifty Years of Emancipation (1913); The Ultimate Effects of Segregation and Discrimination; a volume of essays, The New Negro (1916); and a revised autobiography, Bursting Bonds (1923). His creative works include a collection of stories, The Vengeance of the Gods and Three Other Stories of Real American Color Line Life (1922), and American Aesop: The Humor of the Negro, the Jew, the Irishman and Others (1926). Pickens contributed articles on various aspects of political and sociological matters to The Crisis, The Nation, and other periodicals.

From *Bursting Bonds*

ARKANSAS TRAVELER

I was to journey back from New York to Texas. In the East I had spoken twenty times in two weeks. I was very tired. I hired a Pullman berth to St. Louis and traveled without incident. Out of deference to the color prejudice of the South I took this northerly route from New York to Texas. I also aimed to leave New York City on an early enough train to reach St. Louis next morning in time to take a daylight ride in Jim Crow from there to Little Rock, Arkansas, where I could stay overnight with my father and then take another daylight ride to Marshall. Most prejudiced white people will never know how many sincere efforts intelligent colored people make to avoid disturbing and irritating contacts, even when the colored people would be entirely within their legal and just rights. But the Republican Club of New York, before which my last address was made, kept me so late that I could only catch a train that brought me to St. Louis next afternoon. That left me one choice among three evil alternatives: to stay that night in St. Louis and the next night in Little Rock, thereby losing another twenty-four hours from school and family; or to sit up a night and a day in the unspeakable torture of the Jim Crow car; or to get a Pullman ticket for the night to Little Rock, and so run the risk of trouble with insane prejudiced people. Having been absent from family and pupils so long, I decided to risk the last named evil.

How could I get a Pullman ticket to a southern point out of St. Louis, where they try to refuse colored people such accommodations even into other parts of Missouri and toward the north? I decided to take Pullman for only the sleeping hours to Little Rock, where early next morning I would enter Jim Crow for the rest of the journey. The problem of getting the ticket was easily solved: I simply went into the colored section of St. Louis and got a white Negro friend to purchase it. For just as we have exhibited at world's fairs the phenomenon of white black-birds, so have we in the United States the verbal contradiction of white black-people, many of them being one hundred per cent black, if you please, in their consciousness. But my success in providing myself with this simple human necessity for sleep and bodily salvation brought me an experience on that train which I shall describe for the information of the incredulous.

As I entered the Pullman car, the conductor took my tickets, looked at them, and jerked them back into my hand with a nervous ostentation which clearly indicated that it was his opinion that I had no right to such accommodations. Then the colored porter took my bags, with a humorous smile playing on his features, and conducted me to my section. The porter was walking on air, seemed tickled to death, and was saying by his actions: "Well, brother, and how on earth did you manage to put it over on them?"

My ticket was secured late and I could get only an upper, so that I knew I had a section mate. I therefore boarded the train early, so as to be first in the section and avoid the appearance of being the aggressor in the scene that was probable. I have noticed that when white people of the South (and some of the North) encounter a black man on a Pullman car leaving, say, St. Louis for Chicago, they behave lawfully, even if unkindly, toward him; but when the same white people encounter a black person on Pullman leaving St. Louis for Arkansas, Cincinnati for Alabama, or Washington for Georgia, they sometimes make an unlawful and an awful scene. So I planned to "get there first" in the section, and not seem to be the active cause of this likely scene. I deposited my luggage in the section and busied myself reading a book. Later I decided to deposit my luggage on my seat, and to sit for the time being in another yet unoccupied section toward the rear, from which vantage point I could observe and see what manner of person might enter to be my section mate.

As I sat in this other section, still reading the book, a seedy-looking white man entered the front door, carrying a small worn and rusty bag. Observing him casually, I thought to myself: "Any kind of white person, of any class, character or grade of intelligence, can

buy and claim his accommodations without indirection or embarrassment." Just then I felt, rather than saw, this individual stop short
as he was proceeding down the aisle. He had spied me. It was just
as when a bull suddenly catches sight of a waving red rag. I continued to read, and was apparently unconscious of his presence. After
a few moments of unfriendly staring he went on to his berth, with a
recovered air which seemed to say: "Well, so long as you don't get
any nearer to me than that, maybe I'll behave." Then as bad luck
would have it, he proceeded straight to the section where my coat
and bags were located and deposited his satchel. He had the lower
berth.

The train had not yet started, so he went on out of the car, as
if to cool off a bit from the sudden heat which the sight of me had
aroused in him. I concluded that, while he was out, I would get back
into the section and wait on the issues of the untoward fates. Other
passengers entered, transfixed me with their unwelcoming glances,
and then took their seats,—for luckily I was not in their sections. All
this I saw, and did not see: I had never ceased to read.

The conductor shouted "All aboard!" and my section mate
re-entered. When he espied me where I was now seated, he struck a
posture which could be felt in the very air, strode like a colossus
toward me, mustering into his actions all the possible expressiveness
of resentment, seized his humble-looking bag as if it were the culprit,
and walked out to another part of the train, perhaps the smoking
room, attracting everybody's eyes, except mine: I continued to read,
as if I had seen nothing.

But there was now some tension in my waiting, for I knew well
what was going on. It was a long time before the conductor came
through (from the direction of the smoking room) to take tickets,
and I knew what that meant. As he came to other passengers, he said
"Pullman tickets, please!" But when he came to my seat, he
said nothing,—simply stopped, stood still. I reached coolly into my
left vest pocket, took out my ticket and handed it to him,—not taking
my eyes off the passage which I was reading in the book. He took
my ticket, examined it painfully, then stood and coughed and moved
his feet upon the floor,—then coughed and stirred and stood again.
All the while my hand which had handed him the ticket, was poised
in the air, elbow resting on seat arm, waiting for him to put back
into it my "passenger's check." He wanted me to *say something* or
give some sort of evidence that would enable him to size me up or get
a judgment of me, so that he would know better how to begin the

attack, which I knew he was going to make. I knew what he wanted. He did not get it. I continued to read.

After an age or so he said: "Er—er—is this yo' ticket?"

Then for the first time I turned my face from my book, and looked up at him with an honest puzzling knit upon my brow. I said not a word, but my look said: "Why, man alive! did not I just now hand you that ticket?" He heard the look, and with a little more quandary than at first he resumed: "Well—er—what I mean to say is—er—you can't ride on this ticket: the laws of Arkansas" . . .

I interrupted him with the first words from my mouth: "The laws of Arkansas have nothing to do with the matter. I bought the ticket in Missouri. I am an interstate passenger."

Then in the exasperation of despair he showed his real fangs: "What I mean is, you'll git hurt in this car, an' you better git out o' here while you can!" When I made no response, either by word or movement, he continued to a climax, raising his voice so that every person in the car turned to listen: "You are going to git shot if you stay in here,—you are going to git killed!"—Still I made no response, and still my hand reached for the passenger's portion of my ticket, whereupon he, as if he judged me either hard of hearing or difficult of understanding, reddened and thundered: "I say, you're going to git hurt,—you're going to be killed if you don't git out!'

As if I had suddenly grasped the idea that he was insisting upon some reply, I said naturally and simply: "Well, I'm sorry!" But I made no move, and my hand continued to reach for my check.

In confusion he wheeled and went back to the smoking room,—and I knew why he had gone. He had not given me my check, and I smelt treachery. But it had been advertised to the whole car that I did actually have a ticket, so I waited quietly—and read.

After a while he returned, and other men came behind him and slid into the seats across the aisle opposite me. My temper had risen and my determination was absolutely fixed, but my self-control was still good. With as little excitement as possible I snapped the fingers of my reaching hand and said: "You forgot to give me my passenger's check." And he then screamed out, again attracting the attention of the whole car: "What! are you going to risk it? These Arkansas fellers are going to shoot yo' head off! Are you going to risk it?"

To this I replied, with as little passion as possible but also loud enough to be heard by the whole car, and uttering my words slowly as if counting them: "I am going to stay right where I am,—and attend to my own business!"—He handed me my check with a jerk and strode forward out of the car with a show of passion and a flood of words, among which could be distinguished: "Shot—killed—head shot off!"

It is an awful feeling: desperation *and* determination. I would have it out at once: I called the porter and told him to make down my berth so that I could retire. As I ascended the ladder, I told him in a low voice to apprise me of any hostile movements towards me, so that I might wake up and do my duty. I was surprised and pleased to hear him reply in a loud voice, that rang of indirect defiance: "I'll do it—you bet I will!"

He had had no chance to express himself previously: he could not interfere or meddle in the conductor's business, and now at his first opportunity he showed up fearless and true. I learned later that he had kept his eye and ear on the whole situation and had resolved to sacrifice his job and any thing else to stand with me, if it came to that.—Your Pullman porter is a wonderful being. He understands. Nobody ever fools the porter. No man in all the world can "size" you quicker. He knows who you are and what you are, be you male or female. Your traveling camouflages are nothing to him. You may fool the ticket agent and the station officers, the trainmen, the conductors and your fellow-passengers, and everybody else except God and the Pullman porter.

My resignation caused me to sleep as much as usual: I had no expectation of seeing the light of day again, so I had nothing to worry about. Worry would be useless, so I slept, with the finger of my right hand coiled over the trigger of a deadly weapon.—Can they who have not had the experience, understand that? I think I would not have gone into this car if I had *known* that it would cost me my life and destroy the life of others. But being in was another thing, and being bullied out was impossible. I remembered my boyhood in Arkansas: that just twenty years before I had defied death there, when an officer had drawn a Colt's pistol to shoot me because I was fighting for respect to my sister,—and I had kept right on fighting.

One thing I felt very keenly conscious of—the lies that would be told by the newspapers next day. After I was mobbed and murdered, I would be accused in the whole civilized press of having attacked everybody in the car,—of having abused, insulted, annoyed. As a fact I had uttered less than a hundred words and had molested nobody. But I could see the headlines: "NEGRO TAKEN FROM PULLMAN CAR AND BURNED IN ARKANSAS." Then there were the details: "Negro, said to have been drunk, got on train and began to use insulting language *to the ladies.* Some of the white men tried to quiet him, when he pulled a gun and shot wildly, wounding two or three people. The conductor wired ahead and a posse met the train. The mob which had gathered at the station, overpowered the officers, and the Negro, fighting madly, was chained to a lamp post, saturated with gasoline"—etc., etc. Then all the hundred million people of the United States, except the few thousands who knew me personally, would have thought there was at least some truth in the report about my provocative behavior. "It's too bad, of course— I think Negro criminals ought to be executed by law—but then, *what could he expect?*" This would have been the reflection of the innocent.

Fortunately no attack was made on me that night. The paucity of my words and my seeming indifference to the threat of death had evidently puzzled somebody. Next morning, however, the attack was renewed from another flank. I had risen early and the porter had let me make my toilet in the drawing-room,—still trying to sidestep unreasonable prejudice. In Little Rock I was to get off or go forward into the Jim Crow car, and we were due there at about seven. The train conductor out of St. Louis had evidently not supported the Pullman conductor and the others in their attack on me, but during the night at Bald Knob a new train conductor had got aboard, a real "Arkansas feller." He had heard the awful tidings that I was in Pullman, and had inquired diligently concerning me. He had learned little, for I was an enigma. He therefore took aboard the sheriff of one of the rural counties, stationed the officer in the Jim Crow car, and then came back to the drawing-room, where he tried to irritate me and threatened me with arrest: "I've got a sheriff on this train, an' he says he'll arrest you.—Do you want to be arrested?"

In the bottom of my heart and the center of my soul I had very decided objections to enjoying any such luxury in Arkansas, but I coolly replied "That is for you and the railroad company to decide. All I wanted was *a rest* on this car last night. *The rest* is up to you." He visibly weakened a bit, and I think he mistook my words *a rest* for the word *arrest*, and began to guess that maybe I was some decoy to make a federal case against the railroad.

As we were nearing Little Rock, and not wanting to have to get off the train, so that whatever happened to me would burden the railroad with some responsibility, I called the porter to take my bags and lead me forward into the Jim Crow car. The Arkansas conductor followed us, nagging and shouting: "You had no business in hyeah!" as if trying to draw some further remark from me. In the Jim Crow car was the county sheriff, six feet tall, heavy, red, rough, booted. As I passed in without apparent concern, he addressed no word to me, but remarked defiantly over my shoulder to the conductor who was following me: "Wa-al, I'll arrest him, an' turn him over to the officers in Little Rock."

The sheriff then glared at me, evidently expecting me to answer or acknowledge this indirect statement. I gave neither word nor sign. Passing him in the aisle I took a seat and began to write letters on the back of my suitcase. The conductor and the officer took their seats in Jim Crow, discussed and puzzled over the mystery of me and the greater mystery of the race question. The conductor evidently did not feel sure that it was best to insist upon arrest. When we reached Little Rock, the giant sheriff got up, went to the car door, wheeled around and ran me through with bayonet glances. I looked at him with a "poker face," an absence of all emotion. Then he went out on the station platform, came up beside the window where I sat, and thrust at me the same hostile looks. I looked at him and the passers-by and the trunks and trucks and other scenery with the same interest. Then slowly the boots carried him up the station steps, as he shot back a single glance. My train pulled out for Texas.

Protest to the railroad or Pullman officers in such a case usually means nothing to anybody. They will not incriminate themselves. Letters get lost. If it be registered to them, one may receive a polite reply, saying: "The matter will be investigated." That is the end of the matter.

I had another odd, but pleasant, experience before I reached Texas. Suddenly and unexpectedly I encountered the man who had "pitched headin" to me nearly twenty years before, and who had tried his best to knock my head off with the green oak slabs. We had stopped at a little railway station in southern Arkansas, and I heard outside a voice in command of a gang of Negro railroad workmen who were boarding the train. Strange that, though I could not see the speaker, I recognized instantly the voice of "Dink" Jeter,— stranger still, because I had heard from the mouth of one of his relatives eleven years before, that he was dead, cut to death in a brawl, and I had never heard anything to the contrary. And yet the moment I heard him speak, out in the early night where I could see neither his face nor his figure, I did not think that it was a voice *like his*,—I knew that it was *his* voice and that he was alive.

When he came into the car, I waited, bue he did not recognize me until I made myself known. I had changed more; he was still at twenty years ago. I have never in all my life been happier at meeting a person whom I had known years before, and no such person has ever seemed happier to see me again. This fellow, who had done his uttermost to kill or maim me when I was a child, now put his arms about me, hugged me dramatically and called out to the bewildered railroad hands: "See this boy! I been knowin' him all his life,—this the bes' boy in the whole worl'." This very brutal and very human man, was extravagant in his praises. Nearly a generation before he had used all his demon cunning, endeavoring to catch me off my guard and at least injure me seriously. He asked a thousand questions, simple questions. Perhaps he admired the eternal vigilance with which I had saved myself from him. When he reached his destination, I was loth to part with him. Years ago I had never quite felt that he was a real personal enemy and had felt that he was acting out the natural resentment of the older workmen, who must have regarded me as something of a "scab" for "layin' headin'" at seventy-five cents a day, while grown men wanted a dollar.

This chance meeting with "Dink" Jeter was a test for the sentiment which I had expressed years before, when I thought he was dead: that I could never feel hatred or resentment toward the man, and that as I looked back, he seemed to be one of my appointed teachers who trained me in the art of vigilant self-defense. All summer he had attacked; all summer I had defended.—To me he had been dead for years. He reappeared like a ghost. But for the other men about, I might have regarded him as an apparition. Even now his resurrection seems like a dream.

In 1915 Morgan College, in Baltimore, Maryland, elected me as dean. The position offered many advantages over my situation in Texas, especially for the education of our children. I therefore moved to Baltimore, to the old site of Morgan College at the corner of Fulton and Edmondson Avenues. The president was the Rev. Dr. John Oakley Spencer. The teachers were white and colored. It was a new departure to have a colored man for dean.

WILLIAM STANLEY BRAITHWAITE

(1878-1962)

William Stanley Braithwaite was an astute critic and talented lyric poet whose editorial work gave impetus to the New Poetry movement in American literature. Born of West Indian ancestry in Boston, he had little formal education but taught himself through wide reading and careful observation. In addition to being a poet, Braithwaite became an editor with the Boston Transcript *and* New Poetry Review. *He edited anthologies of Restoration, Georgian, and Victorian verse. From 1913 to 1929 he edited annual anthologies of magazine verse printing the early works of many modern masters. He contributed critical essays to such publications as* Forum, Scribner's, Century Magazine, *and* The Atlantic Monthly.

His own poems are contained in Lyrics of Life and Love *(1904),* The House of Falling Leaves *(1908) and* Selected Poems *(1948). His poems, written in a traditional nineteenth-century lyric style, are slight structures seeking philosophical truth as well as beauty. They are carefully executed, subtle, and often cryptic. They have nothing to do with the life of the black man of that time. Braithwaite felt that racial themes were too limiting for the artist to deal with and that they tended more toward propaganda than toward art.*

Twenty-three years after his first novel, The Canadian *(1901), Braithwaite wrote a second,* Going Over Tindel *(1924). Other prose works are* The House Under Arcturus: An Autobiography *(1940) and* The Bewitched Parsonage, *a biography of the Brontes.*

During the thirties and forties Braithwaite taught English literature at Atlanta University, where he was a colleague of Du Bois.

Philip Butcher is engaged in a study of his career and reputation.

The Watchers

Two women on the lone wet strand,
    (The wind's out with a will to roam)
The waves wage war on rocks and sand,
    (And a ship is long due home.)

The sea sprays in the women's eyes—
    (Hearts can writhe like the sea's wild foam)
Lower descend the tempestuous skies,
    (For the wind's out with a will to roam.)

"O daughter, thine eyes be better than mine,"
    (The waves ascend high as yonder dome)
"North or south is there never a sign?"
    (And a ship is long due home.)

They watcher there all the long night through—
    (The wind's out with a will to roam)
Wind and rain and sorrow for two,—
    (And heaven on the long reach home.)

Rhapsody

I am glad daylong for the gift of song,
For time and change and sorrow;
For the sunset wings and the world-end things
Which hang on the edge of tomorrow.
I am glad for my heart whose gates apart
Are the entrance-place of wonders,
Where dreams come in from the rush and din
Like sheep from the rains and thunders.

The Negro in American Literature

True to his origin on this continent, the Negro was projected
into literature by an over-mastering and exploiting hand. In the generations that he has been so voluminously written and talked about
he has been accorded as little artistic justice as social justice. Ante-
bellum literature imposed the distortions of moralistic controversy
and made the Negro a wax-figure of the market place: post-bellum

literature retaliated with the condescending reactions of sentiment and caricature, and made the Negro a *genre* stereotype. Sustained, serious or deep study of Negro life and character has thus been entirely below the horizons of our national art. Only gradually through the dull purgatory of the Age of Discussion, has Negro life eventually issued forth to an Age of Expression.

Perhaps I ought to qualify this last statement that the Negro was *in* American literature generations before he was part of it as a creator. From his very beginning in this country the Negro has been, without the formal recognition of literature and art, creative. During more than two centuries of an enslaved peasantry, the race has been giving evidence, in song and story lore, of an artistic temperament and psychology precious for itself as well as for its potential use and promise in the sophisticated forms of cultural expression. Expressing itself with poignancy and a symbolic imagery unsurpassed, indeed, often unmatched, by any folk-group, the race in servitude was at the same time the finest national expression of emotion and imagination and the most precious mass of raw material for literature America was producing. Quoting these stanzas of James Weldon Johnson's *O Black and Unknown Bards*, I want you to catch the real point of its assertion of the Negro's way into domain of art:

> O black and unknown bards of long ago,
>   How came your lips to touch the sacred fire?
> How, in your darkness, did you come to know
>   The power and the beauty of the minstrel's lyre?
> Who first from midst his bonds lifted his eyes?
>   Who first from out the still watch, lone and long,
> Feeling the ancient faith of prophets rise
>   Within his dark-kept soul, burst into song?

How misdirected was the American imagination, how blinded by the dust of controversy and the pall of social hatred and oppression, not to have found it irresistibly urgent to make literary use of the imagination and emotion it possessed in such abundance.

Controversy and moral appeal gave us *Uncle Tom's Cabin,*— the first conspicuous example of the Negro as a subject for literary treatment. Published in 1852, it dominated in mood and attitude the American literature of a whole generation; until the body of Reconstruction literature with its quite different attitude came into vogue. Here was sentimentalized sympathy for a down-trodden race, but one in which was projected a character, in Uncle Tom himself, which has been unequalled in its hold upon the popular imagination to this day. But the moral gain and historical effect of Uncle Tom have an artistic loss and setback. The treatment of Negro life and character, overlaid with these forceful stereotypes, could not develop into artistically satisfactory portraiture.

Just as in the anti-slavery period, it had been impaled upon the dilemmas of controversy, Negro life with the Reconstruction, became involved in the paradoxes of social prejudice. Between the Civil War and the end of the century the subject of the Negro in literature is one that will some day inspire the literary historian with a magnificent theme. It will be magnificent not because there is any sharp emergence of character or incidents, but because of the immense paradox of racial life which came up thunderingly against the principles and doctrines of democracy, and put them to the severest test that they had known. But in literature, it was a period when Negro life was a shuttlecock between the two extremes of humor and pathos. The Negro was free, and was not free. The writers who dealt with him for the most part refused to see more than skin-deep, —the grin, the grimaces and the picturesque externalities. Occasionally there was some penetration into the heart and flesh of Negro characters, but to see more than the humble happy peasant would have been to flout the fixed ideas and conventions of an entire generation. For more than artistic reasons, indeed against them, these writers refused to see the tragedy of the Negro and capitalized his comedy. The social conscience had as much need for this comic mask as the Negro. However, if any of the writers of the period had possessed gifts of genius of the first caliber, they would have penetrated this deceptive exterior of Negro life, sounded the depths of tragedy in it, and produced a masterpiece.

American literature still feels the hold of this tradition and its indulgent sentimentalities. Irwin Russell was the first to discover the happy, care-free, humorous Negro. He became a fad. It must be sharply called to attention that the tradition of the ante-bellum Negro is a post-bellum product, stranger in truth than in fiction. Contemporary realism in American fiction has not only recorded his passing, but has thrown serious doubts upon his ever having been a very genuine and representative view of Negro life and character. At best this school of Reconstruction fiction represents the romanticized high-lights of a régime that as a whole was a dark, tragic canvas. At most, it presents a Negro true to type for less than two generations. Thomas Nelson Page, kindly perhaps, but with a distant view and a purely local imagination did little more than paint the conditions and attitudes of the period contemporary with his own manhood, the restitution of the over-lordship of the defeated slave owners in the Eighties. George W. Cable did little more than idealize the aristocratic tradition of the Old South with the Negro as a literary foil. The effects, though not the motives of their work, have been sinister. The "Uncle" and the "Mammy" traditions, unobjectionable as they are in the setting of their day and generation, and in the atmosphere of sentimental humor, can never stand as the great fiction of their theme and subject: the great period novel of the South has yet to be written. Moreover, these type pictures have degenerated into reactionary social fetishes, and from that descended into libelous artistic caricature of the Negro; which has hampered art quite as much as it has embarrassed the Negro.

Of all of the American writers of this period, Joel Chandler Harris has made the most permanent contribution in dealing with the Negro. There is in his work both a deepening of interest and technique. Here at least we have something approaching true portraiture. But much as we admire this lovable personality, we are forced to say that in the Uncle Remus stories the race was its own artist, lacking only in its illiteracy the power to record its speech. In the perspective of time and fair judgment the credit will be divided, and Joel Chandler Harris regarded as a sort of providentially provided amanuensis for preserving the folk tales and legends of a race. The three writers I have mentioned do not by any means exhaust the list of writers who put the Negro into literature during the last half of the nineteenth century. Mr. Howells added a shadowy note to his social record of American life with *An Imperative Duty* and prophesied the Fiction of the Color Line. But his moral scruples—the persistent artistic vice in all his novels—prevented him from consummating a just union between his heroine with a touch of Negro blood and his hero. It is useless to consider any others, because there were none who succeeded in creating either a great story or a great character out of Negro life. Two writers of importance I am reserving for discussion in the group of Negro writers I shall consider presently. One ought perhaps to say in justice to the writers I have mentioned that their non-success was more largely due to the limitations of their social view than of their technical resources. As white Americans of their day, it was incompatible with their conception of the inequalities between the races to glorify the Negro into the serious and leading position of hero or heroine in fiction. Only one man that I recall, had the moral and artistic courage to do this, and he was Stephen Crane in a short story called *The Monster*. But Stephen Crane was a genius, and therefore could not besmirch the integrity of an artist.

With Thomas Dixon, of *The Leopard's Spots*, we reach a distinct stage in the treatment of the Negro in fiction. The portraiture here descends from caricature to libel. A little later with the vogue of the "darkey-story," and its devotees from Kemble and McAllister to Octavus Roy Cohen, sentimental comedy in the portrayal of the Negro similarly degenerated to blatant but diverting farce. Before the rise of a new attitude, there represented the bottom reaction, both in artistic and social attitude. Reconstruction fiction was passing out in a flood of propagandist melodrama and ridicule. One hesitates to lift this material up to the plane of literature even for the purposes of comparison. But the gradual climb of the new literature of the Negro must be traced and measured from these two nadir points. Following *The Leopard's Spots*, it was only occasionally during the next twenty years that the Negro was sincerely treated in fiction by white authors. There were two or three tentative efforts to dramatize him. Sheldon's *The Nigger*, was the one notable early effort. And in fiction Paul Kester's *His Own Country* is, from a purely literary point of view, its outstanding performance. This type of novel failed, however, to awaken any general interest. This failure was due to the illogical treatment of the human situations presented. However indifferent and negative it may seem, there is the latent desire in most readers to have honesty of purpose and a full vision in the artist: and especially in fiction, a situation handled with gloves can never be effectively handled.

The first hint that the American artist was looking at this subject with full vision was in Torrence's *Granny Maumee*. It was drama, conceived and executed for performance on the stage, and therefore had restricted appeal. But even here the artist was concerned with the primitive instincts of the Race, and, though faithful and honest in his portrayal, the note was still low in the scale of racial life. It was only a short time, however, before a distinctly new development took place in the treatment of Negro life by white authors. This new class of work honestly strove to endow the Negro life with purely æsthetic vision and values, but with one or two exceptions, still stuck to the peasant level of race experience, and gave, unwittingly, greater cur-rency to the popular notion of the Negro as an inferior, superstitious, half-ignorant and servile class of folk. Where they did in a few isolated instances recognize an ambitious impulse, it was generally defeated in the course of the story.

Perhaps this is inevitable with an alien approach, however well-intentioned. The folk lore attitude discovers only the lowly and the naïve: the sociological attitude finds the problem first and the human beings after, if at all. But American art in a reawakened seriousness, and using the technique of the new realism, is gradually penetrating Negro life to the core. George Madden Martin, with her pretentious foreword to a group of short stories, *The Children in the Mist*—and this is an extraordinary volume in many ways—quite seriously tried, as a Southern woman, to elevate the Negro to a higher plane of fictional treatment and interest. In succession, followed Mary White Ovington's *The Shadow*, in which Miss Ovington daringly created the kinship of brother and sister between a black boy and white girl, had it brought to disaster by prejudice, out of which the white girl rose to a sacrifice no white girl in a novel had hitherto accepted and endursed; then Shands' *White and Black,* as honest a piece of fiction with the Negro as a subject as was ever produced by a Southern pen —and in this story, also, the hero, Robinson, making an equally glorious sacrifice for truth and justice as Miss Ovington's heroine; Clement Wood's *Nigger*, with defects of treatment, but admirable in purpose, wasted though, I think, in the effort to prove its thesis on wholly illogical material; and lastly, T. S. Stribling's *Birthright*, more significant than any of these other books, in fact, the most significant novel on the Negro written by a white American, and this in spite of its totally false conception of the character of Peter Siner.

Mr. Stribling's book broke ground for a white author in giving us a Negro hero and heroine. There is an obvious attempt to see objectively. But the formula of the Nineties,—atavistic race-heredity, still survives and protrudes through the flesh and blood of the characters. Using Peter as a symbol of the man tragically linked by blood to one world and by training and thought to another, Stribling portrays a tragic struggle against the pull of lowly origins and sordid environment. We do not deny this element of tragedy in Negro life,—and Mr. Stribling, it must also be remembered, presents, too, a severe indictment in his painting of the Southern conditions which brought about the disintegration of his hero's dreams and ideals. But the preoccupation, almost obsession of otherwise strong and artistic work like O'Neill's *Emperor Jones, All God's Chillun Got Wings,* and Culbertson's *Goat Alley* with this same theme and doubtful formula of hereditary cultural reversion suggests that, in spite of all good intentions, the true presental of the real tragedy of Negro life is a task still left for Negro writers to perform. This is especially true for those phases of culturally representative race life that as yet have scarcely at all found treatment by white American authors. In corroborating this, let me quote a passage from a recent number of the *Independent*, on the Negro novelist which reads:

> "During the past few years stories about Negroes have been extremely popular. A magazine without a Negro story is hardly living up to its opportunities. But almost every one of these stories is written in a tone of condescension. The artists have caught the contagion from the writers, and the illustrations are ninety-nine times out of a hundred purely slapstick stuff. Stories and pictures make a Roman holiday for the millions who are convinced that the most important fact about the Negro is that his skin is black. Many of these writers live in the South or are from the South. Presumably they are well acquainted with the Negro, but it is a remarkable fact that they almost never tell us anything vital about him, about the real human being in the black man's skin. Their most frequent method is to laugh at the colored man and woman, to catalogue their idiosyncrasies, their departure from the norm, that is, from the ways of the whites. There seems to be no suspicion in the minds of the writers that there may be a fascinating thought life in the minds of the Negroes, whether of the cultivated or of the most ignorant type. Always the Negro is interpreted in the terms of the white man. White-man psychology is applied and it is no wonder that the result often shows the Negro in a ludicrous light."

I shall have to run back over the years to where I began to survey the achievement of Negro authorship. The Negro as a creator in American literature is of comparatively recent importance. All that was accomplished between Phyllis Wheatley and Paul Laurence Dunbar, considered by critical standards, is negligible, and of historical interest only. Historically it is a great tribute to the race to have produced in Phyllis Wheatley not only the slave poetess in eighteenth century colonial America, but to know she was as good, if not a better, poetess than Ann Bradstreet whom literary historians give the honor of being the first person of her sex to win face as a poet in America.

Negro authorship may, for clearer statement, be classified into three main activities: Poetry, Fiction, and the Essay, with an occasional excursion into other branches. In the drama, until very recently, practically nothing worth while has been achieved, with the exception of Angelina Grimke's *Rachel,* notable for its sombre craftsmanship. Biography has given us a notable life story, told by himself, Booker T. Washington. Frederick Douglass's story of his life is eloquent as a human document, but not in the graces of narration and psychologic portraiture, which has definitely put this form of literature in the domain of the fine arts. Indeed, we may well believe that the efforts of controversy, of the huge amount of discursive and polemical articles dealing chiefly with the race problem, that have been necessary in breaking and clearing the impeded pathway of racial progress, have absorbed and in a way dissipated the literary energy of many able Negro writers.

Let us survey briefly the advance of the Negro in poetry. Behind Dunbar, there is nothing that can stand the critical test. We shall always have a sentimental and historical interest in those forlorn and pathetic figures who cried in the wilderness of their ignorance and oppression. With Dunbar we have our first authentic lyric utterance, an utterance more authentic, I should say, for its faithful rendition of Negro life and character than for any rare or subtle artistry of expression. When Mr. Howells, in his famous introduction to the *Lyrics of Lowly Life,* remarked that Dunbar was the first black man to express the life of his people lyrically, he summed up Dunbar's achievement and transported him to a place beside the peasant poet of Scotland, not for his art, but precisely because he made a people articulate in verse.

The two chief qualities in Dunbar's work are, however, pathos and humor, and in these he expresses that dilemma of soul that characterized the race between the Civil War and the end of the nineteenth century. The poetry of Dunbar is true to the life of the Negro and expresses characteristically what he felt and knew to be the temper and condition of his people. But its moods reflect chiefly those of the era of Reconstruction and just a little beyond,—the limited experience of a transitional period, the rather helpless and subservient era of testing freedom and reaching out through the difficulties of life to the emotional compensations of laughter and tears. It is the poetry of the happy peasant and the plaintive minstrel. Occasionally, as in the sonnet to *Robert Gould Shaw* and the *Ode to Ethiopia* there broke through Dunbar, as through the crevices of his spirit, a burning and brooding aspiration, an awakening and virile consciousness of race. But for the most part, his dreams were anchored to the minor whimsies; his deepest poetic inspiration was sentiment. He expressed a folk temperament, but not a race soul. Dunbar was the end of a régime, and not the beginning of a tradition, as so many careless critics, both white and colored, seem to think.

After Dunbar many versifiers appeared,—all largely dominated by his successful dialect work. I cannot parade them here for tag or comment, except to say that few have equalled Dunbar in this vein of expression, and none have deepened it as an expression of Negro life. Dunbar himself had clear notions of its limitations;—to a friend in a letter from London, March 15, 1897, he says: "I see now very clearly that Mr. Howells has done me irrevocable harm in the dictum he laid down regarding my dialect verse." Not until James W. Johnson published his *Fiftieth Anniversary Ode* on the emancipation in 1913, did a poet of the race disengage himself from the background of mediocrity into which the imitation of Dunbar snared Negro poetry. Mr. Johnson's work is based upon a broader contemplation of life, life that is not wholly confined within any racial experience, but through the racial he made articulate that universality of the emotions felt by all mankind. His verse possesses a vigor which definitely breaks away from the brooding minor undercurrents of feeling which have previously characterized the verse of Negro poets. Mr. Johnson brought, indeed, the first intellectual substance to the content of our poetry, and a craftsmanship which, less spontaneous than that of Dunbar's, was more balanced and precise.

Here a new literary generation begins; poetry that is racial in substance, but with the universal note, with the conscious background of the full heritage of English poetry. With each new figure somehow the gamut broadens and the technical control improves. The brilliant succession and maturing powers of Fenton Johnson, Leslie Pinckney Hill, Everett Hawkins, Lucien Watkins, Charles Bertram Johnson, Joseph Cotter, Georgia Douglas Johnson, Roscoe Jameson and Anne Spencer bring us at last to Claude McKay and the poets of the younger generation and a poetry of the masterful accent and high distinction. Too significantly for mere coincidence, it was the stirring year of 1917 that heard the first real masterful accent in Negro poetry.

In the September *Crisis* of that year, Roscoe Jameson's *Negro Soldiers* appeared:

> These truly are the Brave,
> These men who cast aside
> Old memories to walk the blood-stained pave
> Of Sacrifice, joining the solemn tide
> That moves away, to suffer and to die
> For Freedom—when their own is yet denied!
> O Pride! A Prejudice! When they pass by
> Hail them, the Brave, for you now crucified.

The very next month, under the pen name of Eli Edwards, Claude McKay printed in *The Seven Arts*, "The Harlem Dancer."

With Georgia Johnson, Anne Spencer and Angelina Grimke, the Negro woman poet significantly appears. Mrs. Johnson especially has voiced in true poetic spirit the lyric cry of Negro womanhood. In spite of lapses into the sentimental and the platitudinous, she has an authentic gift. Anne Spencer, more sophisticated, more cryptic but also more universal, reveals quite another aspect of poetic genius. Indeed, it is interesting to notice how to-day Negro poets waver between the racial and the universal notes.

Claude McKay, the poet who leads his generation, is a genius meshed in this dilemma. His work is caught between the currents of the poetry of protest and the poetry of expression; he is in turn the violent and strident propagandist, using his poetic gifts to clothe arrogant and defiant thoughts, and then the pure lyric dreamer, contemplating life and nature with a wistful sympathetic passion. When the mood of *Spring in New Hampshire* or the sonnet *The Harlem Dancer* possesses him, he is full of that spirit and power of beauty that flowers above any and all men's harming. How different in spite of the admirable spirit of courage and defiance, are his poems of which the sonnet *If We Must Die* is a typical example. Negro poetic expression hovers for the moment, pardonably perhaps, over the race problem, but its highest allegiance is to Poetry—it must soar.

Let me refer briefly to a type of literature in which there have been many pens, but a single mind. Dr. Du Bois is the most variously gifted writer which the race has produced. Poet, novelist, sociologist, historian and essayist, he has produced books in all these fields with the exception, I believe, of a formal book of poems, and has given to each the distinction of his clear and exact thinking, and of his sensitive imagination and passionate vision. *The Souls of Black Folk* was the book of an era; it was a painful book, a book of tortured dreams woven into the fabric of the sociologist's document. This book has more profoundly influenced the spiritual temper of the race than any other written in its generation. It is only through the intense, passionate idealism of such substance as makes *The Souls of Black Folk* such a quivering rhapsody of wrongs endured and hopes to be fulfilled that the poets of the race with compelling artistry can lift the Negro into the only full and complete nationalism he knows—that of the American democracy. No other book has more clearly revealed to the nation at large the true idealism and high aspiration of the American Negro.

In this book, as well as in many of Dr. Du Bois's essays, it is often my personal feeling that I am witnessing the birth of a poet, phoenix-like, out of a scholar. Between *The Souls of Black Folk* and *Darkwater*, published four years ago, Dr. Du Bois has written a number of books, none more notable, in my opinion, than his novel *The Quest of the Silver Fleece*, in which he made Cotton the great protagonist of fate in the lives of the Southern people, both white and black. I only know of one other such attempt and accomplishment in American fiction—that of Frank Norris—and I am somehow of the opinion that when the great epic novel of the South is written this book will prove to have been its forerunner. Indeed, the Negro novel is one of the great potentialities of American literature. Must it be written by a Negro? To recur to the article from which I have already quoted:

"The white writer seems to stand baffled before the enigma and so he expends all his energies on dialect and in general on the Negro's minstrel characteristics. . . . We shall have to look to the Negro himself to go all the way. It is quite likely that no white man can do it. It is reasonable to suppose that his white psychology will always be in his way. I am not thinking at all about a Negro novelist who shall arouse the world to the horror of the deliberate killings by white mobs, to the wrongs that condemn a free people to political serfdom. I am not thinking at all of the propaganda novel, although there is enough horror and enough drama in the bald statistics of each one of the annual Moton letters to keep the whole army of writers busy. But the Negro novelist, if he ever comes, must reveal to us much more than what a Negro thinks about when he is being tied to a stake and the torch is being applied to his living flesh; much more than what he feels when he is being crowded off the sidewalk by a drunken rowdy who may be his intellectual inferior by a thousand leagues. Such a writer, to succeed in a big sense, would have to forget that there are white readers; he would have to lose self-consciousness and forget that his work would be placed before a white jury. He would have to be careless as to what the white critic might think of it; he would need the self-assurance to be his own critic. He would have to forget for the time being, at least, that any white man ever attempted to dissect the soul of a Negro."

What I here quote is both an inquiry and a challenge! Well informed as the writer is, he does not seem to detect the forces which are surely gathering to produce what he longs for.

The development of fiction among Negro authors has been, I might almost say, one of the repressed activities of our literary life. A fair start was made the last decade of the nineteenth century when Chestnutt and Dunbar were turning out both short stories and novels. In Dunbar's case, had he lived, I think his literary growth would have been in the evolution of the Race novel as indicated in *The Uncalled* and the *Sport of the Gods*. The former was, I think, the most ambitious literary effort of Dunbar; the latter was his most significant; significant because, thrown against the background of New York City, it displayed the life of the race as a unit, swayed by currents of existence, of which it was and was not a part. The story was touched with that shadow of destiny which gave to it a purpose more important than the mere racial machinery of its plot. But Dunbar in his fiction dealt only successfully with the same world that gave him the inspiration for his dialect poems; though his ambition was to "write a novel that will deal with the educated class of my own people." Later he writes of *The Fanatics:* "You do not know how my hopes were planted in that book, but it has utterly disappointed me." His contemporary, Charles W. Chestnutt, was concerned more primarily with the fiction of the Color Line and the contacts and conflicts of its two worlds. He was in a way more successful. In the five volumes to his credit, he has revealed himself as a fiction writer of a very high order. But after all Mr. Chestnutt is a story-teller of genius transformed by racial earnestness into the novelist of talent. His natural gift would have found freer vent in a flow of short stories like Bret Harte's, to judge from the facility and power of his two volumes of short stories, *The Wife of His Youth and Other Stories* and *The Conjure Woman*. But Mr. Chestnutt's serious effort was in the field of the novel, where he made a brave and partially successful effort to correct the distortions of Reconstruction fiction and offset the school of Page and Cable. Two of these novels, *The Marrow of Tradition* and *The House Behind the Cedars*, must be reckoned among the representative period novels of their time. But the situation was not ripe for the great Negro novelist. The American public preferred spurious values to the genuine; the coinage of the Confederacy was at literary par. Where Dunbar, the sentimentalist, was welcome, Chestnutt, the realist, was barred. In 1905 Mr. Chestnutt wrote *The Colonel's Dream*, and thereafter silence fell upon him.

From this date until the past year, with the exception of *The Quest of the Silver Fleece*, which was published in 1911, there has been no fiction of importance by Negro authors. But then suddenly there comes a series of books, which seems to promise at least a new phase of race fiction, and possibly the era of the major novelists. Mr. Walter White's novel *The Fire in the Flint* is a swift moving straightforward story of the contemporary conflicts of black manhood in the South. Coming from the experienced observation of the author, himself an investigator of many lynchings and riots, it is a social document story of first-hand significance and importance; too vital to be labelled and dismissed as propaganda, yet for the same reason too unvarnished and realistic a story to be great art. Nearer to the requirements of art comes Miss Jessie Fauset's novel *There is Confusion*. Its distinction is to have created an entirely new milieu in the treatment of the race in fiction. She has taken a class within the race of established social standing, tradition and culture, and given in the rather complex family story of *The Marshalls* a social document of unique and refreshing value. In such a story, race fiction, detaching itself from the limitations of propaganda on the one hand and genre fiction on the other, emerges from the color line and is incorporated into the body of general and universal art.

Finally in Jean Toomer, the author of *Cane*, we come upon the very first artist of the race, who with all an artist's passion and sympathy for life, its hurts, its sympathies, its desires, its joys, its defeats and strange yearnings, can write about the Negro without the surrender or compromise of the artist's vision. So objective is it, that we feel that it is a mere accident that birth or association has thrown him into contact with the life he has written about. He would write just as well, just as poignantly, just as transmutingly, about the peasants of Russia, or the peasants of Ireland, had experience brought him in touch with their existence. *Cane* is a book of gold and bronze, of dusk and flame, of ecstasy and pain, and Jean Toomer is a bright morning star of a new day of the race of literature.

(1924)

FENTON JOHNSON
(1888-1958)

Fenton Johnson is included in the annals of black American poetry not only because of his poems themselves, but also because his works anticipated the Harlem Renaissance.

Born and reared in Chicago, Johnson began writing at the age of nine. Later he attended the University of Chicago. He taught school for a year, but then decided that the academic life was not for him and subsequently became a magazine editor and publisher.

In 1912 Johnson collected his poems in a volume, A Little Dreaming. *The poems are conventional; some are in dialect. The most impressive poem is a 300-line blank verse work, "The Vision of Lazarus." The rest are undistinguished.*

Shortly after, Johnson's works underwent a change. Casting aside the conventional mold, he turned to a free form of poetry in which the irregular and unrhymed lines and the rhythms were determined by the theme. In this use of free form, solid imagery, and actual speech rather than romantic bombast, Johnson was related to the New Poetry Movement. His poetry deals with real-life situations, which it conveys in simple, concrete language. In halting rhythms and jagged lines he portrays the chaotic world of the black man, caught in the illogic of racism. He hits existential depths more characteristic of later generations than of his own.

The poems in the later manner are collected in Visions of the Dusk *(1915) and* Songs of the Soil *(1916).*

The Scarlet Woman

Once I was good like the Virgin Mary and the Minister's wife.
My father worked for Mr. Pullman and white people's tips; but he
    died two days after his insurance expired.
I had nothing, so I had to go to work.
All the stock I had was a white girl's education and a face that
    enchanted the men of both races.
Starvation danced with me.
So when Big Lizzie, who kept a house for white men, came to me
    with tales of fortune that I could reap from the sale of my
    virtue I bowed my head to Vice.
Now I can drink more gin than any man for miles around.
Gin is better than all the water in Lethe.

Aunt Jane Allen

State Street is lonely today. Aunt Jane Allen has driven her chariot
to Heaven.

I remember how she hobbled along, a little woman, parched of skin,
brown as the leather of a satchel and with eyes that had scanned
eighty years of life.

Have those who bore her dust to the last resting place buried with
her the basket of aprons she went up and down State Street
trying to sell?

Have those who bore her dust to the last resting place buried with
her the gentle word *Son* that she gave to each of the seed of
Ethiopia?

The Old Repair Man

God is the Old Repair Man.
When we are junk in Nature's storehouse he takes us apart.
What is good he lays aside; he might use it some day.
What has decayed he buries in six feet of sod to nurture the weeds.
Those we leave behind moisten the sod with their tears;
But their eyes are blind as to where he has placed the good.
Some day the Old Repair Man
Will take the good from its secret place
And with his gentle, strong hands will mold
A more enduring work—a work that will defy Nature—
And we will laugh at the old days, the troubled days,
When we were but a crude piece of craftsmanship,
When we were but an experiment in Nature's laboratory. . . .
It is good we have the Old Repair Man.

FOLKLORE
TALE, SONG AND SERMON

The demise of chattel slavery opened another chapter in the black saga of toil and trouble in America. The masses poured forth their experiences in songs which are a valuable source for historians seeking to fathom the truth of blackness. The years following the Civil War saw the development of three types of songs, rooted in slavery but gathering deeper significance in the early chaotic years of "freedom": worksongs, blues and ballads.

Like the spirituals and slave seculars, these songs are a synthesis of African and Euro-American culture, amid the oppression which pervades the life of the black American. The result is a strong body of folk songs, economical in language, warmly emotional, often bitter and ironic, and laced with satiric humor.

The worksongs are direct descendents of the songs which the West African farmers sang as they worked their fields. For the African and for his cultural heirs, songs were a necessary tool, a complement to labor. In Afro-American worksongs, as in West African, the rhythm of the work often sets the rhythm for the song: the swing of the hammer, the hoist of the shovel.

Another African trait in the worksongs is the leader-and-response pattern—the same pattern seen in many spirituals and in the "Amen, Brother!" and "Tell it, Lord!" responses of black congregations. On work gangs the song leader had a vital function in keeping the work going. He would establish a pattern, which would be picked up by the crew and then repeated throughout the song; meanwhile, the work would be getting done. For example, the leader would sing a solo line, each time followed by a set response from the group:

> Leader: *Hyah come de cap'm*
> Group: *Stan' right steddy*
> Leader: *Walkin' lak Samson*
> Group: *Stan' right steddy*
> Leader: *-A big Goliath*
> Group: *Stan' right steddy*
> Leader: *He totin' his talker*
> Group: *Stan' right steddy*

Or, the leader would sing a line, and the group would repeat it throughout the song. Or, the leader and group would sing in unison. There are many patterns, all well known to the workers.

    The subject matter of the worksongs reflects, of course, the harsh life of the worker. Many workers led virtually nomadic lives; they wandered from town to town seeking employment or—since a black man would often be arrested for the most trifling offenses—evading the police. Worksongs reflected their loneliness, their alienation, their longing for home. Other themes were love, religion, weariness, exploits of other workers, and the effects of unceasing poverty and toil. Prison songs comprise a large segment of the worksongs. Men on chain gangs or prison farms could express in songs their hopelessness, their sense of injustice, their worry over loved ones—especially women—on the outside. Often they sang of other prisoners who had escaped. Worksongs, including prison songs, usually have an aspect of social protest.

    The blues are closely related to worksongs in themes, but differ somewhat in treatment and form. Whereas the worksongs involve the feelings of the group, the blues express intensely individual personal feelings. Also, the worksongs are somewhat more varied in mood; the blues almost always express personal misery.

    This, in fact, is what the blues are all about: capturing misery in song and therefore making it bearable. Subjects for the blues are simply those things that would make one blue: love problems, prison, natural disasters, hard times, homesickness and loneliness.

    Blues lyric form is the next step in development after the one-line or two-line repetition of the hollers and the responsive patterns of the worksongs. With variations, the blues stanza basically consists of three lines: The first states the problem or situation; the second repeats the first, often with variation; the third is the punch line which completes the first two. Thus:

*I'm leavin' in the morning, Mama, and I don't know
    where to go.
I'm leavin' in the morning, Mama, and I don't know
    where to go.
Cause the woman I been livin' with for twenty years,
Mama, says she don't want me no more.*

The blues have been popularized and commercialized and synthesized, but the sensitive listener can separate the slick commercial blues package from the genuine passion sung by such greats as Blind Lemon Jefferson, Ma Rainey, Bessie Smith, Josh White, and Huddie Ledbetter (Leadbelly). Worksongs and ballads exist in other cultures; only black people have the blues.

Ballads, like worksongs and the blues, show African traces. The African love of music and penchant for storytelling combine in the wealth of ballads created by black Americans. Many ballads bear the imprint of Euro-American culture. Black variations on white folk ballads exist in "Casey Jones," "Frankie and Johnny," "Barb'ry Allen," and others. Here and there, lines appear in black ballads that have been sung in the story-songs of white America and Europe. But by and large, the ballads of black people are distinctly their own creation. The vast majority of the ballads are black-originated, and all reflect the realities of folk life. They sing the exploits of heroes like John Henry, steel-driving man, or villains like Stagolee, who killed a man over a Stetson hat. Prison, love, and hard times are themes of ballads as is the case in other types of folk expressions. Unlike worksongs and blues, the ballad tells a story chronologically and fairly completely. Also, the ballad lacks the intense personal feeling of the blues, since the song is about somebody else, not the singer.

While not precisely a musical type, the black folk sermon is very close to the song types. Moreover, its recitative mode of presentation and its frequent incorporation of song distinguishes it sharply from the declamatory Euro-American sermon. The black folk sermon has its standard themes and typical rhetorical devices. A study of the folk sermon must draw upon the theory of oral composition developed in recent years to account for epic poetry. The black folk preacher was every inch an artist appealing to a critical but generous audience. His progenitor is the African story teller, sure of his technique and of the responses of his audience.

Folklore is important in a study of black literature for several reasons. In the 1920s black writers began to find in folklore themes, language, and rhythms which they incorporated into carefully wrought works. More important, these works are often infused with the spirit of black experience missing in the dialect poems of the Dunbar school. Sterling Brown wrote particularly effective poems in the style of worksongs and ballads; his Slim Greer has the "feel" of a ballad hero. Langston Hughes adapted the form and content of blues for many poems. James Weldon Johnson turned to the folk sermon for the artistic re-creations of God's Trombones.

Folklore is vital in measuring the accuracy of a writer's image of black experience. The weakness of Dunbar's dialect characters, their lives, and their language is evident when one compares their speech to the actual utterances of the folk. This lore refutes the image of the black man shaped and defeated by an oppressive system, for it is expressive of hardships, and certainly of suffering and injustice—but not of defeat.

T'appin

TOLD BY CUGO LEWIS, PLATEAU, ALABAMA.

BROUGHT TO AMERICA FROM WEST COAST AFRICA, 1859.

It was famine time an' T'appin had six chillun. Eagle hide behin'
cloud an' he went crossed de ocean an' go gittin' de palm oil; got
de seed to feed his chillun wid it. T'appin see it, say "hol' on, it har'
time. Where you git all dat to feed your t'ree chillun? I got six
chillun, can't you show me wha' you git all dat food?" Eagle say,
"No, I had to fly 'cross de ocean to git dat." T'appin say, "Well,
gimme some o' you wings an' I'll go wid you." Eagle say, "A' right.
When shall we go?" T'appin say, "'Morrow mornin' by de firs'
cock crow." So 'morrow came but T'appin didn' wait till mornin'.
T'ree 'clock in de mornin' T'appin come in fron' Eagle's house say,
"Cuckee—cuckoo—coo." Eagle say, "Oh, you go home. Lay down.
'Tain't day yit." But he kep' on, "Cuckoo, cuckoo, coo," an' bless de
Lor', Eagle got out, say, "What' you do now?" T'appin say, "You
put t'ree wings on this side an' t'ree on udda side." Eagle pull out six
feathers an' put t'ree on one side an' t'ree on de udda. Say, "Fly, le's
see." So T'appin commence to fly. One o' de wings fall out. But
T'appin said, "Da's all right, I got de udda wings. Le's go." So dey
flew an' flew; but when dey got over de ocean all de eagle wings
fell out. T'appin about to fall in de water. Eagle went out an' ketch
him. Put him under his wings. T'appin say, "I don' like dis." Eagle
say, "Why so?" T'appin say, "Gee it stink here." Eagle let him drop
in ocean. So he went down, down, down to de underworl'. De king
o' de underworl' meet him. He say, "Why you come here? Wha'
you doin' here?" T'appin say, "King, we in te'bul condition on de

earth. We can't git nothin' to eat. I got six chillun an' I can't git nothin' to eat for dem. Eagle he on'y got t'ree an' he go 'cross de ocean an' git all de food he need. Please gimme sumpin' so I kin feed my chillun." King say, "A' right, a' right," so he go an' give T'appin a dipper. He say to T'appin, "Take dis dipper. When you want food for your chillun say:

> Bakon coleh
> Bakon cawbey
> Bakon cawhubo lebe lebe.

So T'appin carry it home an' go to de chillun. He say to dem, "Come here." When dey all come he say:

> Bakon coleh
> Bakon cawbey
> Bakon cawhubo lebe lebe.

Gravy, meat, biscuit, ever'ting in de dipper. Chillun got plenty now. So one time he say to de chillun, "Come here. Dis will make my fortune. I'll sell dis to de King." So he showed de dipper to de King. He say:

> Bakon coleh
> Bakon cawbey
> Bakon cawhubo lebe lebe.

Dey got somet'ing. He feed ev'ryone. So de King went off, he call ev'ryboda. Pretty son ev'ryboda eatin'. So dey ate an' ate, ev'ryt'ing, meats, fruits, and all like dat. So he took his dipper an' went back home. He say, "Come, chillun." He try to feed his chillun; nothin' came. (You got a pencil dere, ain't you?) When it's out it's out. So T'appin say, "Aw right, I'm going back to de King an' git him to fixa dis up." So he went down to de underworl' an' say to de King, "King, wha' de matter? I can't feeda my chillun no mora." So de King say to him, "You take dis cow hide an' when you want somepin' you say:

> Sheet n oun
> n-jacko
> nou o quaako.

So T'appin went offi an' he came to cross roads. Den he said de magic:

> Sheet n oun
> n-jacko
> nou o quaako.

De cowhide commence to beat um. It beat, beat. Cowhide said, "Drop, drop." So T'appin drop an' de cowhide stop beatin'. So he went home. He called his chillun in. He gim um de cowhide an' tell dem what to say, den he went out. De chillun say:

> Sheet n oun
> n-jacko
> nou o quaako.

De cowhide beat de chillun. It say, "Drop, drop." Two chillun dead an' de others sick. So T'appin say, "I will go to de King." He calls de King, he call all de people. All de people came. So before he have de cowhide beat, he has a mortar made an' gets in der an' gets all covered up. Den de King say:

> Sheet n oun
> n-jacko
> nou o quaako.

So de cowhide beat, beat. It beat everyboda, beat de King too. Dat cowhide beat, beat, beat right t'roo de mortar wha' was T'appin an' beat marks on his back, an' da's why you never fin' T'appin in a clean place, on'y under leaves or a log.

(Collected by Arthur Huff Fauset, 1925)

John Henry

When John Henry was a little fellow,
    You could hold him in the palm of your hand,
He said to his pa, "When I grow up
      I'm gonna be a steel-driving man.
        Gonna be a steel-driving man."

When John Henry was a little baby,
    Setting on his mammy's knee,
He said "The Big Bend Tunnel on the C. & O. Road
    Is gonna be the death of me,
      Gonna be the death of me."

One day his captain told him,
    How he had bet a man
That John Henry would beat his steam-drill down,
    Cause John Henry was the best in the land,
      John Henry was the best in the land.

John Henry kissed his hammer,
   White man turned on steam,
Shaker held John Henry's trusty steel,
    Was the biggest race the world had ever seen,
      Lord, biggest race the world ever seen.

John Henry on the right side
   The steam drill on the left,
"Before I'll let your steam drill beat me down,
    I'll hammer my fool self to death,
      Hammer my fool self to death."

John Henry walked in the tunnel,
   His captain by his side,
The mountain so tall, John Henry so small,
    He laid down his hammer and he cried,
      Laid down his hammer and he cried.

Captain heard a mighty rumbling,
   Said "The mountain must be caving in,
John Henry said to the captain,
    "It's my hammer swinging in de wind,
      My hammer swinging in de wind."

John Henry said to his shaker,
   "Shaker, you'd better pray;
For if ever I miss this piece of steel,
    Tomorrow'll be your burial day,
      Tomorrow'll be your burial day."

John Henry said to his shaker,
   "Lordy, shake it while I sing,
I'm pulling my hammer from my shoulders down,
    Great Gawdamighty, how she ring,
      Great Gawdamighty, how she ring!"

John Henry said to his captain,
   "Before I ever leave town,
Gimme one mo' drink of dat tom-cat gin,
    And I'll hammer dat steam driver down,
      I'll hammer dat steam driver down."

John Henry said to his captain,
    "Before I ever leave town,
Gimme a twelve-pound hammer wid a whale-bone handle,
    And I'll hammer dat steam driver down,
        I'll hammer dat steam drill on down."

John Henry said to his captain,
    "A man ain't nothin' but a man,
But before I'l let dat steam drill beat me down,
    I'll die wid my hammer in my hand,
        Die wid my hammer in my hand."

The man that invented the steam drill
    He thought he was mighty fine,
John Henry drove down fourteen feet,
    While the steam drill only made nine,
        Steam drill only made nine.

"Oh, lookaway over yonder, captain,
    You can't see like me,"
He gave a long and loud and lonesome cry,
    "Lawd, a hammer be the death of me,
        A hammer be the death of me!"

John Henry had a little woman,
    Her name was Polly Ann,
John Henry took sick, she took his hammer,
    She hammered like a natural man,
        Lawd, she hammered like a natural man.

John Henry hammering on the mountain
    As the whistle blew for half-past two,
The last words his captain heard him say,
    "I've done hammered my insides in two,
        Lawd, I've hammered my insides in two."

The hammer that John Henry swung
    It weighed over twelve pound,
He broke a rib in his left hand side
    And his intrels fell on the ground,
        And his intrels fell on the ground.

John Henry, O, John Henry,
　His blood is running red,
Fell right down with his hammer to the ground,
　Said, "I beat him to the bottom but I'm dead,
　Lawd, beat him to the bottom but I'm dead."

When John Henry was laying there dying,
　The people all by his side,
The very last words they heard him say,
　"Give me a cool drink of water 'fore I die,
　Cool drink of water 'fore I die."

John Henry had a little woman,
　The dress she wore was red,
She went down the track, and she never looked back,
　Going where her man fell dead,
　Going where her man fell dead.

John Henry had a little woman,
　The dress she wore was blue,
De very last words she said to him,
　"John Henry, I'll be true to you,
　John Henry, I'll be true to you."

"Who's gonna shoes yo' little feet,
　Who's gonna glove yo' hand,
Who's gonna kiss yo' pretty, pretty cheek,
　Now you done lost yo' man?
　Now you done lost yo' man?"

"My mammy's gonna shoes my little feet,
　Pappy gonna glove my hand,
My sister's gonna kiss my pretty, pretty cheek,
　Now I done lost my man,
　Now I done lost my man."

They carried him down by the river,
　And buried him in the sand,
And everybody that passed that way,
　Said, "There lies that steel-driving man,
　There lies a steel-driving man."

They took John Henry to the river,
    And buried him in the sand,
And every locomotive come a-roaring by,
    Says "There lies that steel-drivin' man,
        Lawd, there lies a *steel*-drivin' man."

Some say he came from Georgia,
    And some from Alabam,
But its wrote on the rock at the Big Bend Tunnel,
    That he was an East Virginia man,
        Lord, Lord, an East Virginia man.

Bad Man Ballad

Late las' night I was a-makin' my rounds,
Met my woman an' I blowed her down,
Went on home an' I went to bed,
Put my hand cannon right under my head.

Early nex' mornin' 'bout de risin' o' de sun,
I gets up-a for to make-a my run.
I made a good run but I made it too slow,
Got overtaken in Mexico.

Standin' on de corno', readin' of a bill,
Up step a man name o' Bad Texas Bill;
"Look here, bully, ain' yo' name Lee Brown?
B'lieve you are de rascal shot yo' woman down."

"Yes, oh, yes," says. "This is him.
If you got a warrant, jes' read it to me."
He says; "You look like a fellow that knows what's bes'.
Come 'long wid me—you're under arres'."

When I was arrested, I was dressed in black;
Dey put me on a train, an' dey brought me back.
Dey boun' me down in de county jail;
Couldn' get a human for to go my bail.

Early nex' mornin' 'bout half pas' nine,
I spied ol' jedge drappin' down de line.
I heered ol' jailer when he cleared his th'oat,
"Nigger, git ready for de deestreec' cote."

Deestreec' cote is now begin,
Twelve big jurymen, twelve hones' men.
Five mo' minutes up step a man,
He was holdin' my verdic' in his right han.'

Verdic' read murder in de firs' degree.
I said, "O Lawd, have mercy on me."
I seed ol' jedge when he picked up his pen,
Say, "I don' think you'll ever kill a woman ag'in.

"This here killin' of women natchly got to stop,
I don't know whether to hang you er not.
Ninety-nine years on de hard, hard groun',
'Member de night you blowed de woman down."

Here I is, bowed down in shame,
I got a number instead of a name.
Here for de res' of my nachul life,
An' all I ever done is kill my wife. . . .

The Remnant
A Sermon

Brothers and sisters, being a duty-bound servant of God, I stand before you to-night. I am a little hoarse from a cold. But if you will bear with me a little while we will try to bring you a message of "Thus sayeth the Lord." If God is willing we will preach. The hell-hounds are so swift on our trail that we have to go sometime whether we feel like it or not. So we are here to-night to hear what the spirit has to say.

It always make my heart glad when I run back in my mind and see what a powerful God this is we serve. And every child . . . Pray with me a little while children—that has been borned of the spirit, I mean born until he can feel it, ought to feel proud that he is serving a captain who has never lost a battle, a God that can speak and man live, but utter his voice and man lay down and die. A God that controls play across the heaven. Oh, ain't He a powerful God? He stepped out on the scope of time one morning and declared 'I am God and there's none like me. I'm God and there is none before me. In my own appointed time I will visit the iniquities of the earth. I will cut down on the right and on the left. But a remnant I will save.' Ain't you glad, then, children that he always spares a remnant? Brothers (pray with me a little while), we must gird up our loins. We who are born of the spirit should cling close to the Master, for he has promised to be a shelter in the time of storm; a rock in a weary land. Listen at Him when He says 'behold I lay in Zion, a stone, a tried stone.' . . . What need have we to worry about earthly things. They are temporal and will fade away. But we, the born of God have laid hold on everlasting life. Every child that has had his soul delivered from death and hell (Pray with me brothers) stayed at hell's dark door until he got his orders is a traveler. His home is not in this world. He is but a sojourner in a weary land. Brothers! this being true we ought to love one another; we ought to be careful how we entertain strangers. If your neighbor mistreat you, do good for evil, for a-way by and by our God that sees all we do and hears all we say will come and woe be unto him that has offended one of these His "Little Ones." I know the way gets awful dark sometimes; and it looks like everything is against us, but listen what Job said, 'All the days of my appointed time I will wait on the Lord till my change comes!' Sometimes we wake up in the dark hours of midnight, briny tears flowing down our cheeks (Ah, pray with me a little longer, Brothers). We cry and don't know what we are crying about. Brother, If you have been truly snatched from the greedy jaws of Hell, your feet taken out of the miry clay and placed on the rock, the sure foundation, you will shed tears sometime. You just feel like you want to run away somewhere. But listen at the Master when he says: 'Be still and know that I am God. I have heard your groans but I will not put on you a burden you cannot bear.' We ought to rejoice and be glad for while some day they think, we know we have been born of God because we have felt His power, tasted His love, waited at Hell's dark door for orders, got a through ticket straight through from hell to heaven; we have seen the travel of our soul; He dressed us up, told us we were His children, sent us back into this low land of sorrows to tarry until one sweet day when He shall send the angels of death to bear our soul from this old earthly tabernacle and bear it back home to glory, I say back home because we been there once and every since that day we have been making our way back." "Brothers! A-ha! Glory to God! The Captain is on board now, Brothers. Sit still and hear the word of God, a-ha; away back, away back brothers, a-ha! Before the wind ever blowed, a-ha! Before the flying clouds, a-ha! Or before ever the earth was made, a-ha! Our God had us in mind. Ha! oh, brothers, oh brothers! Ha! ain't you glad then, a-ha! that our God, Ha! looked down through time one morning, a-ha! saw me and you, a-ha! ordained from the very beginning that we should be his children, a-ha! the work of His Almighty hand, a-ha! Old John the Revelator, a-ha! a-looking over yonder, a-ha! in bright glory, a-ha! Oh, what do you see, John! Ha! I see a number, a-ha! Who are these, a-ha! I heard the angel Gabriel when he answered, a-ha! 'These are they that come up through hard trials and great tribulations, a-ha! who washed their robes, a-ha! and made them white in the blood of the lamb, a-ha! They are now shouting around the throne of God,' a-ha! Well, oh brothers! Oh, brothers! Ain't you glad that you have already been in the dressing room, had your everlasting garments fitted on and sandals on your feet. We born of God, a-ha! are shod for traveling, a-ha! Oh, Glory to God! It won't be long before some of us here, a-ha! will bid farewell, a-ha! take the wings of the morning, a-ha! where there'll be no more sin and sorrow, a-ha! no more weeping and mourning, a-ha! We can just walk around, brother, a-ha! Go over and shake hands with old Moses, a-ha! See Father Abraham, a-ha! Talk with Peter, Matthew, Luke and John, a-ha! And, Oh yes, Glory to God! we will want to see our Saviour, the Lamb that was slain, Ha! They tell me that His face outshines the sun, a-ha! but we can look on him, a-ha! because we will be like Him; and then oh brother, Oh brother, we will just fly from Cherubim to Cherubim, There with the angels we will eat off the welcome table, a-ha! Soon! Soon! we will all be gathered together over yonder. Brothers, ain't you glad you done died the sinner death and don't have to die no more? When we rise to fly that morning, we can fly with healing in our wings. . . . Now, if you don't hear my voice no more, a-ha! remember, I am a Hebrew child, a-ha! Just meet me over yonder, a-ha! on the other side of the River of Jordan, away back in the third heaven.

Backwater Blues

When it rain five days an' de skies turned dark as night
When it rain five days an' de skies turned dark as night
Then trouble taken place in the lowland that night

I woke up this mornin', can't even get outa mah do'
I woke up this mornin', can't even get outa mah do'
That's enough trouble to make a po' girl wonder where she wanta go

They rowed a little boat about five miles 'cross the pond
Then they rowed a little boat about five miles 'cross the pond
I packed all mah clothes, th'owed 'em in, an' they rowed me along

When it thunder an' a-lightnin', an' the wind begin to blow
When it thunder an' a-lightnin', an' the wind begin to blow
An' thousan' people ain' got no place to go

Then I went an' stood up on some high ol' lonesome hill
I went an' stood up on some high ol' lonesome hill
An' looked down on the house where I used to live

Backwater blues done cause me to pack mah things an' go
Backwater blues done cause me to pack mah things an' go
Cause mah house fell down an' I cain' live there no mo'

O-o-o-oom, I cain' move no mo'
O-o-o-oom, I cain' move no mo'
There ain' no place fo' a po' ol' girl to go

(Bessie Smith)

INDEX OF AUTHORS